Democracy and Illusion

Democracy and Illusion

*An examination of certain aspects
of modern democratic theory*

JOHN PLAMENATZ

Longman
London and New York

LONGMAN GROUP LIMITED
London

Associated companies, branches and representatives
throughout the world

Published in the United States of America
by Longman Inc., New York

© John Plamenatz 1973

First published 1973
First appearance in paperback 1977

ISBN 0 582 48575 4

Printed in Great Britain by
Richard Clay (The Chaucer Press) Ltd,
Bungay, Suffolk

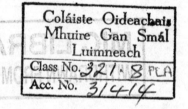

Contents

Acknowledgements

We are grateful to the following for permission to reproduce copyright material:

Dover Publications Inc., for an extract from *Political Parties* by R. Michels, trans. by E. Cedar Paul; Harper & Row Publishers and George Allen & Unwin Ltd. for an extract from *Capitalism, Socialism and Democracy*, Fourth ed. by J. A. Schumpeter; and McGraw-Hill Book Company for an extract from *The Ruling Class* by G. Mosca trans. by Hannah Kahn; ed. by A. Livington.

Preface

Today, almost everywhere, rulers and leaders praise democracy, while their subjects or followers often have doubts about it. This was not so, even quite recently. Mussolini and Hitler did not praise democracy, though they did claim to be popular with their own peoples and even to be, in some exalted and mysterious way, carrying out their will. With their defeat 'democracy' won the second of the two world wars as it had won the first. Or, perhaps I should say, in both wars the victorious powers won their victories in the name of democracy, *in hoc signo*. The symbols and the idiom of democracy have been spreading fast from continent to continent, and so too have some democratic institutions: elected legislatures, universal suffrage, political parties and a variety of other organizations or practices supposed to bring rulers and their subjects closer together.

The champions of democracy around the world do not all recognize one another as authentic spokesmen for it. Some denounce 'democracy' as preached or practised by the others as a sham. They claim that they alone have, or are in process of acquiring, the genuine thing. It is academics, mostly, and then only where it is safe for them to do so, who aspire to neutrality and take it upon themselves to speak of different types of democracy, each as genuine as the others or with as good a title to the common name. The Communist who speaks of *bourgeois democracy* speaks of a type of government or political system which, so he believes, is not truly democratic, though it pretends to be so. Much the same is true of the Western liberal when he speaks of the *people's democracies*.

In this book I have little to say about the actual systems whose apologists claim that they are democratic, and still less about the reactions of these apologists to one another's claims and criticisms, though in my last chapter I do suggest that the claims they make for the systems they favour and their reasons for condemning what they oppose are more alike than they believe them to be. This, of course, does not entail that the differences in practice between the systems have also been exaggerated; for men can appeal to similar ideals and principles to explain and justify dissimilar institutions. No doubt, if they do this long enough, their ideals and principles are likely in the end to diverge considerably because they have been used to explain such disparate things. Nevertheless, there may for a long time be a closer similarity of ideals than of practices.

In this book I confine myself almost entirely to controversies in the West about Western democracy. My purpose is not to give a historical account of them but to look critically at arguments which have attracted wide notice and have been held to be important, at some of their implications, and at the assumptions, many of them tacit, on which they rest. Almost as soon as representative democracy on a large scale appeared in Europe and ceased to be confined to the United States, there were misgivings about it, especially among intellectuals on both the Left and the Right. There were doubts as to whether it was, or could be, true to its own ideals. These doubts took a variety of forms, anarchist, Marxist and sociological or, as the doubters themselves put it, 'scientific', and I discuss them in the first part of the book. Some of them I discuss only in a most general way, while others I look at more closely as they appear in the works of such writers as Mosca and Michels who claimed to be careful students, not just of theories, but of practices, social and political.

My purpose in discussing the ideas of these Sceptics is to consider how far such arguments as theirs can be used to establish that a political system is not democratic. I try to assess the assumptions behind their arguments, the criteria of democracy implicit in their claim that, granted the truth of such facts as they adduce, those facts are good evidence that a political system is not democratic.

The second and longer part of the book deals mostly with the arguments of writers I have called *Revisionists* because they have tried to reconstruct democratic theory on new foundations to meet some of the objections of the Sceptics and also to expose some widely received misconceptions. These writers, from Schumpeter onwards, are by adoption or birth Americans—or at least those whose arguments I discuss are so. They have contributed greatly to a better understanding, not only of Western democracy, but of democratic ideals and practices generally. I have learned much from them: from them and from other writers whose arguments I do not consider because they do not raise so sharply the issues that seem to me crucial. Inevitably, I spend more time explaining where and why I disagree with writers whose books and articles I have read with pleasure and profit than in expressing agreement with them. But I hope that I do not fail to do justice to what is ingenious and illuminating in the arguments I discuss critically. These arguments seem to me defective primarily for two reasons: either they are utilitarian where they ought not to be or they are less precise and less

realistic than their authors suppose. I criticize both particular arguments and, more generally, types of argument or explanation whose
limitations are not sufficiently noticed by the writers who resort to
them.

I devote one chapter of the second part of the book (the part
dealing with what I call Revisionist theories) to discussing some
aspects of the attack on the American political system developed by
Wright Mills in his book *The Power Elite*. Mills might more properly
be called a Sceptic than a Revisionist, but his ways of thinking about
Western, and more especially American, democracy were deeply
influenced by the writers whose accounts of that democracy seemed
to him misleading and complacent. In explaining why the sort
of reasons he gives for holding that there is a power elite in the
United States are not good reasons, I do not question his facts but
only his arguments. Nor do I question his judgment that some groups
in the United States have more power than is good for their country
or for democracy. I argue rather that the judgment could be true
and yet these groups not constitute a power elite; unless calling them
so is merely another way of saying that they have too much power.

In the course of this book I reject a number of arguments purporting
to show either that Western democracy is a sham, or that voters or
leaders in it do not, or cannot, act rationally. The reader may therefore take the book for a defence of a certain type of democracy. But
that is not what it is. I nowhere argue that Western democracy comes
closer to being genuine than its critics say it does. Rather, I argue
that considerations which seem decisive to them are unimportant or
irrelevant because they rest on mistaken ideas about what conditions
must hold if a political system is to be reckoned a democracy. My
reasons, since they concern only ideas and arguments, could all be
sound and yet democracy as practised in the West be as much a sham
as its harsher critics have said it is, though for reasons different from
those put forward by them.

This book, as far as political practices are concerned, is neutral.
This neutrality is no virtue but merely a consequence of its limited
aim. Far from holding that academic students of politics or political
theory should refrain from defending, in the realm of practice, what
they believe in, or attacking what seems evil or harmful to them,
I regret that they do not do it more often. I suspect that one of the
reasons why they hesitate to do it is the sense they have (which is apt
to be stronger in them than in others) that the language of politics,
whether used to describe practices or to define the criteria or the
standards by which practices are identified or assessed, is loose and
confusing. A great deal of discrimination is required to see and to
describe clearly just what it is that is being discussed, whether or not

it is attacked or defended. This business of discrimination is sometimes long and difficult, and though it no doubt sharpens the critical
sense, it also quite often either weakens the urge to attack or defend
or else makes an attack or defence look devious or irrelevant or
unrealistic to whoever lacks the patience to weigh it carefully. If, in
this book, I confine myself to criticizing ideas and arguments, it is
certainly not because I think that in general political theorists ought
to confine themselves in this way. Rather, it is because I believe that
even this limited undertaking is difficult and important, and also large
enough to fill a whole book.

JOHN PLAMENATZ

Oxford,
February 1972

PART ONE Doubts about Democracy

Chapter 1

Types of Democratic Theory

An American writer, Robert Dahl, says in a well-known book that 'it is fashionable in some quarters to suggest that everything believed about democratic politics prior to World War I, and perhaps World War II, was nonsense'.[1] He does not say in just what quarters but presumably he has in mind some of the departments of government or political science at American universities. Professor Dahl, though he is in his own country one of the fashionable writers about democracy, makes it clear that he does not altogether accept this fashionable suggestion. But evidently he has some sympathy with it; he does not dismiss it as absurd and arrogant.

There has certainly been a great change in democratic theory in the West in our century. There has been change at two levels: at a more and at a less abstract level. There have been theories put forward about democracy in general or about Western democracy in contrast with some other kind, and there have been theories about how government functions in one or other of the Western democracies. Also, of course, there have been theories about particular institutions—about parties and pressure groups or about elections and their place in the democratic process. Many of these theories make assumptions and use ideas seldom or never made or used in the nineteenth century. There has been something of a revolution both in how political theorists think about democracy and its typical institutions, taken generally, and in the kinds of explanation they offer of how particular democratic systems or parts of them fuction. This revolution has gone further in the United States than anywhere else where our sort of democracy flourishes—or, perhaps I should say, continues to exist. It has considerably affected everyone in the West who takes the trouble to think seriously and critically about democracy.

I want in this book to try to assess this revolution in Western thought about democracy. I am even further than Robert Dahl—perhaps much further—from holding that everything believed about democracy before the First World War was nonsense. And I suspect

[1] R. A. Dahl, *A Preface to Democratic Theory* (1956), Phoenix Books edition, p. 125.

that I am more inclined than he is to think that some of the theorizing about democracy that has gone on in English-speaking universities since the Second World War is nonsense. But I do agree that there have been important changes in democratic theory, some valuable and some not. Much of the nonsense that spoilt democratic theory in the last century has been shown up for what it is, but not everything that has taken its place is good sense. We too have produced our own brands of nonsense.

I shall not attempt a survey of democratic theory as a whole in the West in our century. I am not competent to make any such attempt. I have read only a small part of the books and articles about democracy and democratic processes written since Hitler's war, not to speak of the Kaiser's war, and I dare say that many that I have not read are as well worth reading as the ones I have read. My reading has been highly selective. My purpose is to examine critically some of the ways in which writers who have made their names as political theorists or political scientists have spoken about democracy in recent times. It seems to me that their ways of speaking about it raise issues of great theoretical importance, and it is these issues, even more than what they have to say about them, that I want to look at.

Several of the books that I shall be discussing, sometimes in considerable detail, are American, and I shall be highly critical of some of their arguments. This does not mean that, in my opinion, democratic theory in recent times has been more simpleminded or more wrongheaded in America than it has been in, say, Britain or France. On the contrary, some of the best theorists of democracy have been Americans. Nowhere in the world are there as many political scientists as in America, and nowhere has democracy—together with its processes and its conditions, social and cultural—been more often and more variously described and explained. In this branch of political theory the Americans in the last fifty years have been more active and bolder than we have; they have put forward the more valuable hypotheses and have made the more interesting mistakes—the mistakes best worth criticizing.

There has been real progress in democratic theory, both in explaining more realistically how democracy works and in defining and elucidating democratic ideals and principles. There have also been misdirected efforts which have, so it seems to me, made democratic theory poorer and more confused than it might be. I believe, among other things, that democratic theory in the West has become too utilitarian. Not that it has gained nothing from this utilitarian bias; I am inclined to think that it has gained considerably. But it has also lost considerably. Or perhaps I should say, more accurately, that it has, because of this bias, moved too far in some unprofitable directions.

Too many political theorists, especially in America, have constructed theories of democracy which borrow more than they contrive to make good use of from the methods and ideas of economic theorists. An example of what I have in mind is Anthony Downs's *An Economic Theory of Democracy* (1965). That book is an extreme case. In it Downs goes further in assimilating political to economic theory than most American political theorists would want to go. But he goes further than they do in a direction in which they too, many of them, want to go. To many of them, as to him, economics seems to have made greater progress than politics has towards becoming *scientific*, and they take it for granted, more or less, that the study of politics, if it too is to make progress, must follow, as far as it can, where economics leads.

Occasionally they admit that the political studies could make considerable progress by using methods different from those of the economist. But, more often, they differ from Downs only in thinking that the student of politics is less fortunately placed than the economist. They assume that, the more he can use methods like those of the economist, the more solid, the more scientific will be the results he achieves. The assumption, conscious or unconscious, is that the methods most likely to produce such results in any of the social sciences are those that the economists have used with conspicuous success. For the social scientist is concerned to explain behaviour that is typical of a social group or category. The economist explains the behaviour typical of the capitalist or the wage-worker or the 'firm' in such and such conditions, and the political scientist explains the behaviour of the voter or leader or party, or of a certain type of voter or leader or party, in situations of different kinds. The methods of the economist are, in the broad sense of the word, utilitarian. Though he may not, as Bentham did, speak of pleasures and pains, he does speak of wants and preferences and costs; he speaks, as Bentham did, of maximizing benefits and minimizing costs, though, unlike Bentham, he does not think of benefits as pleasures or of costs as pains. Ought not the political scientist, as far as he can, to proceed as the economist does, for he too, like the economist, is concerned to explain *typical* behaviour? The assumption is that he ought. This assumption, for reasons that I hope to discuss later, seems to me largely mistaken. Not mistaken altogether but still pretty wide of the mark.

Economics, though it is not reckoned among what are sometimes called the exact sciences, is undoubtedly in some ways more rigorous and precise than what goes by the name of political science. Economists often make different and incompatible predictions about the future, and their explanations of past events sometimes contradict one another. As far as I know, there is no evidence that either their prophecies or their diagnoses are sounder than those of political scientists. Nevertheless, when they construct their theories, they define their assumptions more clearly than political scientists do, they use less ambiguous concepts, and they make larger and more sophisticated uses of mathematics. Their theories are often concise and elegant; they have some of the qualities that natural scientists look for in explanations within their own fields. We can readily imagine a physicist, if he were to turn his attention to the social sciences, finding economics the most congenial to him; feeling more at home with it than with the others. He might well get more pleasure from contemplating the theoretical models of the economist than from any theory put together by a political scientist. As he understands sophistication in matters of theory, economic theory might seem to him more sophisticated than political theory. The natural sciences enjoy an immense prestige; and economic theory, which has more of their rigour and elegance than political theory has, seems to that extent more scientific and superior.

Far be it from me to suggest that economics does not deserve its better academic reputation. I dare say that it does. Certainly, the mere fact that economists make different and incompatible predictions and that their explanations of present and past events sometimes contradict one another, is not in itself strong evidence that their methods are ill adapted to their purposes. I agree that rigour and elegance are desirable qualities in any type of theory. I merely doubt whether political theory has much to gain by following where economic theory has led. Economics differs in some obvious ways from the natural sciences; it cannot test its hypotheses by experiment to anything like the same extent, and the behaviour it studies is subject to historical change. Nevertheless, it can go much further than political theory can in explaining the types of behaviour it studies in terms of quantifiable benefits and costs.

It is not all political theorists indifferently, but above all theorists of liberal democracy, who have been attracted by the example of economics. The reasons for this are, I think, partly historical. The market economy and the modern liberal democratic state arose together in the same parts of the world, in Western Europe and North America. From the beginning individualism has been both political and economic. The Western political theorist, long before he took up democracy, was a kind of egalitarian. He may not have been much concerned that men should in fact be equal, but he found it convenient, for his purposes as a theorist, to assume that in certain respects they were equal. He assumed that they shared certain basic rights and duties, and he explained government as serving to secure these rights and to enforce these duties. Similarly, the economist explained the system of production and exchange as ensuring that men's wants are satisfied as efficiently as possible, given the resources available to them. Indeed, it was the political theorist, as far back at least as Hobbes, who was the first to be conspicuously as individualist —to begin with the individual and his supposed rights and duties, using them to explain either what government does or what it ought to do.

Rights and duties are not wants and preferences. A political theory can be individualist without being utilitarian, without assuming that the proper business of government is to 'maximize' anything qualifiable. The theories of Hobbes and Locke were individualist but not utilitarian. Not till the next century did political theorists take to putting about rights and duties, about social rules, the questions that Hobbes and Locke had put about government: What do they do for the individual? Why should he accept them? What does he gain by doing so? Social rules, and therefore rights and duties along with them, could be shown, they thought, to promote the interests—at least the enduring interests—of the persons required to observe them. Or they could be criticized for not doing so, and changed to ensure that they did. Interests, they thought, could be defined in terms of people's actual wants and preferences.

It is easy to see why this way of thinking should have been attractive to democrats and egalitarians. People's ideas about what is desirable vary. How are we to decide between them? How can we justify democracy, if we admit that some people are better judges of what is desirable than others are? Is it not better to do what Bentham did: to assume that desires or wants are, in themselves, morally indifferent? Is it not better to assume that the function of social rules and institutions is, or ought to be, to maximize the satisfaction of wants? It may, in practice, often be difficult to ensure that they do so. But, at least, if we make this assumption, we treat no man's wants or desires as inherently superior to any other man's. And it follows from our assumption that men should be free to make known their wants, and that governments should have adequate motives for taking account of them.

Democrats attracted by this way of thinking felt that democratic theory in the West had made a false start. It had begun with Rousseau and with Tom Paine. It made use of obscure or empty notions such as 'the general will' or 'the common good' or 'natural rights'. It carried a load of nonsense which had too long stood in the way of clear thinking about democracy.

Rousseau in *The Social Contract* (1762)—the book which, more than any other, had come close to being the bible of the democrats, at least on the Continent—had had in mind only small self-governing communities all of whose citizens take part in what he took to be the main business of government, the making of law and general policy. Partly to explain the working of what he conceived to be the ideal political system, and partly to make it clear why he thought it essentially just, Rousseau produced his doctrine of a *general will* whose end is a good common to all sharers in that will. This doctrine, applied to the sort of community that Rousseau had in mind when he wrote *The Social Contract*, makes better sense than many of its critics have allowed. But, applied to the vast representative democracies that emerged in the West in the last century, it does not make sense. Or at least it seems not to do so.

I happen to believe that there are, implicit in Rousseau's doctrine of the general will, principles by which democrats and egalitarians set great store, though they fail to state them precisely. I also believe that much of the discontent that people now feel with liberal democracy, as we know it in the West, is due more to its failure to realize these principles than to its failure to 'maximize' happiness or welfare or the satisfaction of wants, or anything of that kind. But I cannot deny that the doctrine of the general will has been misapplied, and that some of the blame for this lies with Rousseau. Unless the doctrine can be applied to democracy as we know it, it is of little use to us; and the fact remains that it has been applied to it in ways that seem as perverse as they are obscure. It is not surprising that theorists of liberal democracy should today be suspicious of the doctrine; that they should look upon it, not merely as nonsense, but as dangerous nonsense. They prefer explanations of democracy that discard it altogether; and since the kind of democracy that interests them is in fact representative, they discard it with relief. It is, they think, irrelevant, and the attempt to apply it where it does not apply too often converts democratic theory into an apology for authoritarian government.

The argument for democracy from natural rights, as we find it for example in the writings of Tom Paine, is simpler than the theory expounded in Rousseau's *Social Contract*. It is not obscure, and has not been perverted in the same way. Nor has it been used to excuse the opposite of democracy in democracy's name. But it has other disadvantages. It is based on what many people believe is an unacceptable theory about rights, and it is unrealistic. It asserts that all men everywhere, merely by virtue of being men, have certain fundamental rights, and that among these is the right not to be governed by anyone who has not acquired authority over them with their consent.

If we accept this argument, we have to conclude that only democracy, direct or representative, is legitimate. No matter what the conditions of a people may be, no matter how urgent their need for effective government, no matter how little used they are to democracy, they must have it, for it alone is rightful government. They must have it whatever the consequences to themselves and their neighbours. But this is absurd; for, if they are incapable of it, they cannot have it. There can then be only a pretence that they have it; and sham democracy is not a kind of democracy. Besides, it is often more oppressive than systems of government that make no claim to be democratic; and it may well stand more in the way of the eventual achievement of genuine democracy. Can we take it for granted that sham democracy is a preparation for the real thing?

If we are to make a realistic case for democracy, we must be content to argue that it is the best form of government only when certain conditions hold. We must avoid the absurd conclusion to which Tom Paine's reasoning commits us, that democracy alone is legitimate. Government, especially in large communities, if it is to be democratic, calls for skills and sentiments that are not found always and everywhere. It may be that any people could acquire them in time, that no people are by nature incapable of acquiring them, but we can hardly deny that in fact many peoples have not acquired them. These peoples too need government, even though they are incapable of democracy, and have perhaps never heard of it, or do not care for it if they have. It is absurd to say of their governments, no matter how well adapted to their needs and sentiments, that they are not legitimate. If people are satisfied with the kind of government they have, if they do not question its authority, how can we condemn it as illegitimate merely because it does not secure to its subjects opportunities and rights which are precious to us but not to them? Tom Paine would be surprised to hear his sort of argument for democracy dismissed, not for being unrealistic (for he was perhaps unfamiliar with that objection to it), but for being arrogant and ethnocentric. And yet it has been dismissed for just these reasons.

The doctrine of natural rights, on which Paine's argument for democracy rests, has been rejected on both philosophical and common sense grounds. Philosophers have argued that there is no proper inference from the capacities peculiar to man to any universal human rights. We can say that only creatures having such capacities can make and recognize claims, can be the bearers of rights, but we cannot deduce their rights from those capacities. To the man of common sense, it seems odd that all men, merely by virtue of being men, should have rights that most men had not heard of until the rise of a certain type of moral, legal and political theory in the West. The historian can explain how this type of theory arose, how men came to make and to recognize certain claims and to think of them as universal human rights; he can explain how certain ideas about rights first arose and found wide favour among particular groups or classes in a particular region of the world. He can also show how these ideas spread later to other groups and regions, and may even point to causes which make it likely that they will spread everywhere. The doctrine of natural rights has been, and still is, of great importance. Few will deny it. Nevertheless, it is not acceptable in the form it took in the seventeenth and eighteenth centuries, and it cannot be used, in the way that Paine and others used it, to make a case for democracy. It needs to be greatly qualified—so much so, indeed, that it ceases to be the same doctrine.

For my part, I believe that it is possible to make a case for democracy that is not utilitarian; a case resting on a conception of rights which, though it differs substantially from the traditional doctrine of the rights of man, is yet similar to it in important respects. Why I believe this will, I hope, be made clear gradually during the course of this book. But, for the moment, I am engaged on something different; I am trying to show how a certain type of argument for democracy came to be rejected—primarily in academic and intellectual circles, though not only in them—as both logically absurd and unrealistic. It has been, perhaps, in its time, the most popular argument for democracy, as well as the simplest. It is a different type of argument from the more subtle, as well as more obscure, doctrine of the general will as we find it in Rousseau's *Social Contract*.

I very much doubt whether a sound utilitarian case for democracy can be made, and one of my purposes in this book will be to explain my reasons for doubting it. I am even inclined to doubt whether anyone, not excluding Bentham himself, has ever really believed in democracy primarily on utilitarian grounds. I suspect that the utilitarian case for democracy is one that intellectuals have resorted to because other arguments for it have seemed to them untenable. They have thought of it as both more sophisticated and more realistic than the alternatives to it. Yet I doubt whether it has expressed what puts democracy, in their eyes, apart from and above other forms of government. I suspect that Rousseau's doctrine of the general will and Paine's argument for democracy from natural rights, open to serious objections though they are, come a good deal closer to expressing what it is that democrats care about. Critics of Rousseau and of Paine point to the rhetorical character of their arguments. Rousseau was too subtle and Paine too simple, but they both appealed to the emotions. No doubt they did. It is perhaps worth enquiring what emotions they appealed to.

The theories about democracy that I want to discuss, whether they are critical of it or argue in its favour, or seek to explain it without either condemning or supporting it, all reject or ignore such arguments as those of Rousseau or Paine. Mosca, Pareto, Michels and Schumpeter all do so, and so too do the three or four American writers whose arguments and methods I shall be considering. They do not all put utilitarian arguments in their place. Some of them are merely critics of what they look upon as pretentious theories, but those of them who do venture on alternative (and in their opinion) better explanations have a strong utilitarian bias.

The early Utilitarians, Bentham and his disciples, were as much, or almost as much, economists as they were political theorists. The two Mills, father and son, both produced general treatises on economics that were widely read in their day, and even Bentham's *Economic Writings*, in Werner Stark's New York edition, take up three volumes. Bentham and the elder Mill's case for representative government is strikingly similar to their case for the *laissez-faire* economy in which they believed. The fundamental social problem, as they see it, is to ensure that men get as little as possible in each other's way in pursuing their interests. The proper function of law is to maintain conditions in which men can pursue their interests effectively. In the England of their day the type of government most likely to make laws maintaining such conditions was, in their opinion, a government broadly representative of the people. Though Bentham was more willing than James Mill to move quickly towards universal suffrage, they were both in principle democrats. They also believed that, in their day and their part of the world, government should interfere as little as possible with the production and distribution of wealth, and should confine itself to protecting rights of property and enforcing contracts. John Stuart Mill was less strongly in favour of *laissez-faire* in the economic sphere, and was much less utilitarian in his reasons for preferring representative democracy to other forms of government. But these differences between the three great Utilitarian philosophers of the last century need not detain us, for we shall be concerned with more recent versions of their type of theory. No Utilitarian has been a complete Utilitarian.

A utilitarian argument for representative democracy has obvious and important advantages. In the first place, it is an argument of limited scope. Whoever uses it says only that a certain kind of political system is desirable where certain conditions hold. He may find it difficult to define these conditions fully and precisely but at least he can point to some of them; and he can argue that they are necessary if not sufficient conditions. For example, he can argue that representative democracy, except perhaps on a small scale, works effectively—or, in other words, is in fact what it purports to be—only in communities that are economically advanced, in which both geographic and social mobility are comparatively great and the people generally are literate, and in which there is a large minority of politically active persons, drawn from all social classes, competing for political power and influence and for popular support. These may not be sufficient conditions of large-scale democracy, but it is arguable—and, indeed, has been argued—that they are necessary conditions. Whether they are so or not does not, for the moment, concern us. What I am now saying is merely that, if we make a utilitarian case for democracy, we need say only that it is desirable under certain conditions, economic, social and cultural. We can then proceed to define the conditions and to show that they are realized, or are coming to be so, in that part of the world in which we wish to preserve democracy or to set it up. This advantage is not confined to makers of utilitarian arguments for democracy, but it is an advantage they have over writers who, like Tom Paine, use the sort of arguments that appealed to the American and French revolutionaries, and indeed to most champions of democracy in the late eighteenth and the nineteenth century.

Bentham and James Mill were aware of this advantage. Since they were concerned primarily with their own country, they did not try to define the general conditions of large-scale representative democracy, but they did believe that there were such conditions—confined to certain peoples and certain times. Bentham wrote an *Essay on the Influence of Time and Place in Matters of Legislation* in which he conceded that laws and institutions must be suited to the peoples for whom they are made. He did not mean that the legislator must not try to change established manners and prejudices but rather that what he can hope to achieve is limited by the character and the culture of the people he deals with. Bentham was an ardent reformer long before he became a democrat, and he became a democrat because, so he believed, experience had taught him that the reforms he wanted would never be made except by a government responsible to the whole people. As a young man, he had hoped that at least some of his reforms would be made in Russia by Catherine the Great, whom he knew to be an absolute monarch even though he thought her enlightened. He claimed, of course, that his basic principles applied to all countries everywhere, in the sense that rulers capable of understanding them could use them to improve the lot of the people, to make them happier, to ensure that they acted more effectively in their own best interests. But he did not believe that they justified democracy everywhere. Indeed, it was only rather late in life that he decided that they justified it even in his own country, and presumably in others like it.

Another advantage that falls to the Utilitarian is that he can dispense with the idea that there are basic rights which everyone has or ought to have. In all societies there are many rights confined to particular offices or social roles. Mothers have rights that fathers do not have, and *vice versa*. There are also some rights that everyone in the society is supposed to have. In some societies, especially when they are illiterate and have no regular courts, these common rights are ill defined and insecure. Nevertheless, in all societies there are both common and special rights. The Utilitarian does not deny it. But the common rights of one society differ considerably from the common rights of another. They may not differ altogether. We could, no doubt, distinguish between types of society according to the rights and the duties shared (or supposed to be shared) by everyone. This, I dare say, would be as useful a way of classifying them as most others. If we did this, we should probably find that societies having similar common rights also have similar distributions of special rights—rights attached to specific offices and social roles. In other words, we should probably find that societies having similar economic and social structures, similar divisions of social labour, also have similar ideas about the rights and opportunities that everyone should have. For example, industrial, urban and literate societies, in which the extended family has ceased to exist, are likely to have similar common rights and also a similar distribution of special rights.

Even if we take a number of societies that differ greatly, we may find that there are some rights that they all recognize as rights that everyone should have. Human needs and aspirations, the situations in which human beings find themselves, are in some respects alike all over the world. Just as there are some moral rules common to all societies, so too, no doubt, there are some rights common to them— some claims which it is thought proper for anyone to make, some opportunities which it is admitted that everyone should have. But these claims and opportunities do not coincide with the rights of man, as liberals and democrats have conceived of them in the West. No argument for democracy or a free market economy or a socialist society or a welfare state can be erected upon them. They are compatible with widely different social and economic situations. The Utilitarian or anyone else who rejects the doctrine of natural rights is not committed to saying that, however hard we look, we shall not find any rights that everyone enjoys, or is supposed to enjoy, in all societies; he is committed only to denying that they are fundamental and universal in the sense intended by Paine and the American and French revolutionaries. When a social or political order is challenged on the ground that it denies fundamental rights that all men should have, the rights in question are not in fact claims that a comparative study of a fair sample of dissimilar societies would show to be universally or very widely recognized in them; they are, on the contrary, claims that mean little outside the type of society in which they are made.

Yet another advantage enjoyed by the Utilitarian is that he can make a clear distinction between explanation and justification and also admit a close connection between them. Let me take Bentham and James Mill as examples to illustrate my meaning. They were both economists as well as political theorists. As economists they were more concerned to explain how the economy functioned than to justify it; it served on the whole, so they believed, to maximize the satisfaction of wants or, as they often put it, of happiness. Men want what they find pleasant and avoid what they find painful; and they prefer the more to the less pleasant, and are keener to avoid the more than the less painful. Happiness, so Bentham and Mill believed, is a matter of getting pleasure and avoiding pain, and they therefore took it for granted that to maximize the satisfaction of wants is to maximize happiness. To explain the functioning of the economy they tried to show how, on the whole, it ensured that labour and other resources were put to efficient use to maximize the satisfaction of wants. To justify the economy they showed how, in maximizing this satisfaction, it also maximized happiness. Happiness, they thought, is the one thing that everyone not only desires but agrees is desirable. Though to say that men desire something is not to say that it is desirable, what they think desirable is nonetheless related to what they desire. Their ideas of what is good or right and their wants are intimately connected. Indeed, according to Bentham and James Mill—though they were not absolutely unequivocal on this point—how men use these ideas is determined by their wants and by the problems they face in their endeavours to satisfy them. Both men's actions and the standards they use in assessing them arise out of their wants and the situations in which they endeavour to satisfy them. This does not ensure that they always behave as they should do by those standards. But it does show how the tasks of explanation and justification, though different, are also closely connected. We explain a system of social behaviour by showing how men come to act as they do as they try to satisfy their wants, and we justify or condemn the system by showing how far it ensures or fails to ensure that they get what they want.

On the whole, Bentham and James Mill were satisfied with the economy as they found it. But they were not satisfied with the system of government. They were therefore less concerned to explain it than to criticize it and to argue that it should be radically changed. If government was to do properly what it ought to, if it was to ensure, as far as possible, that its subjects could pursue their own interests

effectively and harmlessly, satisfying their own wants without preventing others from satisfying theirs, it would have to be responsible
to the whole people, or to a much larger proportion of them than it
then was, at least in England. Representative democracy, so it seemed
to Bentham and Mill, was in their day, as it had not been in the past,
both ideally better than the established system and a realistic and
likely alternative to it. It was *realistic* because both rulers and subjects had acquired, or were acquiring, the skills and sentiments needed
for its successful working; and it was *likely* because the unprivileged
classes were beginning to see that they stood to gain by having the
vote. The more convinced they were that they would gain by having
it, the more demanding and the less docile they would be for as long
as it was denied to them. In the end it would become the interest
even of the privileged classes to let them have it, for the cost to the
privileged of resisting popular demands would eventually outweigh
the loss they would sustain by giving up their monopoly of political
power. With the passage of time it can become the interest of a
privileged group to satisfy demands, even though it was originally
against their interest that the demands should be made.

Bentham and James Mill were not political scientists in the sense
that many students of politics, especially in the West, now aspire to
be. They made no empirical investigations, they put forward no
hypotheses which they tested by an appeal to the facts, they prepared
no questionnaires and sent no teams of students out into the streets
to put their questions to ordinary citizens. In constructing their
theories they seem also to have made little use of such history as
they knew. This is less true of John Stuart Mill than of his father and
Bentham, but it is true to some extent even of him. The three great
Utilitarian democrats of the last century were all of them highly
abstract thinkers, who used facts more often to illustrate their arguments than to provide evidence in support of them. If to be scientific
is to put forward hypotheses and to test them empirically, then
Bentham and the elder Mill were scarcely ever political scientists,
and the younger Mill was so only from time to time. But, scientists
or not, they certainly believed that their kind of social and political
theory was more realistic, closer to the facts, as well as more lucid
and better argued, than other kinds.

I am not concerned in this book with utilitarian moral theory for
its own sake. But much of the theorizing about democracy that goes
on in the West today, especially in academic circles (and that is where
most of it does go on), though seldom explicitly or entirely utilitarian,
has a strong utilitarian bias. Though it often purports merely to
explain democracy, it generally does more than this; it also makes a
case for it. There is no reason why it should not. It is no less the

proper business of political theory to justify and to condemn than to explain. Some people, indeed, go so far as to say that in the social studies (which used to be called moral sciences) it is impossible to explain without also, at least covertly, justifying or condemning. While I do not myself share this view, I see no reason why the political theorist should confine himself to mere explanation. Far from objecting to these modern theorists of democracy making a case for it, I regret only that they do not go about the business of arguing for it, as it now is or as it might be if reformed, more openly and systematically.

These theorists, both as explainers and as persuaders (often hidden persuaders), are inclined to be utilitarian. Yet their utilitarianism is not quite that of Bentham. They speak of the satisfying of wants where he speaks of seeking pleasures and avoiding pains, and they do not, as he does, put forward a fundamental utilitarian rule. They make assumptions which, if not exactly tacit, are hurriedly and inadequately defined. But these assumptions, looked at more closely in the light of the consequences drawn from them, turn out to be utilitarian. They take it for granted that the prime function, if not of all important social rules, then at least of those that characterize a democratic system, is, or ought to be, to make it easier for everyone involved in the system to maximize the satisfaction of his wants. It is because I want to do justice to these assumptions and to the explanations and arguments resting upon them, that I go as far as I do—which, after all, is not very far—into the intricacies of utilitarian moral theory.

An advantage sometimes claimed for social and moral theories of the utilitarian type is that they are particularly successful in reconciling man's egoism with his morality. Not all Utilitarians have assumed that man is a consistent egoist who never confers a benefit on someone else except in the hope of himself gaining thereby; many of them have admitted that, at least in his dealings with persons he is fond of, he is often benevolent without hope of benefit to himself. But social rules govern much more than a man's dealings with the few persons whom he cares deeply about; they also govern his dealings with the many people for whom he cares little or nothing. They impose upon him obligations which he carries out, often to his own hurt, for the benefit of persons he is indifferent to or dislikes. He carries them out partly, no doubt, because he is expected to do so and will be blamed if he does not, but he also often does it from a sense of duty, or, in other words, because he requires it of himself. How, then, does it happen that men require of each other and of themselves behaviour which benefits persons they are indifferent to or dislike, often to their own hurt? Because, says the Utilitarian, they accept rules which it is their enduring interest should be generally obeyed. In the long run, they stand to gain more than they lose by this general obedience.

Utilitarianism has been called an economic morality. Now, economics is concerned much less with dealings inside the family, or between friends or close neighbours, than with transactions between purchasers and vendors of easily identified and relatively uniform goods and services. It assumes that purchasers and vendors are indifferent to one another, or rather that they are concerned with each other as sources of benefits to themselves. Men, of course, are not only purchasers and vendors, they are also much more besides. The economist does not deny this; but he happens, professionally, to be concerned with them as purchasers and vendors, and as producers of what can be bought and sold, or bartered. Man, engaged in the transactions which it is the economist's business to study, is predominantly an egoist—or, at least, it is convenient to assume that he is. The purchaser may make the most unselfish and benevolent use of what he buys, but the economist is not professionally interested in this aspect of his activities. He is interested in his relations with the vendor and not in his relations with the persons who benefit from the use he makes of what he buys. Unless, of course, he buys means of production.

Some Utilitarians—for example, James Mill and often (though not always) Bentham too—have agreed with Hobbes that men are complete egoists, in the sense that they confer benefits on others only for their own benefit, but others have not done so. They have agreed with Hume rather than with Hobbes. But Hume, though he denied man's complete egoism, held that a great part of morality and almost the whole of politics could be explained by showing how they arise out of the needs of persons who are out to satisfy their own wants and yet are also mutually dependent. Social rules, as the Utilitarians explain them, serve the needs of rational beings who are indifferent to all but a few of the persons they have to deal with. These rules govern human behaviour, not only within small circles of intimacy and affection, but in much larger and more impersonal spheres—in the vast economies of highly commercial and industrial societies, in political communities whose members are to be counted in millions and tens of millions. The Utilitarians, more perhaps than any social and moral theorists before them, took an interest in the division of labour, in production and government on a large scale, in the working of institutions involving or affecting many people, most of them unknown to one another. To thinkers who are not Utilitarians—for example, to Hegel and to Marx—morality as the Utilitarians explained it has seemed essentially a morality of the market place, a morality which either assimilates all human relations to market relations or else ignores them when they do not lend themselves to this treatment.

Marx spoke contemptuously, not only of the economic, but also of the political and moral theory of his day; he called it bourgeois ideology. He dismissed the idea of man on which it was based as narrow and mean. Though he had little to say about utilitarianism in particular, he no doubt thought of it as one brand among others of bourgeois ideology. His few references to Bentham are all contemptuous; contemptuous and unfair.

For my part, I see nothing essentially bourgeois about utilitarianism, any more than I do about the doctrine of the rights of man. In so far as it has been used to support class interests, those interests have been for the most part bourgeois. But it could be, and sometimes has been, used to support proletarian interests. Utilitarian assumptions and methods are no better adapted to making a case for the kind of democracy that Marxists call bourgeois than to arguments for a classless society. A social theory is utilitarian if it explains social rules and institutions as serving the enduring or long-term interests of individuals or groups considered as subjects of wants or demands that they seek to satisfy as fully as possible, or if it assumes that this is the proper function of rules and institutions. If a utilitarian theory is bourgeois, it is so by virtue of assumptions which are not in themselves utilitarian.

The complaint sometimes made against utilitarianism, that it takes a narrow and mean view of man, seems to me misplaced. No doubt it takes a partial view of him. But, then, so too do other kinds of social theory. The question to ask is whether the view it takes of man is adequate to its purposes, and the answer, in my opinion at least, is that it is so only to some extent. It is often possible to make a strong utilitarian case for one policy in preference to others, for one reform in preference to others, even when the reform involves changing important rules and institutions. It is not always possible to do even this, but often it is. A change of policy, or of law or institutions, takes place within a specific social and cultural context by reference to which the wants and preferences of individuals and groups can often be fairly precisely defined. But a whole system of social rules and institutions can neither be explained nor justified on utilitarian grounds.

Admittedly, these rules and institutions are products of human behaviour, of the actions of men who (to a considerable extent, at least) can define their wants and establish priorities among them. But this does not allow us to assume that a type of reasoning often used to good purpose to explain or to justify changes within a social or political system can also be used to explain or justify the system. I hope to make my reasons for saying this clearer at a later stage of my argument.

The contemporary democratic theorist with a utilitarian bias seeks to explain both democratic institutions and the rules, moral or otherwise, on which these institutions depend as ensuring a fuller satisfaction of wants, or of certain kinds of wants, in a certain type of society. He usually admits, readily enough, that there are many wants as fully satisfied in societies that are not democratic as in those that are. He might even admit, if he were pressed, that there are some wants better satisfied in undemocratic societies. He also, as I said earlier, recognizes that there are peoples who not only lack the skills and sentiments required to work democratic institutions but who would be no better off for acquiring them. Given their circumstances and their wants, democracy, as it is understood and practised in the West, has nothing to offer them. If their circumstances and wants were to change in certain respects, they might then have more to gain than to lose by becoming democratic. But this need not mean that democracy would make them better off—better able to satisfy their wants —than they were before their circumstances and wants changed. If I move from England to Equatorial Africa my circumstances and wants will change considerably, and I shall need to order my life differently if I am to satisfy my new wants adequately. But I may be no better off, no more successful in satisfying my wants, after I have reordered my African life on sound utilitarian principles, than I was before I left England.

The utilitarian democrat claims to make only a limited case for democracy. He need not even be what Bentham was, a believer in progress. He can argue that democracy is the 'wave' of the future only because there are widespread changes producing wants more fully satisfied in democratic than undemocratic societies. He need not say that mankind are the better off for these changes; he need say no more than that, given these changes, they will be worse off unless they establish a democracy. I doubt whether he can make a sound utilitarian case for saying even this much, but he need not, as a Utilitarian, say more.

Democratic theory in the West today is by no means entirely utilitarian; it is much else besides, and I shall be concerned also with several of its non-utilitarian aspects. None of the theorists whose assumptions and arguments I shall discuss speaks of himself as a Utilitarian. Most of them scarcely mention Bentham and his disciples, and when they do they sometimes give the impression of not having read them. Anthony Downs, perhaps the most utilitarian of them all, an economist who decided to try his hand in another sphere, calls his book *An Economic Theory of Democracy*. Among the fifty to sixty authors whose works appear in his bibliography, only four were active before the twentieth century—Plato, Aristotle, Rousseau and Durkheim, none of whom was a Utilitarian. Recent American theorists of democracy use the word *utilitarian* very little and take little notice of the works of the great Utilitarians of the last century. Nevertheless, their writings about democracy often, so it seems to me, have a much stronger utilitarian bias than, say, those of John Stuart Mill.

I shall try, in this book, to do two things: to consider some of the criticisms of democracy made since the larger countries of the West became democratic, and to assess some of the explanations or justifications of it put forward since those criticisms were made. The explanations and justifications have been, to a large extent, answers to the criticisms, and it is they, rather than the criticisms, that have a strong dose of utilitarianism to them. Anarchist and Marxist attacks on liberal democracy have nothing utilitarian about them, at least not unless the word utilitarian is given so wide a meaning that virtually no social philosophy escapes the imputation. Nor were Mosca, Pareto and Michels Utilitarians. In their attacks on democracy, or on popular misconceptions about it, they enlarge upon the role of political elites and minorities. So, too, in his different way, does C. Wright Mills. The explainers and defenders of democracy accept, though with reservations, the distinction made by its critics between active minorities and passive majorities, between leaders and followers, persuaders and persuaded. But they see in the competition of leaders and persuaders for the support or assent of the masses a mechanism ensuring that it pays the leaders and persuaders to exercise their power and influence in the interest of the masses, or else they point to defects in the mechanism and suggest improvements. At the most abstract level, they try to define the competition for popular support most likely to ensure that power and influence are exercised in such ways that the persons subject to them are better able to achieve their own aims.

I shall be concerned with attacks on Western democracy and doubts expressed about it just as much as with utilitarian or partly utilitarian explanations of it—explanations which sometimes come close to being defences as well. My purpose will be to look critically at a number of arguments about a certain type of political system rather than to attack that system or defend it; though, no doubt, as I go about my purpose, I shall reveal, sometimes without being aware that I do so, my own preferences and prejudices.

The fundamental rule of Bentham, its relation to morality and to the self-preference principle

(a) The early Utilitarians, Bentham and his disciples, put forward a rule which they called the greatest happiness principle. They treated it as an ultimate or fundamental rule, but it is not easy to decide its precise status in their eyes. Sometimes they spoke of it as if it were a truth apprehended by reason in the same sense as the axioms of the mathematician were then supposed to be; as if it were a self-evident truth. At other times they spoke as if the rule followed logically from the fact (or what they took to be a fact) that every man desires what is pleasant and avoids what is painful. At still other times, they spoke of it as if it were the one rule that is accepted in all societies. It may not be expressly formulated everywhere but it is everywhere used as a guide to action.

The greatest happiness principle has been much criticized, and has also been amended by critics who believed that Bentham was substantially right and yet also mistaken. He was mistaken in equating happiness with pleasure and the absence of pain, and in speaking of quantities or lots of happiness; but he was right in supposing that the prime function of social rules is, or ought to be, to enable human wants to be satisfied as far as possible in accordance with the preferences of the persons whose wants they are. The greatest happiness principle, *Act so as to ensure, as far as you can, that the persons likely to be affected by your action get as much happiness as possible*, is not a rule that men can use as a guide to action, especially if happiness is taken to be a surplus of pleasure over pain. What is more, it is a rule that most people have never heard of. Far from being an ultimate moral rule, it is not properly a moral rule at all. It is not a rule like *Keep your promises* or *Do not tell lies*.

We could perhaps substitute for Bentham's greatest happiness principle another rule, *Act so as to ensure, as far as possible, that the persons likely to be affected by your action can satisfy their wants in the order of their own preferences*. This rule might be, to use a term now much in favour with social scientists, more *operational* than the greatest happiness principle; there might be many more situations in which it would be possible to act upon it. But this, of course, would not suffice to make it a moral rule, ultimate or otherwise. Even more obviously than Bentham's principle, it is a rule thought up by philosophers or by social theorists for their own purposes. It is a product of sophisticated controversy, and not a rule that people in any society, let alone all societies, use to guide or to control action, or to assess other rules. It is not a rule of the sort that people call moral even in advanced societies where moral rules are distinguished from rules of other kinds.

There is no ultimate moral rule or principle of the kind imagined by Bentham, and few moral theorists would now claim that there is. There are, to be sure, some rules (about keeping promises, not betraying friends, and so on) accepted in all, or nearly all, societies, and it can be plausibly claimed for them that their general observance is in everyone's interest. We can, if we like, call them universal moral rules. But none of them is like Bentham's general happiness principle or any other rule that a Utilitarian moralist might formulate to meet the objections to Bentham's principle. None of these applies on all occasions, which is what Bentham claimed for his principle. For though he admitted (whenever he remembered to do so) that the circumstances and wants, and therefore also the social rules, of different peoples can differ greatly, he ordinarily took it for granted that a rule is not properly moral unless it is in keeping with the greatest happiness principle. He assumed that any rule that men are obliged (or have a duty) to keep can be deduced from the greatest happiness principle together with their wants and circumstances. He appears also to have believed that the greatest happiness principle is everywhere accepted, even by people who cannot formulate it correctly and often fail to observe it.

Today the moral theorist, even the Utilitarian, puts forward no 'master' rule of this kind, though he often assumes that rules which are generally accepted and about which people 'feel strongly', as they do about moral rules, serve or are believed to serve some common interest. He assumes that people who 'accept' a rule as a moral one believe that it is everyone's interest that everyone should observe it, and respond to the breach of it in ways that differ from their responses to breaches of other kinds of rules; they 'condemn' the breach of it in others, and feel 'guilty' when they break it themselves even when nobody else knows they have done so. Their acceptance of the rule as moral consists of much more than their merely thinking it desirable that there should be sanctions to discourage breaches of it.

But 'condemnation' and 'guilt' are not simple ideas. Just what attitudes, what responses to the actions of others or of ourselves, have we in mind when we speak of 'moral' condemnation and 'moral' guilt? And cannot people be trained or otherwise brought to respond in these ways to breaches of rules that do not, and perhaps are not even believed to, serve common interests?

Bentham seems to have had more than one opinion about what constitutes the morality of a moral rule. Sometimes he spoke of moral obligation as if it consisted merely in being liable to suffer a certain kind of penalty, not legal punishment but the 'disapproval' of others. This disapproval, presumably, would not be an unthinking response but would consist of some kind of hostile behaviour directed towards someone believed to have broken some rule. There is, presumably, no disapproval unless whoever 'feels' it would, if challenged, say of the person he disapproved of: 'I condemn him because he did *this*', *this* being some action or failure to act that breaks a rule. But, clearly, there can be disapproval in this sense though nobody believes that the rule in question serves a common interest.

Even if we suppose with Bentham that actions and omissions are not ordinarily disapproved (in whatever way *moral* disapproval differs from other kinds) unless they are breaches of rules which are in the common interest, we cannot be sure that this is always the case. Some rules outlive their utility, and some perhaps never were useful, despite the widely held belief that they were and still are. We must suppose that Bentham was aware of this, for he did not preach unquestioning obedience of accepted moral rules.

If we insist that a rule, to be moral, must not only be used in certain ways (to justify certain kinds of condemnation, including self-condemnation), but must also be *believed* by those who use it to serve a common interest, we may find ourselves having to admit that in some societies there are few, if any, moral rules, or that the rules whose breach is most strongly condemned are not moral. For though in all societies some of the rules the breach of which is strongly condemned do in fact serve common interests, there may be societies in which people are not aware that this is so or take little account of it. In these societies the importance of rules held to be important may consist in the belief that they are of divine (or some other) origin. And the response to breaches of rules believed to serve common interests and accepted merely on that account may fall far short of this strong condemnation.

Even where actions that are strongly condemned do break rules believed to serve important common interests, the belief—as Bentham knew—may be mistaken. Must we then say that a rule can be moral, even though this belief about it is mistaken? Bentham and his disciples did not, I think, raise this question. Bentham sometimes spoke as if the morality of a moral rule consisted in how people respond to breaches of it, or in these responses together with certain beliefs held to justify them,˙ and sometimes as if it consisted in certain consequences of the rule's being generally observed. He never, I think, went so far as to combine these opinions by saying explicitly that a rule is not moral unless it serves some important common interest and is generally believed to do so, and breaches of it are strongly condemned.

Bentham was primarily a legal reformer, but a Utilitarian may also be a moral reformer. He may want people who do not yet do so to recognize that certain rules serve important common interests, and may expect their coming to recognize it to move them to condemn strongly what they had until then been indifferent to. If the morality of moral rules consists, not merely in their being in the common interest, but also in the belief that they are so and in the responses to breaches of them generated by this belief, then the arguments of the moral reformer, if they are found convincing, make rules moral which were not so before. But moral reformers, even the Utilitarians among them, do not speak as if they were trying to make rules moral that are not so, or trying to deprive moral rules of their moral character; they speak as if they were trying to get people to recognize the moral character of rules that are moral independently of this recognition.

James Mill in his *Fragment on Mackintosh*, though he often calls moral approval and disapproval *feelings*, also at times calls them *judgments* and implies that these judgments are not so much responses to breaches of rules serving to discourage such breaches as invocations of rules which are effective because of people's feelings or beliefs about the rules.[1] This implies that the moral character of rules consists, in part at least, not in the response to breaches of them, but in the way they are used deliberately to control behaviour, other people's and one's own. James Mill does not, I think, say enough about moral judgments to explain how the use of moral rules to control behaviour differs from the ways in which rules that are not moral are used for the same purpose. But even if he had done this, the objection could still be made that moral reformers, and in general people who dispute about moral principles, do not speak as if they were trying to induce others to use or to cease using rules in the special ways that make them moral rules, but speak of the rules as if they were moral independently of how they are used.

On the other hand, if the morality of a moral rule consists merely in its serving some important common interest, someone who recognizes that it does so may yet ask why he is obliged to observe it. For its serving a common interest is one thing and his being obliged to observe it is another. Is he obliged to observe it by virtue of some rule requiring him to observe rules serving common interests? But why should he observe this rule about rules? And what is involved in his being obliged to observe it? To *recognize* that a rule is in the common interest is merely to admit that its general observance has certain consequences; it is not to *recognize* an obligation to observe it. Recognizing an obligation is different in kind from recognizing a fact. What can this recognition be if it is not a readiness to use rules in certain ways, or a disposition to respond to the breaking of them in certain ways, or both the one and the other? But if this is so, people engaged in disputes about morals must have illusions about what they are doing; for they speak as if they were trying to induce each other to recognize the morality of rules whose moral character is independent of the ways in which people use them or respond to breaches of them,

[1] *Fragment on Mackintosh*, 1870 edition, pp. 363ff.

whereas what they are in fact doing is trying to get one another to begin or to cease using and responding to rules in these ways.

The idea of a basic rule or principle requiring people to observe rules that serve common interests is, just as much as Bentham's greatest happiness principle (or any substitute for it which improves on it by rejecting its unrealistic hedonism), an invention of the philosophers. Ordinary people know nothing of it. To be sure, they often respond favourably to invitations to promote a common interest, though they also quite often respond unfavourably on what they believe to be moral grounds. It is by no means obvious that the best way to get people to recognize that a rule is a moral rule is to persuade them that it serves a common interest, especially if a common interest is thought of as Utilitarians think of it, as something that enables people to satisfy their wants more efficiently.

Nobody (not even Bentham) denies that men's wants are affected by their moral standards. Thus, even if it were true that they come to 'accept' (that is to say, to invoke and to respond to invocations and breaches of) the first moral rules to arise among them so as to make it easier for them to satisfy wants as yet unaffected by moral standards, this would no longer be true of rules accepted by them after they had acquired such standards. To be sure, these later rules might also in their turn come to be accepted because they made easier the satisfaction of wants, but the wants would then no longer be morally 'neutral'. Thus, even if this account (which is not the only plausible one) of the origins of particular moral rules were true, it would not follow that we could say of any society's moral code, taken as a whole, that it either was or was not better adapted than some other code to satisfying men's wants; for, if there were any considerable change in the code, there would also be a considerable change in the wants.

It is only among beings who 'accept' moral rules, who use and respond to the use and breach of them in specific ways, that arguments about what is and what is not morally obligatory have any point to them. In a community (if any such were possible) in which there were no beings capable of 'accepting' rules in these ways, there would be no moral rules, though there might be rational beings who observed rules from motives of prudence. That a rule is, and is recognized to be, in everyone's interest is not enough to make it a moral rule.

(b) Not only Bentham, but others too, have taken it for granted that, if it is someone's interest that a rule be generally obeyed, it must also be his long-term interest to obey it himself. This, in strict logic, is not true. For example, if a man has been for a long time a successful thief, and has good grounds for confidence in his own skill and continued success, it is not his interest, not even his long-term interest, to observe the rule requiring him to abstain from what belongs to others. Yet it is his interest that the rule be generally obeyed. For if it is not obeyed by the great majority of people the social order on which he, as much as the honest man, depends to achieve his purposes (or to maximize the satisfaction of his wants), will disintegrate. His long-term interest is that the rule be generally obeyed, except by himself and his partners in crime, if he has any. It is not much to the purpose to say that crime is a risky business. So, too, is keeping a grocery store. Crime, let us hope, is more risky than most honest occupations, but there are some honest occupations more risky than most crimes. And, in any case, it is not irrational to take risks. If a rational action is one correctly designed to maximize the satisfaction of wants, dishonesty can be as rational as honesty.

Of course, if it is a man's interest that a rule be generally obeyed, it is also his interest that anyone inclined to break it should be liable to suffer if he does so. Nor can he reasonably expect an exception to be made in his own favour, for it is against other people's interest that it should be made. Besides, their willingness to obey the rule would be weakened if an exception were made in his or anyone else's favour, unless it could be shown to be in the general interest that it should be made. Therefore, it is his interest that the rule be generally observed and enforced, even though, as in the case of our imaginary thief, it is also his interest himself to break it from time to time—for this is how he makes his ample and dishonest living, how he (given his wants and preferences, his abilities and his temperament) effectively maximizes the satisfaction of his wants or, as some contemporary social and political scientists prefer to say, his 'goal achievement'.

The dishonest man, no less than the honest one, needs to make use of social rules, especially those general rules whose breach evokes the strongest feelings of resentment and disapproval, the moral rules. It is often his interest, just as it is the honest man's, to invoke one or other of these rules against someone else. This he cannot do effectively unless he does so in a way which implies that in like circumstances the rule may be invoked against anyone, himself not excluded. He would fail of his purpose if he invoked the rule in such a way as to suggest that he himself was not bound by it. He would act irrationally were he to claim for himself an exemption which he could not, if challenged, show to be in the general interest, or justify by appealing to some principle accepted by the persons he was trying to influence. But he would not act irrationally were he to break the rule whenever, to the best of his information and taking the future into account as far as he reasonably could, he stood to gain by doing so.

There are successful criminals who owe their success more to judgment than to luck, and we cannot say that they act irrationally merely because their success depends on most people keeping rules which they themselves, from time to time, prudently and secretly, break. No doubt, if everybody acted as they do, they would be much worse off than they are. But then most people do not act as they do, and it is reasonable for them (the criminals) to act on the assumption that criminals are, and are likely to remain, a relatively small minority. Provided they have good reason to believe that most people will keep the rules which it is the interest of both criminals and honest men should generally be kept, and that they themselves, by taking care, can sometimes break them with impunity, they act rationally in their own interest. We cannot deny that they act rationally merely because they cannot themselves effectively invoke the rules against others without implying that they too are bound to keep them. Admittedly, their behaviour goes against the principles they profess; or, as we sometimes say, it 'contradicts' their principles. But to say this is to speak metaphorically. Though you contradict yourself if you say that *everyone* is bound by a rule and then claim not to be bound by it yourself, you do not act irrationally if you invoke a rule against others while yourself breaking it from time to time to your own advantage.

APPENDIX B

Democracy misconceived: a paradox

I have already quoted Professor Dahl saying that 'it is fashionable in some quarters to suggest that everything believed about democratic politics prior to World War I, and perhaps World War II, was nonsense'. The suggestion here, presumably, is not that it was absurd of these people (whoever they were) who wrote about democracy before 1914 to believe that government ever had been or could be democratic; it is rather that they had absurd beliefs about what makes government specifically democratic. Democracy as they described it never did exist and probably never could exist; but then they quite misconceived its nature. They were victims of illusion, but their illusion consisted, not in the mistaken belief that democracy could or did exist, but in their misguided claim to have explained it.

This suggestion, as soon as we examine it closely, seems rather odd, or at least puzzling. Political behaviour is not like a physiological process. If we hear someone say that everything believed about the functions of the heart in the human body before Harvey published his *De Motu Cordis* was nonsense, we may think that he exaggerates but he makes a statement that could be true. A man need not know that he has a heart for his heart to behave normally, and when he first hears that he has one, he may have quite mistaken beliefs about what it does. But democratic politics is a system of behaviour which cannot be defined apart from the intentions of the persons whose behaviour it is and the rules they consciously observe. It is a highly complicated and sophisticated system of deliberate behaviour and it could not function as it does unless the persons engaged in it had many true beliefs about what they were doing when they acted politically, and at least some of them had some true beliefs about the system as a whole. The system can, of course, subsist though no one has a clear and full understanding of how it operates as a whole. It can subsist though the persons involved in it have false beliefs about it.

Indeed, it has sometimes been argued, not implausibly, of a particular system that it could not function as it does *unless* people had false beliefs about it. This is what Marxists often say of bourgeois democracy; and we cannot dismiss the assertion as too absurd to be taken seriously. But it hardly makes sense to say of a highly sophisticated system of deliberate and rule-directed behaviour that everything believed about it before a certain school of theorists set about trying to explain it was false. In the social sciences, theory waits on practice, not only in the obvious sense that it seeks to explain it, but also in the less obvious sense that many of the ideas it uses to define and to explain the behaviour it studies are ideas already involved in that behaviour. The man engaged in democratic politics does not stand to the democratic theorist as a bird stands to an ornithologist. The theorist cannot explain the politician's behaviour without taking into account how that behaviour appears to the politician, how he conceives of the political world in which he acts. But how a man's behaviour appears to him in a social context is his theory about that behaviour; it is not a set of visual and other sensuous images, or reflexes, or tendencies to act. It is something that can only be expressed in words; it is essentially descriptive and explanatory.

Democracy is a highly sophisticated political system. This is true not only of the democracy practised in the West in the last century or so; it is true even of Athenian democracy. Indeed, democracy and political theory were almost born twins; they were born in Athens in quick succession. The two great political theories of antiquity that have come down to us, Platonic and Aristotelian, were both reactions to democracy; the first altogether hostile and the second more moderate and impartial. But theories as sophisticated as these do not emerge suddenly in an intellectual desert; they are fruits of controversy. They appear in highly articulate and self-critical societies. Democracies are politically very self-conscious societies. They exist only where citizens have a fairly elaborate image of the political community they belong to. It is to some extent because they have this image that they want to be active politically, true though it is that they acquire the image in the process of formulating their political aspirations and endeavouring to realize them. Democratic societies are politically self-absorbed; they do not take themselves for granted. They are introverted, sometimes self-satisfied and sometimes anxious about themselves. Systematic political theory is in them more abundant, more influential, more intimately bound up with practice than in all others— with only one important exception.

The exception is the self-styled revolutionary state, as France was under the Jacobins or Russia has been under the Bolsheviks. But the revolutionary state, though it is seldom democratic, is nevertheless a phenomenon of the democratic age. As often as not it claims to be democratic, and in any case is a product of the kind of widespread discontent which finds expression in equalitarian and democratic slogans.

In studying democratic theory we are studying something which is of the essence of democracy. This is true, even though the theory may seem to us seriously inadequate. Inadequate though it is, it gives us an insight, not just into what people have thought and think about democracy, but into what democracy is. Democratic theory is of the essence of democracy in much the same way as a man's conception of himself is of his essence. The conception is partly true and partly false, but even what is false about it can help us to understand what sort of man he is. A man's false beliefs about himself often reveal his aspirations, and we do not understand him fully unless we understand what he aspires to be. We misunderstand him equally if we take his false beliefs for true and if we neglect them on the ground that they tell us nothing about him.

I must not take too seriously Professor Dahl's quip about what it is fashionable in some quarters to suggest about old-fashioned democratic theory. He was no doubt pulling the legs of some of his colleagues in the political science and government departments of American universities. He never meant to be taken literally, and I have quoted him only to introduce some remarks I want to make about the relation of social theory to social practice generally, and of democratic theory to the practice of democracy in particular. In recent times in academic circles, above all in America though in Western Europe as well, it has been the fashion to question the use of studying political theory, especially the political theories of the past, even the recent past. This fashion has been understandable, even excusable, because many of these studies, often in marked contrast with the theories they study, are poor and thin. But even when they are good of their kind, they are apt to be dismissed as mere 'intellectual history'; the implication being that this kind of history, though it may at its best tell us a great deal about what people have thought in the past, has virtually nothing to tell us about how they behave in the present. The implication is, I believe, false. The political theories of the past, even when they purported to explain how governments were organized and how they functioned, and not to tell them what they should do, were often grossly inadequate, even the best of them. But they did help to formulate the aspirations which in part moved men to make the changes that produced the political systems we know today. The modern state is to a considerable extent a product of political theory, and especially of democratic theory. But the theory which helped to produce it is not the theory of the persons who now in some quarters suggest that old-fashioned democratic theory is nonsense; it is rather this old-fashioned theory. If then this old-fashioned theory is nonsense, the modern democratic state is at least in part a product of nonsense. If that is so, then it is nonsense we do well to study, not just to discover how foolish political theorists could be in the past, but the better to understand our own political behaviour.

As a matter of fact, old-fashioned democratic theory, even when it seeks to explain how democracies function, has a great deal of sense to it. But this, I hope, is not a point I need insist upon. Nobody is seriously concerned to deny it, not even teachers of political science in the United States. I suspect that what these critics of old-fashioned theory have in mind is not that there is no truth or sense to it, nor even that there is only a little, but rather that it has been superseded by a type of theory superior to it. There was a good deal of sense to Ptolemaic astronomy as also to Galen's beliefs about the heart and the blood-vessels, and yet the Ptolemaic theory was altogether superseded by the Copernican and Galen's theory by Harvey's. Once the newer theories appeared, the older ones could be safely ignored by someone whose only concern was to understand the behaviour of the planets or of the heart and the blood.

But old-fashioned political theory cannot be safely ignored in this way. Not so much because it has affected political behaviour as because of the way it has done so. There have been many theories produced about animals, some of them a long time ago. These theories have affected the breeding and training of animals; they have helped to produce new species or new forms of behaviour among old species. Some of these theories are now obsolete and are no longer studied, except by historians of science, even though in their day they had a considerable influence on farming and stock-breeding and therefore on the behaviour of animals. Nevertheless, we can explain adequately how animals behave even though we know nothing of these obsolete theories. We need to know about these theories only if we want to explain when and how certain new species came into being or new forms of behaviour appeared. Theory, old-fashioned and new, has affected the behaviour of many more animals than just men.

But man alone among the animals known to us is a maker and user of theories and of the ideas they contain. He alone is an ideological animal, and is therefore affected by ideology in ways that other animals are not. To understand his behaviour we must understand how he uses the ideas and the rules whose use makes it the kind of behaviour it is. In primitive societies these ideas and rules are not products of theory, even though, in the eyes of the social anthropologist who studies them, they may constitute a coherent system in which is implicit an ordered view of the world. But in advanced societies they are, to a greater or less extent, products of explicit theory. This is never more true than of the ideas and rules involved in political behaviour, especially when that behaviour is democratic politics.

Let me give an example to illustrate my meaning. Almost everyone admits that, if a country too large to practise direct democracy is to be reckoned democratic, the men who have the final say in making law and policy must be popularly elected and the elections must be free. Stalin, Krushchev and Tito have admitted this as readily as any political leader in the West. That is why they have always claimed that in Russia or Yugoslavia under their rule elections have been free. Whether in fact they have believed what they said is here irrelevant. The point is that they would not have said it unless they had taken it for granted that in a democracy elections are free. But what are we to understand by free elections? How are we to decide what it is about elections that makes them free?

If we make a comparative study of elections in all countries that claim to be democratic (or whose rulers make this claim on their behalf), we will no doubt find that they have a good deal in common. Shall we then take what is common to them, or some part of it, and say that it is in this that the freedom of elections consists? But we in the West do not admit that elections in the Soviet Union really are free. Shall we then make a comparative study of elections in the countries that are genuine democracies? But how do we decide in the first place which those countries are? We must surely have some idea of what free elections are before we can make this decision. No doubt, our comparative study of these elections will enrich and make more precise our idea of what constitutes the freedom of free elections, but we must have some idea before we decide what to include in our comparative study.

The proper method, when we pursue our study, is not to make a list of the features common to these elections and then conclude that they are the essential features of free elections. For we may find that some of them are superfluous in the sense that if they were lacking the elections would be none the less free on that account. They may serve some other purpose without contributing to the freedom of elections. Of other features we may say that, though they are needed in all these countries to ensure that elections are free, they might not be needed in others whose circumstances were different. These features would not be superfluous where they exist but equally they would not be essential to democracy; they would merely be necessary in all countries which happen to be genuine democracies. We may conclude also that in some of the countries included in our study elections are freer than in others, or freer under some conditions than others. Finally, we may conclude that elections in none of these countries are as free as ideally they might be.

In reaching our conclusions, we should not be appealing to principles and ideals that just happened to be ours. On the contrary, we should be appealing to the principles and ideals of the peoples whose political behaviour at elections we were studying. We should not be judging them in the light of standards peculiar to ourselves; we should be seeking to define the standards implicit both in their own behaviour *and* in their explanations and criticisms of that behaviour. We should be engaged necessarily in conceptual analysis and in the critical appraisal of arguments whose purpose is to justify or to condemn. For, unless we were so engaged, our comparative study of political practice would not help us to find out what we want to know. The ideas analysed and the arguments appraised would be in large part inspired, directly or indirectly, by a variety of systematic theories. The people using the ideas and making the arguments would no doubt, many of them, have an uncertain grasp of these theories, and the theories themselves would not be fully compatible with one another nor fully consistent internally. But to understand the ideas and the arguments we should have to know something about the theories.

If we want to decide what it is that makes elections free, we must not, of course, confine ourselves to studying political theory any more than to making a comparative study of political practices. We cannot get the criteria we want merely by looking at what theorists of democracy, working in the privacy of their studies, have had to say about free elections. Not even what they are agreed about gives us the criteria we need, for some theorists have been less perceptive than others and have missed some of the essentials. We can get our criteria only by seeing how elections are conducted, by examining critically what is said for and against the ways in which they are conducted, and by considering the theories which have inspired these attempts to justify and to condemn. We must do all this even though our purpose is not to tell people how they should conduct elections; even though our aim is only to define that sense of the term free elections which enables us to understand both how people behave at elections and how they appraise that behaviour.

Chapter 2

The Attack on Democracy as an Illusion

The writers who in the last thirty years and more have taken what might be called a new look at Western democracy, discarding what seemed to them the grosser misconceptions about it, took up the business of explaining (and often also justifying) it after it had been under attack for a considerable time as a sham. The attackers have been mostly Europeans and the theorists and apologists coming after them mostly Americans. The 'new look' began with Schumpeter, who moved to the United States from Central Europe, was familiar with German and Italian doubts about democracy, and produced a summary account of a democratic system which made many of the doubts seem irrelevant or less serious than before. Schumpeter was not perhaps as much an innovator as some of his disciples or admirers have supposed him to be. But he has inspired, especially in his adopted country, a long train of ingenious and realistic theorizing about democracy.

In this chapter and the next I want to discuss the attack on democracy as a sham or an illusion. This attack has taken two different though related forms, one more popular and cruder than the other. The cruder attack, which I shall call *anarchist* or even *anarcho-Marxist*, is important both historically and because it expresses sentiments which are still widespread and strong. The other attack I shall call *academic*, partly to distinguish it from the first and partly because the three writers (Michels, Mosca and Pareto) whose ideas and arguments I shall be discussing claimed to be, and were recognized by others as being, social and political scientists. The academic attack is important, not because it expresses popular attitudes and feelings, but because what I have called the new look at Western democracy is largely a response to it.

In the present chapter I shall consider the attacks of the sceptics and their significance generally, contrasting the academics with the anarchists, and I shall also discuss briefly a few of the arguments of the anarchists. In the next chapter I shall look rather more closely at some of the arguments of the academic sceptics, and in particular at assumptions and implications not noticed by the writers who used the arguments. If I spend more time on Michels and Mosca, and even Pareto, than on the anarchists, it is not because, in general, they were more influential. On the contrary, the anarchists and Marxists came closer than they did to expressing doubts and resentments that were (and still are) widely shared and politically important. But my concern in this book is primarily with ways of explaining and assessing Western democracy which have become the fashion in intellectual and academic circles in the West, and above all in English-speaking countries, since the Second World War. These ways are much more a response to the attacks of the academic than of the anarchist sceptics.

Robert Michels produced a pioneer study of political parties; and if he was concerned mainly with parties of the Left, it was because in his day they were the ones that prided themselves most on being democratic. Michels questions their pretensions, and in the course of doing so uses arguments implying that democracy is impossible in the modern world. If he does not say it in so many words, he does suggest it. Mosca, in *Elements of Political Science* (a work better known in this country under the title, *The Ruling Class*, English translation, 1939) reaches this conclusion quite explicitly; and so too does Pareto in his *Treatise on General Sociology* (1916), of which the English translation is called *Mind and Society* (1935).

I shall not attempt even the briefest summary of these well-known (or, rather, often mentioned) books. They are all long, and one of them very long; and I shall deal only with some of their arguments because they raise points that I want to consider. Robert Michels in his sociological study of political parties speaks of what he calls 'the iron law of oligarchy'; he discerns in the large democracies of the West tendencies to oligarchy which, in his opinion, greatly weaken, if they do not destroy, their claim to be democratic. Though he does not call them sham democracies, some of his arguments, if they are sound, imply that this is precisely what they are. Michels, who took pride in studying society scientifically, no doubt thought it improper for a scientist to come to such a bald conclusion. In the Preface (written in 1915) to the English translation of his great book, he thinks it enough to say, 'democracy, at once as an intellectual theory and as a practical movement, has today entered upon a critical phase from which it will be extremely difficult to discover an exit', and to claim that his 'general conclusions as to the inevitability of oligarchy in party life, and . . . the difficulties which the growth of this oligarchy imposes on the realization of democracy, have been strikingly confirmed in the political life of all the belligerent nations immediately before the outbreak of the war and during the progress of the struggle'.[1] Michels has a great deal to say about this critical phase and its attendant difficulties, and barely a word about how to get over the difficulties. The main, or at least the most striking, argument of his book is that the organizations needed to work mass democracy develop in ways that make it very difficult indeed to achieve the ideals of democracy. Though he does not go so far as to exclude all hope of genuine democracy in the modern world, he points to no reasons for being hopeful.

Mosca is bolder than Michels; he does not stop at saying that democratic ideals are difficult to achieve but implies quite clearly that they are unattainable; he speaks of a 'political class' that dominates the majority even where there is a parliamentary system. But, as we shall see later, he points to this conclusion cheerfully enough and is not sorry that the ideals of naïve democrats should be out of reach. Far from disliking the parliamentary regimes of his day, he defends them with considerable energy; he merely argues that they too are run by a political class. It is as simpleminded, apparently, to want to get rid of them on the ground that they do not live up to democratic ideals as to suppose that they do. Democracy may be an illusion, but the peoples who are victims of this illusion are nevertheless among the more fortunate.

Mosca, Pareto and Michels all three take it for granted that, even in the Western democracies, it is the leaders who really matter politically and not the masses they lead. Michels, purporting to give the gist of Mosca's opinion, says that the majority are 'pre-destined . . . to submit to the dominion of a small minority, and must be content to constitute the pedestal of an oligarchy'.[2] But the doctrine of 'the elites' in relation to the masses is associated more with Pareto even than with Mosca, and I shall discuss it along with another doctrine of Pareto's, that human behaviour is much less *logical* (or, as we should say, *rational*) than is ordinarily supposed. This doctrine, too, is not peculiar to Pareto, nor even original with him; but he makes more of it, perhaps, than anyone before him, drawing larger and more varied conclusions from it. I shall not follow any of his arguments in detail; I shall merely use two of his most widely known doctrines as points to start from in discussing the role of leaders in political communities. Everywhere, so Pareto tells us more elaborately even than Mosca does, the passive majorities are dominated by the elites; and everywhere human behaviour is largely non-logical or non-rational—though, apparently, not equally so in every sphere of human

---

[1] Robert Michels. *Political Parties, A Sociological Study of the Oligarchical Tendencies of Modern Democracy*, translated by Eden and Cedar Paul, Dover Publications, pp. viii, ix.

[2] Michels, *Political Parties*, p. 377.

activity. For example, it is more logical in the sphere of production and exchange than in the political sphere. Pareto was an economist before he took up sociology in general, and political sociology in particular; and we must allow him the prejudices of his profession.

I must confess that I do not share the admiration often expressed for Pareto as a political sociologist. He seems to take it more or less for granted that, if political behaviour is predominantly non-logical and the initiative belongs to leaders rather than to the people they lead, democracy is impossible; though this, as we shall see, is by no means obvious. He therefore devotes his energies much more to showing that human behaviour is largely non-logical, especially in the political sphere, and to showing that always and everywhere there are leaders busy doing the leading, than to explaining how all this, even if true, justifies his scepticism about democracy. His distinction between logical and non-logical behaviour is open to serious criticism, and his ideas about elites and their social functions are none too clear; but for my purpose, I need not consider them. I shall confine myself to giving reasons why we cannot conclude that democracy is an illusion because political behaviour is largely non-logical, or because there are elites everywhere.

When, in the second part of this book, I consider what Schumpeter and American writers who build on the foundations he laid have to say about democracy, I shall argue that they do not so much deny the facts of political life, as Mosca and Michels (and even Pareto) present them, as explain them differently. Of course, they reject some of their pretended facts but others they do not question; they merely incorporate them into their theories. These writers, Schumpeter and his intellectual posterity, I shall call *Revisionists*. Far from denying that democracy is possible they offer an explanation of it, but one that is radically different (so they think) from the explanations demolished by the doubters. The revisionists assume that what they have to say is newer than in fact it is. For example, Schumpeter dismisses the idea of 'the will of the people' as an absurdity, forgetting (or perhaps not knowing) that, long before he was born, Bentham had poked fun at the notion that there is such a will: a will that governments, if they are democratic, ought to give effect to. Bentham at that time was not yet a democrat, but later when he became one, he did not change his mind on this point. A representative government, he then argued, can be relied upon better than other kinds to promote the people's interests because it owes its power to a popular vote at free elections, and because such elections are held at regular intervals. But Bentham was not, as Schumpeter was, putting forward a theory of democracy designed to meet, or to set aside as irrelevant, the objections of a Mosca or a Pareto; he was not *revising* democratic theory to bring it closer to the facts of political life in countries that prided themselves on being democracies; he was merely arguing for universal (or at least manhood) suffrage at a time when only a small minority of his compatriots had the vote.

The Revisionists have indeed been innovators, though less so than they imagine. They have wanted to produce a more realistic theory of democracy, one that takes account of the facts of political life in the great democracies of the West, and especially in the United States, which is not only the largest of them but the one to which most of the Revisionists belong. To take only the writers whose arguments I shall be discussing: Schumpeter emigrated to the United States and there produced *Capitalism, Socialism and Democracy* (1942), while Dahl, Lindblom and Downs are all native Americans. So too is C. Wright Mills, whose conception of an elite I shall discuss in some detail. Wright Mills, of course, had his doubts about American democracy, which he expressed in his book *The Power Elite* (1956). He might therefore be reckoned a Sceptic rather than a Revisionist; and yet I shall put my assessment of his arguments into the second part of this book, if only because the Sceptics whose ideas I discuss in this chapter and the next all wrote before the Revisionists produced their theories, whereas Wright Mills was familiar with Revisionist theories and critical of them.

The writers I call Revisionists, unlike the Sceptics before them, are all, in the broad sense of the term, Utilitarians. They do not call themselves so; they never refer to Bentham and very seldom to John Stuart Mill, and they see themselves as bringing not utilitarianism but democratic theory up to date. Yet most of the time, they take it for granted that the proper business of government, or at least of democratic government, is to make it easier for people to pursue their own interests successfully; and some of them even speak of 'maximizing' 'goal achievement' or 'want-satisfactions'. Three of the writers whose arguments I shall discuss, Schumpeter, Lindblom and Downs, are or were economists, and economics is the most utilitarian in method of the social sciences. I have therefore decided to follow up my discussion of certain aspects of these revisionist theories with an assessment of utilitarian explanations of political behaviour, enquiring how far, within what limits, such explanations are possible. This assessment of utilitarian political (and especially democratic) theory makes up the sixth chapter of this book. The seventh and last chapter, after a brief summary of what has gone before, puts forward suggestions for an alternative and (I hope) simpler and sounder method of explaining and even justifying democracy; for in the sphere of political theory explanation and justification, though they are distinct, are also closely related operations. Democracy, I shall argue, is best defined as a political system in which people have certain rights and obligations; and their having the rights must be justified not on utilitarian but on quite different grounds. The responsibility of rulers to subjects, which is the essence of democracy, can be defined realistically only in terms of these rights and obligations; indeed, it consists in being able to exercise rights and carry out obligations that cannot be justified on utilitarian grounds.

Mosca and Michels, and Pareto too, when they say or imply that democracy is impossible or very difficult to achieve, presumably have in mind democracy as believers in it imagine it to be. These believers think of it as a system in which the people decide what they want done about the larger issues that face the community and choose deputies to put their decisions into effect. Where there is democracy, according to this idea of it, there is a will of the people, and the business of the government is to carry it out. But, so these doubters in their different ways say, there is no such will, and there could not be in our vast modern societies; and therefore democracy is an illusion. The reply of the Revisionists is that, though democracy according to this idea of it is indeed impossible, the idea is a misconception. This misconception they sometimes call the 'classical' theory or idea of democracy; it must, they say, be abandoned and something more realistic put in its place.

Though I agree that the idea is largely misconceived, and that there is a need for something better, I fail to see why it should be called 'classical'. It does not come to us from the Greeks; for it is an idea of representative democracy, and the Greeks knew only the direct kind. Nor does it come from Rousseau, the first of the great modern champions of popular government; for he was also the first to argue that where the people choose representatives to make law and policy in their name, they have no political will. Nor, lastly, does it come from Bentham and James Mill, the earliest utilitarian champions of representative democracy. Already a hundred years before the attack on the classical theory of democracy was launched Bentham was making fun of the term 'the will of the people'. This theory or idea is I suggest, much better called *popular* than *classical*; it is to be found much more in the speeches of radical politicians, in newspapers and journals with a wide circulation, and in ordinary talk about politics than in the works of serious students of government, not to speak of books that are recognized 'classics'. It is an idea (or set of ideas) that belongs much more to political rhetoric than to systematic, political theory. What political scientists, especially in America but not only there, call 'the classical theory of democracy' is, I suggest, an invention, or rather construction out of bits and pieces, of the writers who attack it. To set up for demolition a straw theory made up of popular illusions is, I admit, sometimes a good way of putting across one's own ideas; but it is, I think, less than generous to foist the theory on poor Rousseau or on other early champions of popular government or parliamentary democracy. It may even be imprudent in a world, even an academic world, in which the 'classics' of political theory are still sometimes read.

I have thought it best, before looking at the attitudes and arguments of the Sceptics, to indicate what I mean to do in later chapters, so that the reader can see how what I say about the Sceptics fits into my argument as a whole. The recent theories of democracy that are my main subject, the theories of the writers I call Revisionists, of whom Schumpeter is the first, are a response to attacks on a certain type of democracy, or rather on ideas widely accepted in countries claiming to be democracies of that type. They are, of course, more than just a response to these attacks; but a good way of getting at the gist of what they say about representative democracy is to consider how far they meet the objections of the Sceptics. What they call 'the classical theory of democracy' is really, at bottom, their interpretation of ideals that such writers as Mosca and Pareto dismiss as unrealizable; and these ideals are implicit in popular ways of talking about democracy. And yet, as we shall see, these ideals and the misnamed 'classical theory' made out of them do, after all, owe something to Rousseau; they are, if you like, perversions or misapplications of what he said. If Rousseau, instead of saying that the people's will cannot be represented, had been in favour of representative democracy and had spoken of it as he in fact spoke of direct democracy, then he would have produced a theory not unlike what Schumpeter called the 'classical theory of democracy'.

Before I move on to discuss the arguments of the Sceptics, I should point to a difference between the anarchists and Marxists, on the one hand, and the academic Sceptics (Pareto, Mosca and Michels), on the other. Though they all agree that democratic ideals cannot be realized in society as it is, the anarchists and Marxists, unlike the others, have hopes for the future. They do not say that the ideals can never be realized. Indeed, in their own way, they accept the ideals; they want the individual to have the liberties that the liberal and the democrat claim for him, and they agree that decisions that affect the people should be taken either by themselves collectively or by persons answerable to them for what they do. The illusion, as the anarchist or Marxist sees it, is the belief that these ideals can be realized in bourgeois society; for they are necessarily out of reach while the economy and the social order remain as they are in the West. But if they were to change in certain ways, and they may and probably will do so, then these ideals could be achieved. Therefore, it is reasonable to aim at achieving them by transforming society. But Pareto and Mosca, and also (though less boldly) Michels, speak of these ideals as if they were forever unattainable. They admit, of course, that the social order will change in the future but not in ways likely to bring genuine democracy within reach.

The anarchist and Marxist attack on bourgeois democracy

It may seem odd now, more than fifty years after the October revolution, to put anarchists and Marxists together, especially when talking about democracy. Most avowed Marxists today are members of the Communist Party or are sympathizers with it, and the state is nowhere more powerful and more careless of the mere individual than where Communists are in control of it. But we must remember, not only that there are Marxists who dislike the Communist Party and what it stands for, and whose right to call themselves disciples of Marx is as good as anyone's, but also that the doctrine of the 'withering away' of the state is still an article of faith (at least officially) among Communists. This doctrine is essentially anarchist; it is the anarchist ingredient in Marxism.

What exactly will disappear when the state does so, just what institutions and practices will then cease to exist, is not explained in detail by those who predict or long for this disappearance. They seem to agree that there will then be no organized force to ensure that people obey social rules or to punish them for failing to do so, and that such public authority as survives will be exercised either collectively by those subject to it or by agents closely responsible to them. The anarchist ideal is not a rejection of democracy but of organized force and remote and irresponsible authority. There must be no forcing people to do what they do not want to do, and as little directing them what to do as possible, and such directing as there is should be done either by the entire community or by persons whom they authorize to do so and from whom they can withdraw the authority as soon as they please.

If by democracy we mean some such political system as we have in Britain or the United States, or even Switzerland, then, of course, the anarchist does not think much of it; he does not want what is called democracy in the West, though for the time being, for lack of anything better, he may put up with it. Yet there is a sense in which he is the most extreme of democrats, going further than anyone else in insisting that such government as there must be should be truly popular. Thus, he challenges other democrats to be true to ideals they share with him rather than rejects those ideals; he wants them taken further, perhaps much further, than most people believe they can be taken.

You will have noticed perhaps that I have passed from speaking of the anarchist and the Marxist to speaking of the anarchist alone. This is because the anarchism of Marxists, and especially of Communists, is today suspect. It is difficult to believe that Communists take seriously the doctrine that the state must eventually disappear, and with it the organized use of force and all irresponsible authority. If they took it seriously, they would surely be embarrassed by what they do, and change their ways. And yet the doctrine still has its attractions for them; it came into the world long before they got power anywhere, and was used then, as it still is now, to attack the 'bourgeois' governments of the West. Freedom and truly popular authority—the avowed ideals of the 'bourgeois' liberal and democrat—are impossible (according to this doctrine) while the state survives, and can be achieved only after it has ceased to exist. Therefore the institutions that 'bourgeois' liberals point to as evidence that in the West the individual is free and that governments are responsible to the people can be dismissed by the Communist as no evidence at all; for he claims to know (by the light of his doctrine) that where the state survives there can be neither freedom nor truly responsible government. The absence in countries controlled by his party of institutions that mean so much to the Western liberal leaves the Communist unmoved, for this absence does not mean (as he sees it) that these countries are less democratic or free than the so-called democracies of the West.

The point of the anarchist (and even Marxist) attack on 'bourgeois democracy' as a *sham* is not really that bourgeois governments, even when they are popularly elected, do not in fact govern in the general interest, though they claim to do so. Anarchists no doubt believe this also, but it is not the real point of their calling bourgeois democracy a *sham*. Even a direct democracy can govern badly, can fail to govern in the general interest, even though that interest is by definition the people's interest and it is the people who do the governing or some of it. Just as an agent can act with the consent of his principal, and yet act against his interest. The point of calling 'bourgeois' democracy (or any other kind) a *sham* is presumably that it is not what its name implies that it is; it is not government responsible to the people.

The anarchist holds that all forms of 'government' are bad. All forms claim to govern in the general interest when in fact they do not do so. Only in the society of equals with no state in it will the general interest no longer be sacrificed to some partial interest. Now, aristocracies and oligarchies claim to rule in the general interest just as much as 'bourgeois' democracies do; but the anarchist (and the Marxist too) ordinarily thinks it enough to call them 'oppressive' without calling them 'shams' as well. Their claim to govern in the general interest may be false, but in another respect they are what they pretend to be; they are governments responsible only to a small part of the people, which is precisely what is implied by the names given to them. But the 'liberal democracies' of the West belie their name, for they are not democracies. In the eyes of the anarchist (and the Marxist too), they are oligarchies dressed up to look like democracies.

The reasons that anarchists, and others who think as they do, give for holding that 'bourgeois' democracy is a sham are by this time familiar. I shall not consider them now in detail because, as we shall see, the more important of them recur, in rather more sophisticated forms, in the doubts about democracy in general expressed by such writers as Pareto, Michels and Mosca. Perhaps four of these reasons stand out among the others: (1) where there are great inequalities of wealth, then, whatever the form of government, power and influence always belong mostly to the wealthy, if only because they alone can afford to provide their children with the expensive schooling needed to fit them for positions carrying power and influence; (2) where the political system, to work effectively, calls for large organizations, power and influence belong to their leaders rather than to the rank and file; (3) where there are great social inequalities, leaders, no matter how modest their social origins, soon acquire the attitudes and ambitions of the privileged and lose touch with their followers; and (4) power and influence depend greatly on information, and the wealthy are better placed than the poor both to get information and to control the distribution of it.

These are, at least in the West, old and familiar objections to representative democracy; and though the earlier and simpler versions of them came from anarchists and others on the extreme Left, they have been repeated, qualified and elaborated upon by more academic students of society and government. The writers I call Revisionists take large account of them; though, in their eyes, they are not defects peculiar to 'bourgeois' democracy but tendencies that we must expect to see operating in every great democracy of the industrial age.

If we look at the anarchist attack on 'bourgeois' democracy, not in detail but in a general way, we see that it is an attack on two fronts. This type of 'democracy', we are told, is a sham because there is implicit in it an absurd, an impossible, claim: that there can be political equality where there is not social equality. But 'bourgeois' democracy is also a sham, so it would appear, for a quite different reason: because it assumes that government can be responsible to the people even though only a small fraction of holders of public office are popularly elected. Even where, as in the United States, this fraction includes not only the legislative but some of the highest executive officers, holders of public offices who are appointed to them outnumber the elected by hundreds, if not thousands, to one. What is more, among the elected, the greater an officeholder's authority, the larger usually his electorate and the more tenuous therefore his responsibility to his electors, and the less say electors have in choosing candidates for the office.

We have here two different objections to our sort of political system, of which only the second implies that it is the very structure of government, as we know it, which is incompatible with genuine democracy. Anarchists insist as much on this second objection as on the first; they want to abolish, not just social inequalities, but all authority (except perhaps over children) not exercised by or responsible to the persons subject to it. That is why they want to abolish the state. Though they seldom explain just how the business of the community is to be done when the state has disappeared, they insist that equality of income and opportunity is not enough; that public authority (or what survives of it when the state disappears) must belong to the people collectively or to their mere agents.

Michels, who was familiar with the writings of Marx and Engels, and therefore with the anarchist element in their thinking, more or less agreed that the sheer size of the modern state, with its very complicated machinery of government, makes genuine democracy virtually impossible. The simplemindedness of which he accused the Marxists and anarchists consisted, not in their distrust of the modern state as essentially undemocratic, but in their (in his eyes) absurd belief that it could be abolished. The 'bourgeois' state, as they called it, owed its structure, not to its being an organ of class rule or to social inequality, but to the needs of industrial society. He did not deny the fact of social inequality, nor even that the state helps to maintain it; he merely rejected the idea that the state arises from this inequality and will disappear with it.

There are anarchists who, like some of the early socialists, condemn industrialism on the ground that it is incompatible with the equality and truly popular authority they believe in. But they do not all condemn it; and the Marxists, of course, accept it as a condition of progress. They want the blessings of modern industry without its defects; they want high productivity *and* authority exercised either directly by the people or by their mere agents. Or at least they ought to want all this if they really mean what they say when they dismiss 'bourgeois' democracy as a sham. If this is really what they want (and most anarchists if not Marxists seem really to want it), then they want more than is possible. They want—to adapt an old formula from the early days of socialism—no *government* and not too much *administration*; no class rule or organized use of force, and no authority 'remote' from the people. But how is the efficient administration of a highly industrial society to be reconciled with the requirement that everyone who takes official decisions must be responsible to the persons affected by his decisions? And how are the people to make or alter important social rules and take important decisions of policy? One reason, so the anarchists say, why force needs to be used to maintain order is that authority is remote from the people subject to it. How, then, must authority be organized to be brought close to them or placed collectively in their hands? How ensure that it is used sparingly, and not oppressively, when it is in their hands? What limits are to be set upon it, seeing that an advanced industrial society cannot do without it altogether?

Presumably, in an advanced industrial economy there must be a good deal of 'administration' on a large scale; that is to say, affecting everyone over a wide area or large categories of persons. How will this kind of administration, when the state has disappeared, differ from government as we know it today? Even if it deals only with the production and distribution of goods and services, its scope is wide. For services include, presumably, such things as education and the care of the sick and the old. And why not also, in a complex society where there are so many transactions between persons distant from and scarcely known to one another, the settlement of disputes? It is by no means easy to decide what activities at different levels of government could be dispensed with in an industrial society that was classless and without crime. Anarchist and even Marxist critics of our 'sham' democracies tell us much too little about the society of equals in which the state has disappeared. They tell us what principles are to be realized in it but not how they are to be realized: what the institutions of a highly productive society of equals would be like.

Rousseau was the first among modern political theorists to argue that some kinds of authority must be exercised directly by the people. He was no anarchist; and yet, like the anarchists after him, he attacked the large, the 'overgrown' state. And though, unlike the anarchists, he did not condemn the use of force to ensure obedience to social rules, he did care deeply for social equality. Indeed, one of his two reasons for disliking the large state was that (in his opinion) it leads necessarily to social inequality; the other being that inside it truly popular government is impossible. Both these reasons would seem good to anarchists. But Rousseau, unlike later critics of the bourgeois state and bourgeois democracy, made it quite clear what he wanted, and the price that would have to be paid for it. Truly popular government, he thought, is possible only in small and economically self-supporting communities without industry or commerce on a large scale. If the citizen is to be politically a man of independent judgment, he must be a man of property, and yet must not have so much property as to make other citizens dependent on him. Rousseau's ideal community consists of men who own the means of production they use, and who are equals in the sense that none can use his wealth to buy another's vote; or, as political scientists today might put it, in the sense that they are all of roughly equal strength as bargainers. Only in a community of equals of this kind can the people rule themselves.

Rousseau tells what popular government is. The people must themselves make the laws; for, if they elect representatives to make laws on their behalf, they have no political will. And if they have no such will, he implies, then their representatives cannot be responsible to them. The people can elect magistrates to administer the laws and to settle disputes according to law, and these magistrates can be responsible to them; for the people, having made the laws themselves, are competent to decide whether they are being properly administered. Rousseau does not discuss the taking of major decisions of policy as distinct from the making of laws, but it would be quite in the spirit of his general argument that such decisions should be taken by the people collectively. Only if the people keep for themselves the most important business of government, which is the making of law (and, I suggest, policy), can the persons to whom they entrust the rest of that business be responsible to them. If they leave it to others to transact *all* public business, doing nothing themselves except decide who is to transact it, they exercise no real control over their rulers, and there is *no will of the people* or, as Rousseau has it, *no general will.*

To guard against the assembly of the people being improperly influenced by special interests, Rousseau forbids what he calls 'partial associations' within the state; that is to say, groups organized to promote group interests. Thus, truly popular government, as he conceives of it, requires that there should be, to use terms invented since his day, neither pressure groups nor political parties. Organizing to push special interests makes it, not easier, but more difficult to take decisions in the common interest; and giving citizens the vote does not ensure that they understand the business done by the persons they vote for or exert real control over them.

Quite deliberately, I have put Rousseau's meaning in my own words, so as to bring out more clearly what he has in common with anarchist and Marxist critics of the modern state, and of 'democracy' as it is practised in the West. To be sure, in his day there was as yet no democracy in the West (except in small parts of Switzerland), but there were already large states with powerful central governments remote from the people and, in Britain at least, there was a partly elected legislature. Anarchists (and Marxists also in their anarchist moments) share Rousseau's fear of authority remote from the people and his passion for equality, but they are less specific than he is when it comes to explaining how what they think desirable is to be achieved.

Though Rousseau was no anarchist, anarchism owes a good deal to him. The two things that he cared most about, and to which he gave new meanings and a new urgency (social equality and freedom from remote authority) have also been supremely important to anarchists: to Godwin, to Proudhon, to Bakunin and even (in their anarchist moments, which were not few) to Marx and Engels. Though Rousseau has been called, not unjustly, an idolator of the state, the state he idolized is the community small enough to be so organized, economically and politically, that its members are equals and can together decide what obligations are to be laid on them all. He did not believe, as most anarchists do, in equality between the sexes, and he spoke, as no anarchist does, of the citizen being forced to be free when compelled to obey laws that are pronouncements of the general will; but he was also the first enemy of the state grown too large for the freedom of its citizens, and of the representative system as necessarily a sham.

The academic sceptics contrasted with the anarchists

The anarchists, like Rousseau before them, have in mind a society of equals in which men are really free in the sense that social rules are entirely acceptable to them, and nobody feels himself bound by a will alien to him; a society in which the ideals of the democrat are achieved as they never can be while the established order endures. They outdo other democrats, and especially the ones they call 'bourgeois', in their devotion to these ideals; for, when they attack 'democracy', it is not these ideals that are their targets, but a political system for which it is claimed (in their opinion falsely) that it achieves the ideals, or comes close to doing so. These ideals, they believe, can be achieved; and many, if not all of them, also believe that they can be achieved in developed industrial societies.

It is this belief that the writers I call academic sceptics dismiss almost with contempt. Indeed, it seems at times to follow from their ways of speaking about society and social change that neither equality nor democracy is possible. These ideals arise only in relatively advanced societies, necessarily so organized that equality and popular government, as Rousseau and others have imagined them, are unattainable. This might seem, to many people, a sad, even a bitter, doctrine; for, if it is true, it follows that ideals that have come to mean more to us than they meant to our ancestors are out of reach; it follows that industrial society, our kind of society, produces aspirations that cannot be satisfied because that society is as it is and cannot be otherwise. Old forms of inequality disappear but new ones arise. People may say that there is less inequality than there was, but this is because there is less of the old kinds of inequality which they have learnt to resent as obstacles to progress. Progress they associate with the rise of new organizations and institutions, whose purposes they still approve or have not yet learned to challenge. It is the generations after them who notice and resent the new forms of inequality that come in with these organizations and institutions. For example, radicals who for years have seen the trade unions as champions of equality are apt not to see the inequalities that arise with their growing power. People who have learnt to associate harmful social inequalities with the division of society into classes take it for granted that, as that division grows less sharp, social inequalities decrease or become less harmful; which is by no means obvious.

If government is to be efficient in an industrial society, if it is to provide what is expected of it, it must operate on a large scale; it must govern communities whose populations are reckoned in tens and even hundreds of millions. There may be local and regional governments, but there must be, if government taken as a whole is to do what is expected of it, a great concentration of power at the centre. Organizations outside the government, if they are to exert much influence over it, must either be large or else recruited from the wealthy or the powerful. If they are small and influential, they speak only for small sections of the community, and then their influence, being out of all proportion to the numbers they speak for, is a danger to democracy. If they are large, then what happens within the vast apparatus of government happens also inside them. Effective power in them soon comes to belong to leaders remote from the rank-and-file and influenced much more by the small number of persons having access to them than by the much larger number who do not have it.

There are, in arguments like these, two elements which are perhaps worth distinguishing, a *social* element and a *political* one. In a complex society (and industrial societies are extraordinarily complex) there is a wide diversity of functions. The community of the interdependent is vast; the number of persons on whom any one person depends for the goods and services he needs to live as he is accustomed to do is enormous, and most of these persons are unknown to him. He is not, as he would be in a primitive community, dependent only on a small company of kinsmen and neighbours. Not only are the occupations of the persons he depends on many and varied, but some carry much greater prestige and influence than others do. This is true, not only of societies in which class divisions are important, but also of societies in which they are not. Even in societies where a man's or a woman's opportunities are neither much restricted nor much enlarged by the social status of his or her parents, there can be a wide diversity of occupations of which some attract much greater deference than others.

Apart from these inequalities not directly connected with the political system, there are others involved in that system. The machinery of government is vast and intricate, and some holders of office not only have much greater official power than others but are much better placed to exert influence unofficially and to manipulate opinion. So we have here, even in a society which is more or less classless, as the word class is used by Marxists and by others who look forward to the disappearance of classes, two powerful causes of inequality: an extensive division of labour and the size and complexity of the machinery of government. The two, of course, go together; for there is no need of a vast apparatus of government in a simple society with no great division of labour, and the division of labour cannot go far unless society evolves methods of interpreting, enforcing and changing an intricate system of rights and obligations. Nevertheless, it is possible and useful to distinguish inequalities that arise directly out of the structure of government and politics from other kinds.

Anarchists and socialists, not least among them Marx, have seen in the division of labour the prime cause of inequality, and have sometimes even spoken as if this division could be abolished. Presumably, they have not meant to be taken literally, and it might be closer to their meaning to say that what can be abolished is less the division of labour than its harmful effects. In an industrial society, however organized, there are many different kinds of work done, many of them highly skilled; and everyone depends for his living on the work of an enormous number of people, of whom all but a few are unknown to him. The socialist or anarchist who deplores the evil effects of the division of labour (the inequalities and restraints arising from it) believes, presumably, that an industrial society can be so organized that everyone has varied and congenial work to do, and can pass easily from one occupation to another. This must be what he means by getting rid of the division of labour in some future society that is to be as productive as ours, or even more productive. Unfortunately, he seldom explains how this is to be achieved, and merely takes it for granted that it will be in what he calls 'the classless society' or 'the society of equals'.

It was this socialism, still closely related to anarchism, which to Pareto and Michels seemed absurdly simpleminded. And in their time there was still a large dose of it in Marxism. No doubt, even in those days, socialist leaders, especially if the parties or groups they led were large and politically important, were not in practice much concerned with it; but they spoke of it respectfully on what they thought were appropriate occasions. Michels, who studied the German Social Democratic Party (at that time still officially Marxist) in great detail, was keenly aware of this separation of practice from theory. In practice, the German Socialist leaders accepted the established order, social and political, and confined themselves to getting greater benefits inside it for their supporters. They went on speaking of revolution and of the eventual transformation of society, but their words meant little, either to others or themselves. They were not self-seeking, and Michels does not suggest that they were; they wanted better pay, better conditions of work, better education, greater security for working men and their families. They also wanted, as socialist leaders still do, no matter how practical and hardheaded they may be, greater equality of opportunity.

But equality, as most socialists (not excluding Marx) understood it in the days when there were as yet no powerful socialist (or Marxist) parties in the world, involves a good deal more than we today, even the socialists among us, understand by equality of opportunity. Equality of opportunity, as we speak of it, is consistent with some occupations carrying much greater power and prestige than others, and with a division of labour that makes it difficult for people to move from one occupation to another. There is probably more equality in this sense in Britain today than there was before the First World War, and more also in Russia; it is easier now than it was then for the child of poor parents to get the education needed to qualify him to do work earning a high reward or otherwise attractive to him. But, once he has had his education and has started to work, it is perhaps no easier than it used to be for him to pass from one kind of work to another. Nor are different occupations markedly more equal in respect of the power or prestige, as distinct from the net income, they bring to those who enter them.

Equality of status among people engaged on widely different work depends, so the old socialists of the era before the rise of massive socialist parties believed, above all on two conditions: on the material benefits that a man gets having nothing to do with the kind of work he does, and on everyone being able to pass easily from one kind of work to another. The old socialists (including Marx) mostly took it for granted that these two conditions are compatible with industrial efficiency. Since their day it is widely admitted, even among socialists, that they are not. It is admitted also that industrial society requires a vast, and for some purposes, a highly centralized, and therefore hierarchical, machinery of government. Industrial society, capitalist or not, is unavoidably highly competitive because its efficient working calls for a wide variety of skills, many of them acquired only after long courses of expensive training, from which some people benefit much more than others do.

The kind of equality by which highly industrial societies set great store because it promotes efficiency is not only unlike the equality of Marx's communist society but incompatible with it. It is equality as most people today conceive of it, not only in the West, but in the Soviet Union. It allows of quite fierce competition for the better paid and otherwise more attractive jobs. In other words, it allows of considerable inequalities, and not only in capitalist countries. The question is: Are they inequalities compatible with democracy, with government genuinely responsible to the governed?

The answer to this question of the writers I call academic sceptics is that they are not. To this extent they agree with Marx (if not with the powerful men who in our day still call themselves his disciples) and with the anarchists. But in another way they differ from them, from Marx, from the Marxists of the pre-Bolshevik era, and from most anarchists; they differ from them in believing that nothing much can be done in industrial societies to reduce these inequalities. Socialism, in their opinion, can do little or nothing to reduce them. Or, if socialism is defined in such a way that a society cannot be socialist while it tolerates these inequalities, then it follows that an industrial society cannot be socialist. For, according to these sceptics, an industrial society is *necessarily* so organized that these inequalities arise. Of its very nature, it cannot be a society of equals, if equality is understood as most socialists still understood it in Marx's time; and so too it cannot be democratic in spite of the lip-service it pays to democracy. Indeed, it may not all be lip-service; aspirations to democracy may be genuine enough though the thing itself is out of reach.

Chapter 3

The Academic Attack on Democracy

The academic attack might almost be called the Italian attack, for Robert Michels was greatly influenced by Mosca and Pareto, and worked for a time in Italy. Though he was the youngest of the three, I shall look at some of his arguments first because I want to consider his iron law of oligarchy before passing on to examine the notions of 'a ruling class' and of 'elites', as Mosca and Pareto used them.

Michels and the iron law of oligarchy

I shall look only at some of the implications of one or two of Michel's general arguments and not at his whole account of how government operates in the larger Western states. I shall contest, not his facts, but the conclusions he draws from them.

In his book *Political Parties* (1911), one of the pioneer works of its kind, Michels quotes some sentences from Chapter IV of Book iii of Rousseau's *Social Contract*: 'Taking the word in its strict sense, there has never existed a true democracy, and there never will. It is against the natural order that the larger number should govern.' These sentences could serve as a text, not only for Michels, but for Mosca and Pareto as well.

As a matter of fact, Rousseau, in this chapter, is using the word *democracy* in a peculiar Aristotelian sense, different from ours. He means by it a political system in which all public offices are open to all citizens on the same terms; he has in mind what we should call the executive and judicial spheres of government. He is not denying, in this particular chapter, that the people can themselves make law and policy; he is not denying the possibility of what we should call direct democracy or direct popular government. He did, of course, believe that direct democracy is possible only when certain conditions hold, and that these conditions did not hold in Western Europe in his day. Nevertheless, the particular sentences that Michels quotes use the word *democracy* in an old Greek sense, which is not the sense in which Michels, Mosca and Pareto use it when they say or imply that democracy is virtually impossible. For they, by *democracy*, do not even mean direct democracy, or the making of law and policy by the people; they mean representative democracy. And when Michels says or implies that it is impossible, he means that representative government, however wide the electorate, cannot be (or is most unlikely to be) genuinely responsible to the people. He implies that representative democracy *on a large scale* is impossible. It is the scale of the operations, and not merely the fact that makers of law and policy are elected, that makes this type of democracy virtually a sham.

The sentences quoted from *The Social Contract* come from a chapter in which Rousseau discusses a tendency for power, no matter how it is legally distributed, to pass from many into few hands. This is Rousseau's version of what Michels, some hundred and fifty years later, was to call 'the iron law of oligarchy'. Power tends to pass from large bodies to small ones, and from persons who exercise it occasionally to others whose occupation is to exercise it, the holders of office, the professionals. In *Political Parties* Michels seeks to show how this law operates in a large political community, even when it aspires to democracy. His position, therefore, is different from Rousseau's; he does not say that representative democracy is a sham merely because it is representative. He does not argue that holders of authority cannot be responsible to the people, unless the people retain in their own hands one kind of authority, the right to make law and general policy. He argues that, given that representative democracies are in fact large political systems, the iron law of oligarchy operates strongly in them, destroying or seriously impairing their democratic character.

Now, clearly, in a representative democracy there is no question of the larger number governing. What, then, is the point of saying that this tendency to oligarchy, noticed by Rousseau, undermines even representative government? The point, presumably, is that it weakens, if it does not wholly destroy, the *responsibility* of elected officials to their electors. If you say to the citizen in a representative democracy that he is not actually a law-maker, he will not contradict you, even if he believes in the system. It is only if you go on to tell him that the persons elected to make the law are not in fact *responsible* to him and his fellow-citizens that he is likely to take issue with you.

Clearly, then, the crucial question here is, what is to be understood by responsibility? But this is a question that Michels ignores. By this I mean, not that he fails to put it in so many words and to give a definite answer, but that there is no inferring from his argument how he would answer such a question, if it were put to him. Though he concludes that representative democracy, organized as it was in his day (and still is now), can hardly be anything but a sham, he says nothing to indicate what conditions must hold if elected officials are to be responsible to their electors.

The gist of Michels's argument, by now a very familiar one, is this: representative democracy, especially where citizens are counted in millions, is possible only where there are organizations, political parties and other bodies, to nominate candidates and to formulate demands on behalf of the classes and groups whose votes they seek. The larger an organized body, the greater the tendency to oligarchy inside it. But where organizations indispensable to the functioning of a political system are oligarchies, the system itself cannot be genuinely democratic. Michels, in his book, is concerned chiefly with political parties, and with the German Social Democratic Party in particular, though he does also take notice of some pressure groups, especially the trade unions. What he calls 'the iron law of oligarchy' applies presumably to all organized bodies, except perhaps to very small ones, and not just to political parties and pressure groups, but it is above all its application to parties and pressure groups that concerns the theorist of democracy.

Parties and pressure groups do not have the same functions, and it could be argued that the political effects of their being oligarchic are different; for example, that whereas oligarchic political parties are a danger to democracy, oligarchic pressure groups are not, or are much less so. But Michels does not put forward this argument, and I shall not consider it.

Michels's book is not really a systematic study of the organization and functioning of parties and pressure groups in several of the larger democracies. It attends mostly to Germany and Italy, which were not, in Michels's day, widely acknowledged to be the most democratic of Western states. Nor indeed does Michels claim for them that, despite appearances to the contrary, they were as near to being democratic as, say, France or the United States. He was interested primarily in parties of the Left, especially socialist parties, and in working-class organizations, presumably because they took a special pride in being democratic. The German Social Democratic Party, about which he has much more to say than about any other single organization, was at the time that his book appeared much the most important party of its kind in the world. Being a Marxist party, it denounced bourgeois democracy as a sham; and it was often called, by its friends as well as its enemies, a state within the state. Its leaders claimed for it that it was genuinely democratic in a way that the German state was not.

To Michels, no doubt, it seemed that there could be no better way of driving home the point he wanted to make, that the iron law of oligarchy operates in all organizations, than to show it at work in trade unions and in socialist parties, and especially in the greatest socialist party of them all.

There are two parts to Michels's general argument: first he tries to show how all large organizations, no matter what their avowed principles or aims, tend to become oligarchic and authoritarian, and then he concludes that a political system unable to function without such organizations is not a democracy. But while the first part is a developed argument with copious (though not always convincing) evidence deployed in support of it, the second is little more than a bare assertion often repeated in rather different words. Michels gives reasons why we should expect his iron law to operate, and points to many examples (mostly, but by no means always, German and Italian) of its doing so, and then merely takes it for granted that where it does operate, the political system is not a genuine democracy. The conclusion seems to him so obvious as not to be worth an argument. All that needs to be established by argument is, he thinks, that the iron law does operate, even in popular and proletarian organizations. But this, so it seems to me, is a mistake; for a political system, though it includes organizations, is not itself one, at least not in the same sense as what it includes. We cannot simply take it for granted that it must be undemocratic if important organizations indispensable to its functioning are so.

Before I explain more fully why I think this cannot be taken for granted, I want first to look at some of Michels's reasons for holding that there is this tendency for all large organizations to become oligarchic. My purpose is not to deny the tendency but merely to suggest that some of the reasons that Michels gives (and thinks inmportant) are not good reasons.

Michels's book was the first of its kind, and there are confusions of thought and of purpose in it. There are even times when he comes close to suggesting that there is something undemocratic about the mere fact of leadership. He does not say this in so many words but some of his arguments imply it. On several occasions he accuses the socialists of being politically simpleminded, and he says of the German Marxists that they make the absurd claim that 'socialism knows nothing of leaders'. Their party, they say, since it is democratic has only *employees*, 'the existence of leaders being incompatible with democracy'.[1] In the eyes of Michels the claim is absurd, not because it suggests that democracy is incompatible with leadership, but because it implies that socialist parties and organizations are somehow exempt from the common lot of all large organized bodies. The leaders of the SDP are, he insists, *leaders* in just the same sense of

[1] R. Michels, *Political Parties* (Dover Publications Inc., N.Y.), p. 35.

the term as the leaders of any other party; it is no more true of them than of the others that they are the agents of their followers, carrying out their will.

In fairness to Michels I must say that the main thesis of his book is not that organizations having powerful leaders are undemocratic; it is rather that in large organizations leaders tend not to be responsible to their followers. These two assertions are not equivalent, and neither entails the other. And yet there are times when Michels comes close to treating the two assertions as if they were equivalent. He attacks the German Marxists, not for misconceiving democracy, but for claiming that their party was democratic.

On the face of it, it is odd to suggest that there is anything undemocratic about leadership. Democracy is a form of government, and all government involves leadership. Where there is government, and not just collective action for a short time and on a small scale, there are always some people set apart from the others because their recognized function is to take decisions that the others are expected or required to act upon. Whoever argues that large organized groups are incompatible with (or detrimental to) democracy must show, not that they involve leadership, even powerful leadership, but that the leadership they involve is of a kind that precludes leaders being responsible to their followers. Therefore, if he is really to make his point, he must distinguish between kinds of leadership and must show how some kinds exclude genuine responsibility while others do not. This Michels does not do, or indeed even attempt. He really does little more than give examples of undemocratic behaviour on the part of German and other leaders of socialist and proletarian organizations.

The idea that there is something inherently undemocratic about the mere fact of leadership is not confined to Michels and the SDP leaders of his day. It has attracted both democrats and sceptics about democracy. There are traces of it in the writings of Rousseau and Marx, and even larger traces in the writings of Mosca and Pareto, for whom democracy is only a myth, though not necessarily a harmful one.

I doubt whether any of these writers would, if challenged, have gone so far as to say that democracy is a contradiction in terms, though some of their arguments, taken literally, imply that it is. I suspect that what they really believed can be expressed in these words: leadership cannot be professional and continuous, with leaders clearly set apart from those they lead (or, in other words, authority cannot be regular and official) except in conditions which, if they do not preclude democracy altogether, are a standing threat to it. They are seriously concerned to suggest, not that all leadership is undemocratic (which really is absurd) but that, human nature and the conditions of effective leadership being what they are, almost as soon as stable leaders arise relations between them and their followers develop in ways which make it extraordinarily difficult for them to be responsible to their followers. This contention may or may not be true, but at least it is not obviously absurd. And yet, if there is to be any substance to it, if it is to be possible to draw useful conclusions from it—for example, if it is to help us decide how close we can get to democracy, how we can extend or strengthen it, or what we must forgo in order to get it—it must be put more clearly and carefully, more elaborately, than any of these writers have put it.

Suppose that there are a hundred men who, from time to time, have to take decisions which affect them all, and that nearly all the proposals and arguments put before them are made by some ten of them, who have no more authority than the others to make them but who just happen to do so. These ten men are, in a quite usual and proper sense of the word, *leaders*, and it is admitted by the others that they are. The others have noticed that all the proposals and arguments they listen to before they take their decisions are made by these men, and they do not mind this in the least. They could, if they wanted to, make proposals themselves and take part in discussing them. They could be talkers but they prefer to be mere listeners, except for the words they utter to express simple consent or dissent. Nobody would deny that in this community of a hundred men decisions are taken democratically, even though there are ten among them whose influence is much greater than that of the others. For the others choose to be silent when they could speak; they have learnt to trust the ten, to look to them to take the initiative both in putting proposals and in arguing for and against them. Even Rousseau would not deny that this community was democratic; nor, I suspect, would the American political scientists of our day who speak of what they call *political equality*, or the principle that no member of a community should have greater control or influence than another over decisions taken on behalf of the community. I doubt whether these theorists mean quite what they say; I suspect that equality of influence is only another word for some kind of equality of opportunity or right. Clearly, in the case I have imagined, the ten men who do all the proposing and discussing have, man for man, much more influence than the ninety who choose to be silent. But it is not clear that each of the ten has as much influence as any other. For a man's influence depends on how much other people listen to him and take account of what he says. Even if the hundred men in our community all made proposals and spoke for an equal time, it would not follow that each had as great an influence as any other on common decisions.

If, in our imaginary community, some of the silent ninety were to cease being silent—if the politically active minority were to increase to, say, forty—the hundred men might find that they were having to listen to more than they wanted to hear, that it was more difficult for them than it used to be to follow the argument and to make up their minds how to vote, and that the business of taking decisions in common was far too long. They might then agree to confine the right of making proposals and discussing them to ten of their number— perhaps the ten who were originally the talkers among them. Would this agreement make the community less democratic than it was before? All the men would still be voters and listeners, proposals would still be put to them, and they would reject or accept them by voting on them. They would merely be reverting deliberately to what had long been the practice among them before that practice had changed (in their opinion) for the worse. They would, of course, be making a rule of what used to be merely a practice, and in the process would be depriving nine out of ten of their number of rights they had long possessed but had also, until quite recently, refrained from exercising. Their reason for doing so would be that they thereby made it easier for them all to think clearly about issues of common concern and to take decisions without too much loss of time.

Why, then, should the community be any the less democratic? Rousseau, one of the most egalitarian of political theorists, would not have denied that the decisions of this community were expressions of the general will merely because only ten men out of the hundred had a right to make proposals and to discuss them. More than once in his political writings, he suggests that it might be desirable to confine the right of making proposals of law to only a few citizens. He had Greek examples in mind. According to him, what really matters, if the general will is to find expression, is that all the citizens should listen to the arguments for and against the proposals put to them, and should then vote on them. They should come to the assembly with open minds, and should then make up their minds in the light of what they hear there. What matters, presumably, is that the citizens should understand the issues at stake and should then make up their minds what should be done in the common interest. This, so Rousseau sometimes suggests, they are more likely to do if the majority confine themselves to listening and voting.

Rousseau was a champion of popular sovereignty, and in the community that I have imagined the people are sovereign in his sense. In it there are leaders and followers, an active minority and a less active majority. The functions and rights of each are clearly defined, and yet there is no equality of political influence, unless that is merely another name for the political rights that everyone has.

Michels quotes Rousseau with approval, though his own position is by no means the same and is less clearly stated. He does not, as Rousseau does, say that representative government cannot be genuinely responsible to the people; he says rather that the organization indispensable to that form of government in large communities makes it virtually impossible that it should be responsible. Rousseau's clear (though perhaps mistaken) indictment of representative government is quite different from Michels's doubts about the Western democracies of his day. That he should quote Rousseau in support of his own position suggests that his ideas about it are far from clear.

If we disagree with Rousseau, we do at least know what it is that we are rejecting. According to him, it is only when the people have a collective will that they can elect magistrates to act on their behalf who really are responsible to them for what they do; and the people have a collective will only when they make the laws and major decisions of policy. If they depute this, the fundamental business of government, to others, they fail to create the minimal conditions of genuine political responsibility. They may, of course, if they follow public affairs closely, have definite opinions about them, though few of them are likely to do this in the circumstances. But this is not the real point of Rousseau's rejection of representative democracy. Even if the citizens were all keenly interested in politics, there would still, according to him, be no political will of the people and therefore no genuine responsibility of rulers to their subjects. If the people merely decide who shall make law and policy, and do not make them themselves, those who do make them are not their agents. This argument of Rousseau's may not be convincing but at least it is clear.

Rousseau, of course, also believed that, even where the people do make law and policy, the magistrates (their agents) will be tempted to gain power at their expense, and that the odds are in favour of their eventually succeeding. The price of popular sovereignty is eternal vigilance, and in the world as it is this vigilance will always, sooner or later, be relaxed. The magistrates are few and the people many, even in a small community; the magistrates are busy at their official work every day, while the people, having other business to attend to, are politically active only from time to time. All officeholders, elected or not, try to increase their power. Being relatively few in number, organized and wholly taken up with the business of government, they (and especially the more powerful of them) are well placed to accumulate power at the expense of the sovereign assembly. The people's control over their agents, when those agents are organized bodies or full-time officeholders, is always precarious. This, if you like, is Rousseau's version of 'the iron law of oligarchy'. It differs in several ways from Michels's version but is in two crucial respects the same: Rousseau agrees with Michels that power tends always to pass from larger to smaller bodies and from part-time to whole-time wielders of authority.

I do not agree with Rousseau that a representative government cannot be responsible to the people. He takes too narrow a view of what is involved in holders of power being responsible to others for how they exercise it. Why this is so will, I hope, be made clear when I consider the accounts of democracy of the men I have called Revisionists. But I do understand Rousseau. I can see what criteria must be used to decide whether in any particular case the people are *sovereign* in Rousseau's sense of the word. I can see why, in his opinion, the people are not sovereign when they elect representatives to make laws and decisions of policy binding on them. I do not understand Michels nearly as well. I understand him, of course, when he says that organization, especially on a large scale, reduces the responsibility of persons elected to offices of any kind to their electors. I not only understand him; I also agree with him to some extent. But I do not see the force of several of his reasons for saying this, and I do not know what criteria he would use to establish whether or not a person elected to office was responsible to his electors. I suspect that some of his reasons are irrelevant, and that his ideas about political responsibility are more muddled than Rousseau's.

I shall not go into Michels's arguments in detail; I shall confine myself to some comments which will, I hope, be useful as preliminaries to the rather closer analysis that I shall make of some of the arguments of the Revisionists. Michels speaks of organization and its effects. All government is an organized activity; it is a form of collaboration governed by rules; there are established ways of taking decisions and of carrying them out. This is as true of direct democracy as of any other form of government; and the rules prescribing how decisions are to be taken and implemented inside it can be very elaborate.

As we have seen, Michels's argument is not that all organized collaboration for political (or indeed other) purposes eventually becomes undemocratic, no matter how democratic it was to begin with; it is that organized collaboration on a large scale does so. There are, so it seems to me, two main reasons why political writers come to this conclusion: one is that business can be done effectively only by a small number of people, so that the larger an organization the smaller the proportion of its members who take an effective part in running it; and the other is that the more complicated the rules of an organization, the greater the opportunities that leaders have of 'playing the rules' to impose their wishes on the rank and file. These are two different reasons, though they often go together; for, on the whole, the larger an organization, the more complicated its rules.

For obvious reasons, a direct democracy has to be small, whereas representative democracy, as we know it today, operates on a vast scale. But it need not do so. A community whose adult members were about as numerous as our House of Commons could be a representative democracy. It might even gain in efficiency by becoming one and ceasing to be a direct democracy. It would need, in any case, to elect executive officers to enforce its laws and carry out its policy decisions, and it might well choose to elect a small number of deputies to make its laws and decide its policies. Rousseau would say that, if it did choose to do this, it would cease to be a democracy. Or rather—since he used the word democracy in a special sense of his own—he would say that a people who chose to do this would be abdicating their sovereignty; and this, for him, would entail that persons exercising political authority in the community would no longer be responsible to the people for how they exercised it. It would entail, therefore, that the community had ceased to be democratic in our sense of the word, which is also the sense in which Michels uses it. Whether the citizens numbers six hundred or six million, whether or not there are parties and pressure groups among them, makes no difference here; if they choose to elect deputies to make their laws and to take major decisions of policy, they abdicate their sovereignty. They cease to be persons to whom holders of public offices can be genuinely responsible. Six hundred citizens need not make this choice, they need not abdicate politically, whereas six million have no choice but to do so. Nevertheless, so Rousseau implies, if the six hundred were to make this choice, it would have the same nullifying effect as if six million had made it.

It is perhaps a mistake to hold, as Rousseau was logically bound to do, that the choice is equally fatal to democracy, no matter how small the community that takes it. Still, whoever does hold this view does at least make his position clear. But Michels never goes so far as to say that government, if it is representative, cannot be democratic. He does not point to anything about the way in which a representative democracy, whatever its size, must be organized that precludes its being genuinely democratic. Such a democracy, if it were small enough, could be simply organized. It could operate without either parties or pressure groups. For example, there might be a rule requiring that candidates for office be nominated by any two or three citizens meeting for that purpose, and yet the number of candidates competing for any office might still be small enough for electors to be able to listen to them all and make up their minds which they preferred. The number of citizens nominating candidates might be small, so that the great majority of citizens would merely choose between candidates, having had no part in nominating them, just as they do in the vast democracies of our day, with their gigantic parties and innumerable pressure groups. What is more, in the democracy I have imagined, citizens might not be much better placed than they now are in Britain and the United States to get to know candidates' views about matters of public interest. Radio, television and the newspapers can as easily make a candidate and his opinions known to a hundred thousand electors as to a thousand. Why, then, should the small representative democracy I have imagined, without parties and pressure groups, be any nearer to being genuinely democratic than is the United States? Would Michels have said that it was nearer? Presumably he would, for he was committed to doing so by his thesis that it is primarily 'the iron law of oligarchy' operating in the parties and pressure groups indispensable to large democracies which greatly weakens, if it does not altogether destroy, their democratic character. But he would, I suspect, have been hard put to it to explain why.

In a country of several millions, democratic or not, there will be a wide variety of groups having different interests. If the country, besides being populous, is also industrial, literate and quickly changing, this variety will be greater still, and many of the groups will be organized to promote their interests. The business of reconciling these interests, of devising policies taking account of many and diverse claims that can only be partly satisfied, is intricate and difficult. The citizen who considers these policies will often not understand them, or will not understand how they affect his interests or the interests of groups and communities he is attached to or cares about strongly. If the country is democratic, and he is called upon to choose between rival candidates for office who support different policies, he may be incapable of making an intelligent choice. But— and this is the simple point I want to make here—this incapacity, while it has much to do with the size of the country and the complexity of the problems that governments have to settle, may have nothing to do with the size of parties or pressure groups. It is one thing to say that public business in the representative democracies of our day is so complicated that most of it is unintelligible to the vast majority of citizens, so that the persons who do this business cannot be genuinely responsible to those on whose behalf they do it. It is quite another to say that it is organized parties and pressure groups and their oligarchic character which have this effect.

Though the same causes—the size of the country, its political system, and the variety of group interests inside it—make public business complicated and also give rise to parties and pressure groups, it may be the first of these effects rather than the second that greatly reduces the responsibility of governments to the people. It has been argued, since Michels's time, that pressure groups and parties, especially large parties, by helping to moderate demands and to express them more clearly, by making realistic bargains and compromises, by proposing alternative policies and arguing for and against them, may make public business considerably more intelligible to the citizens than it would otherwise be. But the more intelligible that business to citizens whose votes can make or destroy governments, the more genuine, presumably, the responsibility of rulers to their subjects. How does the fact (if it is a fact) that all or most parties and many pressure groups are oligarchic affect their capacity to perform these services essential to large democracies? Michels does not really face this question and therefore does not answer it. He takes it for granted that, given that parties and pressure groups, like all organized bodies of any size, are oligarchic and bureaucratic, they cannot but undermine democracy. Democracy on all but the smallest scale cannot do without them, and yet they stifle the spirit of democracy.

Taking it for granted that where political parties are undemocratic, the political system must be so too, Michels devotes his energies mostly to showing that large parties are undemocratic, not excepting the German Social Democratic Party which prides itself on being the opposite. Some of his arguments, if we take them generally (without considering how far they apply to the SPD in particular) are sound enough. That there is a tendency for power to pass from the many to the few, and from occasional to frequent wielders of authority, is not to be denied. And, certainly, I have not wished to deny it or to suggest that the danger is small. Michels's book is important because it is the first close study made of this tendency; indeed, the first attempt to go further than Rousseau went in a few brief sentences of *The Social Contract*.

My objections to Michels are, firstly, that his general conclusion, that representative democracy on a large scale is impossible, rests on the premise, which he takes for granted though it needs to be argued, that a political system cannot be democratic unless the parties and pressure groups inside it are so too; and, secondly, that some of the evidence he points to in support of his iron law is irrelevant. Not everything that he takes to be a sign that democracy inside a party has disappeared or is disappearing needs to be interpreted as he interprets it. He is, I suggest, as he piles up evidence that this law is operating in that citadel of German democracy, the SPD, sometimes taken in by popular misconceptions. In saying this I question, not his facts, but the conclusions he draws from them. I accuse him of what many political scientists (I regret to say) seem to think are trivial faults, of irrelevance and confusion of thought, and not of being so unscholarly as to get his facts wrong.

Two charges often made against a political party (especially when

it is radical), and always resented by its leaders, are that it has ceased
to care for its principles and has grown bureaucratic. Though it is not
obvious that this indifference and this bureaucracy are evidence that
the party is undemocratic, they are often taken to be so. Both Michels
and the German socialists took it for granted that they are, so that
Michels, when he set about showing that the SPD cared little or
nothing for the Marxist ideology it professed and was also bureaucratic, was hitting where it hurt.

Michels, of course, does not assume that a party whose members
care deeply for its principles is democratic, for that would be an
absurd assumption easily disproved. He assumes rather that a party,
and especially an 'ideological' party, is unlikely to be democratic if
its leaders are not seriously concerned to promote its principles. This
is a belief still widely shared among radicals, who for the most part
think of themselves as democrats and men of principle. A radical
party can hardly be democratic, they think, unless it is 'ideologically'
sincere. Though all parties, as distinct from pressure groups, put
forward some principles, professing to do more than merely push the
interests of their supporters, it is radical and egalitarian parties that
are the most sensitive to the charge that their lack of 'sincerity'
proves that they are not democratic.

Speaking of the SPD during the years of its rapid growth before the
First World War, Michels shows how little its ideology meant to its
leaders. What the leaders were really concerned about was to preserve
the unity of the party, to maintain their own authority inside it, to
win over or to silence or make harmless those who opposed them, and
to get the votes on which the party's influence, and therefore their
own, depended. The Marxism they professed meant very little to the
leaders of the largest and presumably the most powerful socialist party
in the world. The intellectuals were intent on their doctrinal disputes
and the party leaders paid little attention to them, except when they
went so far as openly to challenge supposedly fundamental doctrines
to which the leaders had long subscribed without understanding them.
Though its creed was still revolutionary, the party had to all intents
and purposes ceased to be so, if indeed it ever had been so. Challeng-
ing the creed was, in the eyes of the leaders, not really heresy so much
as disloyalty; it was like disrespect for the flag, and had to be put
down to preserve party discipline and class solidarity. And Michels
might have added that a revolutionary creed can be a great asset to a
party that has ceased to be revolutionary, just as it can be a great
embarrassment. It can be an asset to the party by setting it apart from
other parties and giving it a sense of mission that they lack, and therefore a stronger hold over its members and supporters. Whether it is an
asset or a liability depends, of course, on circumstances.

Michel's assessment of the German Social Democratic Party, as it was in the years before he wrote his book and prehaps as it always had been, may well be substantially true; and if it is true, it is certainly important. It helps to explain why the party behaved as it did when war broke out, and again later when the Bolsheviks seized power in Russia. But how is it evidence that the party had ceased to be democratic? If Michels had shown that the rank and file still remained true to an ideology or to principles that the leaders no longer cared about, this would be some evidence that the party was no longer democratic. But, far from arguing that this was so, he admits that the rank and file were as indifferent as the leaders to Marxism.

Michels was himself no Marxist, and yet this argument of his, that a radical party which has ceased to take its ideology seriously has ceased to be democratic, has a Marxist ring about it. According to the Marxists, a proletarian party whose leaders care nothing for the theory which alone throws light on the real interests of the class cannot promote those interests effectively, and will eventually lose the confidence of the class and cease to be the party of the class, even though the workers continue to vote for it. This is a mysterious doctrine, and I forbear from commenting on it. But we have, I think, to accept some such doctrine as this, if we are to treat a party's indifference to its own ideology as evidence that it is undemocratic.

If the bulk of the German workers cared (as most historians seem to agree) even less than their leaders did for the Marxist principles of the party they voted for, the indifference of the leaders does not prove that they were unresponsive to the demands of the workers or that their power did not depend on the workers' support. If the leaders of an organization take no notice of the demands of its members, or these members are prevented or discouraged from making demands, this is evidence (as far as it goes) that the organization is undemocratic. But their caring little or nothing for an ideology or for principles, or even for 'real interests', that their followers care about even less than they do, is no evidence at all.

Nor is it clear why a party's being bureaucratic should make it internally undemocratic or subversive of democracy in the political system. An organization is bureaucratic when it has a hierarchy of officials to run it. But Michels, presumably, when he calls large organizations bureaucratic, is not just pointing to this feature in them; he is pointing rather to some of its consequences. Social and political theorists have differed considerably in their accounts of these consequences, but one consequence often noticed by them is that, in a large organization, the persons who run it spend a great deal of time discussing how it should be run, and are often intent on keeping to its rules without stopping to enquire what purposes the rules serve. The larger the organization, the more likely it is to be bureaucratic in this sense.

This we can admit and yet hold that the larger an organization the more desirable that it should be bureaucratic in this sense. It cannot operate unless it has many rules, and it is unlikely to operate efficiently if the rules are continually called in question. There is a division of labour among its officials, and it may be a good thing that some of them should devote most, or even all, of their energies to seeing to it that the rules are kept. The managers of a large organization cannot run it as an experienced driver drives his motor-car; they cannot keep their eye all the time on the road that leads to where they want to get to and not watch themselves driving.

No doubt, managers can frustrate the avowed purposes of the organization they run by excessive attention to the running of it and by too great a respect for its rules, and it is often this excessive attention and respect that we have in mind when we call the organization bureaucratic. We then use the words to pass an adverse judgment and not just descriptively. But excessive bureaucracy sacrifices the purposes of an organization to its internal politics and to its rules, no matter what the purposes are. It still has to be shown that when its purpose is to secure the election to public office of candidates responsive to the wishes and careful of the interests of the electors who vote for them (that is to say, when it is a political party), or when its purpose is to persuade the government to look after the interests of some part or other of the people (that is to say, when it is a pressure group), the organization is then most apt to sacrifice its purposes to its rules; or, in other words, to be bureaucratic in the bad sense. Was the German Social Democratic Party, when Michels wrote his book, more bureaucratic, in this sense, than, say, the German State Railways? Were the German trade unions more so than the vast organization controlled by Krupp?

Perhaps they were. It may be that organizations having political or quasipolitical purposes are in general more apt to be bureaucratic in the bad sense than even the largest organization whose purpose is to make as big a profit as it can, or to produce something as efficiently as possible, where efficiency can be measured in money or in some other precise way. Since the purposes of parties and pressure groups and the costs of achieving them are not easily measured, there is perhaps not much point in comparing these bodies with non-political organizations in this respect. Still, to the extent that it does make sense to compare them, it may be that they are, more often than non-political organizations, excessively bureaucratic. But this is not the point that Michels is trying to make. He seems rather to suggest that, if an organization claiming to be democratic (to have leaders responsible to its members) is bureaucratic, it is likely to be so in the bad sense. He produces a good deal of evidence to show that leaders (and not least the leaders of the SPD) spend much of their time trying to hold the organization together and to maintain their own positions inside it. He then concludes that they are more concerned about these things than they are about what the organization is supposed to stand for or about the interests of the groups which support it. But, surely, if the organization is to promote what it stands for, and if it is to further the interests of the groups which support it, it must hold together and must have a stable leadership. Michels makes no attempt to distinguish between situations in which holding a party together and maintaining one's position inside it frustrate its aims and harm the interests of its supporters, and situations in which they do not. He merely shows that in a large party leaders do spend a great deal of time on these holding and maintaining operations, and then concludes that they are sacrificing its aims and the interests of its supporters to their ambitions. He produces a whole lot of facts and then uses them indiscriminately to support a conclusion they do not support. Careful scholarship and careless logic!

Towards the end of his book Michels writes:

> The party is created as a means to secure an end. Having, however, become an end in itself, endowed with aims and interests of its own, it undergoes detachment, from an ideological point of view, from the class which it represents. In a party it is far from obvious that the interests of the masses which have combined to form the party will coincide with the interests of the bureaucracy in which the party becomes personified.[1]

As a matter of fact, as Michels no doubt knew in spite of what he says here, it is never the masses who combine to form a party; it is always a small number of persons who form a party in the hope that it will attract wide support. Presumably if a party does attract wide support it is the interest of its supporters that candidates put up by the party should get elected and should promote policies beneficial to the supporters or of which they approve. The interests of the party bureaucrats, as distinct from those of the mass of its supporters, consist, presumably, not in the private interests of the bureaucrats, but in the interests common to them as managers of the party. It is their interest to keep the party going, to retain their authority inside it, to get party candidates elected, and so on.

Michels says that it is far from obvious that their interests will *coincide* with those of the party's supporters. But just what does he understand by the word *coincide*? No doubt it is the business of the

[1] Robert Michels, *Political Parties*, p. 389.

party bureaucrats rather than of the party supporters to run the party, to hold it together, and to get its candidates elected. And yet it is the interest of the supporters and not only of the bureaucrats that the bureaucrats should do this. It may not be the interest of the supporters that the bureaucrats should retain their authority inside the party; it all depends on whether or not their retaining it is a condition of the party's doing efficiently what its supporters want it to do. Bureaucrats and supporters have some interests in common, and bureaucrats also have interests peculiar to them. Moreover, bureaucrats and supporters may not have the same order of preferences among the interests they share.

Obviously, the interest of party bureaucrats and party supporters do not coincide; for they have distinct as well as common interests, as people always do in any large organization with a wide diversity of functions. And people who have distinct interests may also have interests that are incompatible. Indeed, in any community or organization, even a small one, that lasts for a considerable time, there are bound to be not only distinct but also incompatible interests. What, then, is Michels concerned to say?

Presumably he is not just uttering a commonplace; he is not saying that in all organizations, and especially large ones, even when they claim to be democratic, there are incompatible and not merely distinct interests. He is saying that the managers of a large organization soon acquire interests incompatible with those of the mass of its members or supporters, and are so placed that they can promote these interests to the detriment of the interests of the mass. He is also implying that they could not, or could not for long, sacrifice the interests of the members to their own, if they were in fact responsible to them, if the organization were democratic.

Nobody would deny that organizations that purport to be democratic often become undemocratic, and that they do so because of the way that those who run them promote their own interests. But someone who, like Michels, is arguing that this happens always, or nearly always, must do better than just point to the fact of bureaucracy and show (what is no doubt true) that bureaucrats always have interests distinct from, and even incompatible with, the interests of the organization or community they claim to serve. Michels, as a matter of fact, has a great deal to say about how people who run an organization acquire interests and attitudes that are peculiar to them, and much that he says was new or not much noticed at the time that he said it. There is plenty to be learned from reading his book. But what he does not do is show how the pursuit of their peculiar interests by the managers of an organization purporting to be democratic prevents its remaining so for long. He quite often fails to distinguish between mere difference and incompatibility, between *distinct* and *conflicting* interests; and he seems to take it for granted that, where the interests of the managers conflict with those of the members of a democratic organization, the managers, simply because they run the organization, always can and nearly always will subvert its democratic character in order to get their way. But this is not obvious, and must not be taken for granted.

Political scientists now make a distinction, seldom made when Michels wrote his book, between the members of a party and supporters who are not members. Theorists of democracy fifty years ago mostly ignored this distinction, and this no doubt made it easier for them to assume that parties must be democratic if the political system is to be so. But we, who make the distinction, are aware that a party can be internally democratic, and yet the aims of its leaders diverge widely from those of the mass of its supporters. We are aware, too, that a party can be internally *un*democratic, and the aims of leaders and supporters diverge very little.

An *un*democratic party can, but need not, be dangerous to democracy. Whether or not it is must depend on its aims and the methods it uses (and is prepared to use) in gaining support and competing for power. Let us suppose, though only for the sake of argument, that the Conservative Party in this country is less democratic in its internal organization than is the Labour Party, and that the wishes of party members have considerably less influence in determining who the leaders of the party will be and what policies will be officially adopted. It might still be the case that the Conservative Party was just as successful as its rival at choosing candidates trusted by its supporters and mindful of their demands and interests, and that it contributed just as much to providing the country with governments enjoying wide support among the people, and to ensuring that they lost power when they lost that support. It might also happen that neither party had much success in promoting the interests of its supporters or of the people generally, though the leaders of each promoted their own and the party's interests with considerable success. What is more, their failure to promote more general interests might have little to do with their success in pursuing their own or the party's interests. They might have done much for their supporters and for the people and still have done as much for themselves and their party. All this is possible, but Michels's account of parties and their place in the political system takes no notice of it. He devoted his energies to showing that large organizations soon become undemocratic, and never seriously enquired how they must function in a political system to sustain democracy.

A political system is democratic if it operates in such a way as to

ensure that makers of law and policy are responsible to the people. It
may be difficult to assess just how far they are responsible. It is not
easy to define precisely the criteria of political responsibility; or at
least it would seem so, seeing how far political theorists have dis-
agreed about how they should be defined. It is possible so to define the
criteria that no country claiming to be a democracy satisfies them, and
to uphold the definition by appealing to common ways of speaking
about democracy and insisting that they be taken literally. But this
taking the rhetoric of democracy literally in order to explain democracy
away, though it can be amusing, is not enlightening. It also has the
disadvantage of dismissing political systems that differ greatly from
one another as equally undemocratic, though some come much nearer
than others to securing to the individual the rights that democrats
really care about.

Michels, in his pioneer work, appeals from time to time to the
authority of Mosca and Pareto. Socialists, he says, believe that some
time in the future there will be 'a genuinely democratic order', and
even the wretched conservatives, though they deplore its coming, admit
that it can and may come. The hope of the socialists is the bogy of
the conservatives. Only in what Michels calls the scientific world are
there already a few clear-eyed men 'who deny resolutely and once for
all that there is any such possibility'. These sceptics are to be found
especially in Italy, where they are led 'by a man of weight, Gaetano
Mosca, who declares that no highly developed social order is possible
without a political class, that is to say, a politically dominant class,
the class of a minority. Those who do not believe in the God of
democracy are never weary of affirming that the God is the creation
of a childlike mythopoeic faculty.'[1]

His own study of parties and trade unions seemed to Michels to
bear out the truth of what Mosca said:

> It would seem to prove that society cannot exist without a 'domin-
> ant' or 'political' class, and that the ruling class, while its elements
> are subject to a frequent partial renewal, nevertheless constitutes
> the only factor of sufficiently durable efficiency in the history of
> human development. According to this view, the . . . State cannot
> be anything other than the organization of a minority. It is the aim
> of this minority to impose on the rest of society a 'legal order',
> which . . . can never be truly representative of the majority. Even
> when the discontent of the masses culminates in a successful attempt
> to deprive the bourgeoisie of power . . . always and necessarily
> there springs from the masses a new organized minority which
> raises itself to the rank of a governing class. Thus the majority of
> human beings, in a condition of eternal tutelage, are predestined

[1] Michels, *Political Parties*, p. 377.

by tragic necessity to submit to the dominion of a small minority, and must be content to constitute the pedestal of an oligarchy.[1]

The political class or elite

The passage I have just quoted, though Michels presents it as a summary of the main thesis of Mosca's *The Ruling Class*, is equally in the spirit of Pareto's reflections on politics. It seemed to Michels that his own study of political parties bore out this thesis. But here, surely, he was mistaken. The thesis may or may not be true, but we certainly do not have to accept it if we accept the facts of political life as Michels presents them to us. It is a far cry indeed from showing that there is a tendency to oligarchy and bureaucracy in all organizations, and especially large ones, to proving that in every society, except perhaps the simplest, there must be a dominant minority who impose a legal order on a majority 'in tutelage' to them. It does not even follow that, where many of the organizations indispensable to the working of a political system are oligarchic, the system must be so; for a political system is not an organization in the sense that a party or pressure group or government department is one. It includes such organizations but is not one itself. Nor does it follow that, if a political system has many such organizations, the men who 'control' them form a dominant class or elite or group of elites who together 'control' society.

In any society, except the most primitive, we can distinguish the people whose acknowledged business is to exercise authority from the rest of the community; and if the society is at all developed, we can find surrounding these holders of public office other people whose business is to influence them or to comment on their activities or to promote successors to them. These 'professionals' in the sphere of government and politics are always a minority, though in recent times a much larger one than they used to be. Political relations among them, whether they are actively engaged in government or in activities ancillary to it, differ in important respects from political relations between them and ordinary citizens. It is these professionals, these political leaders and these persuaders (as American political scientists call them), who between them do the public business of the community. They are the active minority whose activities are nowadays studied in much greater detail than ever before.

But why call them, as Mosca does, the political class? What is the point of calling them a *dominant* minority? What are the implications of calling them, in the manner of Pareto, an 'elite'? It is true that Pareto often speaks of elites in the plural, and admits that there are

[1] *Ibid.*, p. 390.

conflicts between them; but he also speaks as if the elites, despite these conflicts, somehow collectively dominate the rest of the community. If the political class or elite or group of elites excel, it is presumably in power and influence. They may perhaps excel in other ways, but it is, presumably, their excelling in these ways that makes them a dominant minority. What then does this dominance of theirs, so fatal to democracy, consist in? It cannot consist merely in their exercise of the authority and influence which is theirs by reason of the offices they hold, whether they are public offices or offices in such bodies as parties and pressure groups. For, even if these elites, or at least some of them, were what Mosca and Pareto deny that they are, even if they were leaders genuinely responsible to the people, 'true representatives of the majority', they would still, presumably, have this authority and influence. The point of voting for them at elections would be to ensure that they had them; and if they were elected and failed to use them, they would be failing in their duty and could hardly be said to be representing or acting for the people who elected them.

Michels speaks of 'a scientific world' in which it is 'resolutely denied' that democracy is possible. This is the world of the 'political scientists' of his day, with Mosca occupying a high place in it, at least in the estimation of Michels. But, unfortunately, in this scientific world, several questions that need to be answered before we can decide whether or not democracy—and I have in mind, as Michels had, representative democracy—is possible were almost entirely neglected; as much by Mosca as by Michels, as much by Pareto as by Mosca. To say this is not, of course, to deny that a case can be made for holding that the political systems of the West fall so far short of being what their apologists claim they are that they hardly deserve to be called democracies; it is not even to deny that, if such a case were made, it would not owe something to Mosca and Michels, and perhaps Pareto as well. It almost certainly would; or, rather, its arguments would overlap considerably with theirs. It is to suggest only that their attacks on the pretensions of Western democracy, though perceptive and disturbing in some ways, are also to a large extent misdirected.

To call the groups who share authority a 'ruling class' or a 'ruling elite', to say that whenever one such 'class' or 'elite' disappears, another arises inevitably to take its place, is to use language which already inclines your audience or your readers to accept your conclusion before you have established it. It is to suggest that democracy is impossible before you have put yourself to the trouble of explaining what it would be like, if it could exist, and why it is out of reach.

Though Mosca, Pareto and Michels seem at times to be preaching a political sermon on the text, *plus ça change, plus c'est la même chose*, this is not quite what they are doing. True, it is always a minority who rule and a majority who are ruled, and therefore always a minority who 'impose their will' on a majority; and yet, after all, elections and other things do make a difference. The ruling minority do not always impose their will by the same methods. Nor is the minority formed or recruited—or however you like to put it—always in the same way. There is, to use an expression of Pareto's, a circulation of the elites. The sort of people who get to the top, the ways they get there, the principles to which they appeal to justify their authority or their policies, the methods they use to get people to do what they require of them: all these things change. The structure of authority, the rules that define it, the social order of which it forms a part, are never for long the same. Nor are the aspirations and the standards unchanging of those subject to authority, even though they lack a political will and have the will of others imposed on them. Neither the shepherds nor the sheep remain the same. It is not just a question of the generations succeeding one another, of old sheep and old shepherds dying and new ones taking their place. The new sheep differ in manner and spirit from the old, and so do the new shepherds. Or, to vary the metaphor, it is not a question of unchanging roles and changing actors; the roles change as well as the actors. The human comedy changes continually. Or, rather, it changes in some ways and remains the same in others. One of the ways in which *it never changes* is that there is always in it an active minority *imposing* their will on a passive majority.

There is nothing odd or unacceptable about the belief that in human affairs there are some things that remain the same and others that change. It is a commonplace that nobody challenges. Aristotle and Burke, Marx and the anarchists, all accept it. What we want to know, what Mosca and Pareto fail to tell us (though they think otherwise), is just what it is among the things that do not change that makes genuine democracy impossible. Everyone, not excluding the democrat, has always agreed that in all societies in which government is a whole-time business, it must be confined to a minority who take many decisions which the rest of the community must accept, though they have no part in taking them. Even Rousseau agreed that this must be so. He wanted the people, the generality of citizens, to take only certain kinds of decisions; he saw that, even in the most favourable circumstances, they could take only a small part in the business of government as a whole. In the *Social Contract*, he tried to explain what that small part was, and why it was supremely important that the people should take it.

Mosca, as a matter of fact, has a good deal to say in favour of the system which, so he argues, is not and cannot be what its champions say it is; and some of the things he says are, oddly enough, very like what these same champions say. For example, though he assures us, on one page, that when it is said that voters choose their representatives, the language used is 'very inexact', and that it is much nearer the truth to say that the representative *has himself elected* by the voters, or, better still, that *his friends have him elected*, he then, on the next page, goes on to say that

> the great majority of voters . . . have not so much freedom to choose their representatives as a limited right to exercise an option among a number of candidates. Nevertheless, limited as it may be, it has the effect of obliging candidates to try to win a weight of votes that will serve to tip the scales in their direction, so that they make every effort to flatter, wheedle and obtain the good will of the voters. In this way certain sentiments and passions of the 'common herd' come to have their influence on the mental attitudes of the representatives themselves, and echoes of a widely disseminated opinion, or of any serious discontent, easily come to be heard in the highest spheres of government.[1]

The style is the style of Mosca, on both these pages, but on the second the thoughts might have come from Schumpeter or even from A. D. Lindsay.

'In elections,' says Mosca, 'as in all other manifestations of social life, those who have . . . the moral, intellectual and material means to *force their will* upon others take the lead over the others and command them.' He then says, this time only a few lines down the same page:

> If each voter gave his vote to the candidate of his heart, we may be sure that in almost all cases the only result would be a wide scattering of votes. When very many wills are involved, choice is determined by the most varied criteria, . . . and if such wills were not coordinated and organized it would be virtually impossible for them to coincide in the spontaneous choice of one individual. If his vote is to have any efficacy at all, therefore, each voter is forced to limit his choice to a very narrow field, in other words to a choice among the two or three persons who have some chance of succeeding; and the only ones who have any chance of succeeding are those whose candidacies are championed by groups, by committees, by organized minorities.[2]

To take a lead is not quite the same thing as to *force your will on others*. These two phrases, in Italian as in English, have different meanings, though Mosca uses them here as if they had not. And why should he suggest that candidates have a chance of succeeding *only*

---

[1] Gaetano Mosca. *The Ruling Class*, translated by Hannah Kahn, edited by Arthur Livington, pp. 154–5.
[2] *Ibid.*, p. 154 [my italics].

because they are championed by organized minorities? Do these minorities champion candidates regardless of their popularity? Can they ensure that the candidate of their choice gets the votes without considering how the voters feel about him? Or can they ensure that the voters feel about him as they, his champions, want them to? If they can do that, why then should candidates, as Mosca admits they do, try to win votes by obtaining the good will of the voters? Here again we find Mosca, confident though his manner is, shifting uncertainly between two positions, of which one would seem reasonable enough today to many academic apologists for Western democracy.

Mosca, though he was no democrat, was a liberal and a believer in constitutional government. He distinguished between political systems according to the rights they secure to the individual. He preferred the modern state, which he called 'bureaucratic', to feudalism on the ground that in it the rights of the individual are more precisely defined and better protected. He spoke with approval of what he called 'juridical defence', by which he meant security under the law and also something more, I think, than bare security. The extent to which 'juridical defence' is achieved depends, above all, on how authority is exercised, on the quality of political intercourse between rulers and subjects and between superiors and subordinates within the ruling hierarchy.

> The existence of an honest government, a government that is based on integrity and justice, a government that is truly liberal in Guicciardini's sense of the term, is the best guarantee that one can have that the rights commonly known as private will be effectively upheld. . . . Guicciardini defines political liberty as 'a prevalence of law and public decrees over the appetites of particular men'.[1]

Mosca agrees that the honesty of a government, its concern for justice, depends on more than the moral character of the men who happen to control it; it depends also, and above all, on how government is organized, on the structure and the ethos of the political system. If there is to be security under the law, it is not enough that the law should be respected in the letter; it must be respected also in the spirit. There must be principles of morality and justice that legislators, judges and bureaucrats respect. How can these principles be respected unless citizens are free to appeal to them against their rulers, and subordinates against their superiors in the hierarchy?

The perfecting of 'juridical defence' requires, according to Mosca, a fairly high level of intellectual and economic development. It requires, further, that Church and State should be separate, that there should be many well-to-do people in the community who do not owe

---

[1] *Ibid.*, p. 130.

their wealth to being employed by the state or to getting contracts from it, and a political 'system in which all governmental acts are subject to public discussion'.[1]

So Mosca, after all, comes down strongly in favour of the system which he says pretends to be what it fact it cannot be; he speaks out boldly for parliamentary or representative government. In his opinion:

> The only demand that it is important, and possible, to make of a political system is that all social values shall have a part in it, and that it shall find a place for all who possess any of the qualities which determine what prestige and what influence an individual, or a class, is to have. Just as we do not combat a religion because its dogmas seem far-fetched, so long as it produces good results in the field of conduct, so the applications of a political doctrine may be acceptable so long as they result in an improvement of juridical defence, though the doctrine itself may easily be open to attack from a strictly scientific standpoint. It cannot be denied that the representative system provides a way for many different social forces to participate in the political system and, therefore, to balance and limit the influence of other social forces and the influence of bureaucracy in particular.[2]

What Mosca now says really comes down to this: it is not the representative system that is unacceptable but the theory behind it. And the theory is unacceptable only in the sense that it is mistaken. It does no harm, or very little. Indeed, to the extent that it sustains a system which has more to be said for it than any likely alternative to it, it does a power of good. The democratic myth may be only a myth, but the believer in 'juridical defence', even though he is too shrewd to be taken in by the myth, may congratulate himself on living in a part of the world where most people are taken in by it.

The defects of parliamentary government, says Mosca, almost all come from improper interference with elections.[3] Democracy is impossible and all government is the imposing of a minority's will on the majority; and yet, for all that, it does matter greatly that the voter should not be intimidated or bribed. It is also important that there should be freedom of speech and association. What is more, where there is a limited suffrage, 'one of the chief assumptions of the liberal system can be made, we do not say complete, but not wholly illusory —namely, that those who represent shall be responsible to the represented.'[4] This, presumably, is because a limited electorate consists of relatively well informed and educated persons better able than the masses to understand what their representatives are doing. Yet Mosca does not suggest that citizens should qualify for the vote by passing

[1] *Ibid.*, p. 257.   [3] *Ibid.*, p. 265.
[2] *Ibid.*, p. 258.   [4] *Ibid.*, p. 413.

tests designed to ensure that only persons of better than average political judgment (however that is to be measured) take part in elections to public offices. The limited electorate he has in mind is limited much as it used to be in the West before the coming of universal suffrage; it consists of persons who own certain kinds of property, or have not less than a certain income, or are householders. But what reason is there to believe that they are endowed with better judgment than the people generally? It may be that in Mosca's time and in Italy they were better educated and better informed politically than the rest of the community. But this was a state of affairs that could be, and to some extent has been, remedied. Why then assume that only a minority of the people can have the capacities needed to make their rulers responsible to them? Mosca does not say.

He might have argued that it is the size of the electorate rather than its quality that matters here; that where there are vast numbers of electors, the business of organizing elections and choosing candidates is such that the kinds of interference he condemns as improper cannot be prevented. But this, though it could be argued, is not in fact the argument of Mosca. When he says that it is the friends of a representative who 'have him elected' and that only candidates 'championed' by 'organized minorities' have a chance of being elected, he is speaking of the representative system as he thinks it always has been and not as it is only where there is manhood or universal suffrage. He nowhere considers how methods of selecting candidates and conducting elections vary with the size of the electorate, nor does he enquire how far some methods are better adapted than others to preventing improper interference with voters or to ensuring that candidates are congenial to them or are able and willing to explain their intentions clearly and realistically.

As a critic of representative democracy Mosca is more specific, and therefore in some ways more instructive, than Pareto; and the same can be said (and perhaps even more so) of Michels. Mosca in *The Ruling Class* and Michels in *Political Parties* attack, not so much a political system, as the claims made for it and the assumptions that lie behind the claims—the theory used to explain and justify it. Both Michels and Mosca were, in the broad sense of the word, liberals, and they were also closely acquainted with socialist theories and socialist movements. They were familiar both with socialist attacks on the bourgeois parliamentary system and with the claims of the socialists that their own movements and aims were genuinely popular. They were suitably impressed by what the socialists had to say *against* the bourgeois state, but not by the claims they made *for* themselves and the working class. Some of the arguments they used to show that democracy is impossible were used later by the men I have called Revisionists to attack what they thought were illusions about democracy; illusions for which they wanted to substitute better theories of their own.

Michels lived and wrote in Germany and Italy, and Mosca in Italy alone. They saw representative democracy at work in the two countries in which eventually it gave way to fascism. They were not familiar with it at its best, or perhaps I should say in its quieter, more self-confident and more solid forms. Germany did not have full parliamentary government until after the First World War, and Italy, though for different reasons, was only half a democracy when Mussolini put an end to parliamentary government in 1922. In the southern part of Italy, and especially in Mosca's native Sicily, parliamentary elections were virtually a farce. I am not now suggesting that the beliefs about democracy of Michels and Mosca are not worth taking seriously; I am suggesting only that, if they had lived in countries with a longer and stronger parliamentary or democratic tradition, their beliefs might have been different.

The Fascists, when they came to power, had no use for Mosca. Pareto they admired and honoured, or at least their leader, Mussolini, did so. But though Pareto, who died in 1923, accepted the honours thrust upon him in the last year of his life, there is no reason to believe that Fascism was congenial to him. He was not, any more than were Mosca and Michels, an apologist for authoritarian government. He merely produced a social and political theory that denied some of the assumptions about human nature dear to socialists and radicals. He was a mathematical economist before he turned his mind to other things; he then wrote a book attacking socialism, and finally produced what is now perhaps his most famous work, his *Treatise of General Sociology*, published in 1916, and better known in English-speaking countries under the title, *Mind and Society*.

It can be said of Mosca that, in a way, his heart was always with what he attacked. He was a liberal who believed that representative government, though it was not and could not be what its champions said it was, was nevertheless, judged by liberal standards, better than any alternative to it. Of Pareto it could not be said that he was at heart a liberal, though he was something of a *laissez-faire* economist. Politically, he was a conservative; and fascism, which is in some ways a subversive creed as well as a perversion of both democracy and socialism, would almost certainly not have appealed to him, had he lived long enough to get to know it. It was not his fault that Mussolini admired him.

Pareto is of less direct interest to us than either Mosca or Michels because he does not, as they do, take institutions essential to democracy and then argue that they cannot do what, according to democratic theorists, they should do. He does not try to show how particular instruments of democracy stand in the way of its alleged purposes; how elections are so managed that voters do not really choose who shall represent them, and parties so organized that members and supporters have very little influence on leaders. His great treatise puts forward a general theory of social action and social change. It has been said that this theory weakens faith in democracy in two ways: it argues that only a small part of human behaviour is logical or rational, and it holds that in every society it is the elites that matter, the masses merely following where they lead.

I shall consider only in a general way the relevance for democratic theory of these two theses: that a large part of human behaviour is *not* rational, and that it is the elites and not the masses who matter politically.

Notice, in the first place, that it is faith in democracy and not in other forms of government that is weakened by this belief that human behaviour, for the most part or in large part, is not rational. Nobody, to the best of my knowledge, has argued that oligarchy or monarchy is an illusion because so much of human (or political) behaviour is not rational. Indeed, this dearth of rationality seems to rule out, not so much democracy in general, as representative democracy. I have yet to come across the argument that direct democracy is impossible because most people much of the time are not rational. Why then should we suppose that representative democracy is a sham for this reason? It may be a sham for other reasons—as, for example, for the reasons given by Rousseau. But why for this reason, or even for this reason among others? It is not obvious that political behaviour is less rational than other kinds. But even if we assume that it is, why should this make representative democracy *impossible* any more than the direct kind, or than any other form of government?

Those who deny that direct democracy is possible do so on quite other grounds; they say, for example, that a community large enough to be economically self-supporting and sophisticated enough to aspire to democracy is already too large to be a direct democracy. Even Periclean Athens, they say, was too large to be one, and was in fact an oligarchy of citizens who formed only a small part of the whole population. Only very primitive societies are both self-supporting and small enough for all the adults, or all the grown men, in them to meet together to take decisions in common; and they are patriarchal. In more advanced societies, communities not too large to take decisions in common are not self-supporting; they can therefore take only some of the important decisions that affect their members. Most of the really important decisions that affect them are taken outside the community. This is the kind of argument ordinarily used to show that direct democracy is impossible; and it has nothing to do with the extent to which human behaviour is rational.

In a representative democracy, citizens take political decisions different in kind from those they would take in a direct democracy. They elect candidates to public offices and do not make either law or policy. Everyone agrees that representative democracy is a sham unless persons elected to public offices are *responsible* to those who elect them. But what is to count as *political responsibility*? This is the crucial question, and one not easily answered. The political theorist who tries to answer it and to give a clear answer may find himself having to conclude that responsibility, to be effective, requires that electors are better informed about the intentions of candidates or parties and about the likely consequences of their carrying out their intentions than most electors can be. In that case, he will conclude that representative democracy, in the world as we know it, is impossible. But if he goes that far, he may well find that consistency obliges him to go further: to conclude that government responsible to the rich or to the bourgeois is also impossible.

Or, alternatively, he may contrive so to define political responsibility as to avoid such conclusions and yet make sense of many of the claims that believers in representative democracy make for it. Provided that his definition allows him to discriminate between governments, and does not require him to call any elected body or person *responsible*, no matter how candidates are selected or how ignorant the electors or how much subject to coercion, he may have reason enough to be satisfied with it. But, even if the conclusions he reaches about what constitutes political responsibility require him to say that representative democracy, except perhaps on a small scale, is virtually impossible, he need pass no judgment on human behaviour in general. He need neither deny nor affirm that most or much of it is rational. In a large community whose most foolish member was as wise as Socrates, it might still be true that most electors could not be as well informed as they would need to be to ensure that the men they elected were effectively responsible to them.

The authors of *Voting*, a well-known American study of an election campaign, quote a passage from an essay on democracy written by an eminent American judge, Learned Hand:

> I do not know how it is with you, but for myself I generally give up at the outset. The simplest problems which come up from day to day seem to me quite unanswerable as soon as I try to get below the surface. . . . My vote is one of the most unimportant acts of my life; if I were to acquaint myself with the matters on which it ought really to depend, if I were to try to get a judgment on which I was willing to risk affairs of even the smallest moment, I should be doing

nothing else, and that seems a fatuous conclusion to a fatuous undertaking.[1]

Judge Hand is here making, in his own vivid way, a point quite often made by writers on democracy. The criteria of what constitutes a rational use of the vote can be set so high that virtually no one, not even the learned and the wise, can make a rational use of it. Yet responsibility, political as well as moral or legal, presupposes a capacity to make rational decisions. To vote at an election is to do more than just put a mark on a piece of paper or a ball into a box, for a monkey can be trained to do that. It involves making a deliberate choice, and anything that deserves to be called a deliberate choice requires *some* understanding of the situation in which it is made and of the alternatives open to the chooser. The question is, How much understanding? The answer must vary both with the kind of choice and the kind of responsibility we have in mind.

Political responsibility differs in some obvious ways from both moral and legal responsibility. When we enquire whether a man was morally or legally responsible for what he did, we consider how far he understood the situation in which he acted and the likely consequences of his action. Whether other people understood what he did is not relevant, unless their understanding was part of the situation in which he acted. But when we enquire how far someone in authority is politically responsible for his actions, the extent to which others (those he is responsible to) understand what he does is of the essence of the matter. How far do they understand actions of the kind for which he is responsible to them? How far can they assess his performance? If an elected official is to be responsible to his electors, they must understand what they are doing when they elect him, which they cannot do unless they understand the nature of the office to which they elect him. But there are degrees of understanding. How much understanding is a condition of this kind of responsibility? How far should electors be able to assess an officeholder's performance? If they are bad judges, is he any the less responsible to them? These are questions not easily answered.

And understanding alone is clearly not enough. The College of Cardinals are an unusually intelligent and well-informed electorate, but the Pope whom they elect is not responsible to them for his official actions. For someone to be responsible to others, they must either be able to deprive him of his office, even if only after a period of time, or else must be able to invalidate his official decisions or forbid their

---

[1] Berelson, Lazarsfeld and McPhee, *Voting* (1954), Phoenix Books edition, p. 312, from an essay by Judge Learned Hand in '*Democracy: its presumptions and reality*'.

being carried out. This may be obvious enough; and yet, when we are considering large constituencies to which officeholders are supposed to be responsible, it may be difficult to define precisely the conditions of this responsibility. Thus mistakes as to whether or not the conditions are met are easily made. But all this has nothing to do with man's being, as Pareto says he is, predominantly non-logical or non-rational.

Those who, like Pareto, pass this kind of wholesale judgment on human behaviour, ordinarily do not say that human beings can never, or scarcely ever, be *morally* or *legally* responsible. Nor do they deny that it makes no sense to say of any but a *rational* being that it is morally or legally responsible. Why, then, should they conclude that this judgment of theirs, if it is true, virtually excludes *political* responsibility? There may be good reasons for the conclusion. But, before we can decide whether or not there are, we must look more closely than they do at political responsibility and its conditions. Democracy is not to be argued out of existence quite so easily, quite so carelessly, as that.

Let us admit that there are conspicuous and powerful minorities in all societies, even the most democratic. Let us admit also that when we make distinctions between societies, we pay attention to these minorities out of all proportion to their size. When we try to explain how, for example, Elizabethan England differed politically or culturally from Victorian England, we are ordinarily more concerned with the behaviour of 'elites' than with the behaviour of 'masses'. Even when we compare the two societies socially or economically, we attend to the elites considerably more than to the masses, though in these cases the disproportion is not nearly as great. This, perhaps, is part of what those writers mean who say that it is the elites and not the masses that are important. If it is, then the believer in democracy can agree with them without more ado, and without fear that he has conceded a point that can be used against him.

As for the assertion that the masses merely follow where the elites lead, I do not see its relevance to democratic theory. It is too broad and too vague for any political consequences to be drawn from it. No doubt, where there are leaders, there are followers too. But human followers do not follow their leaders as dogs do their masters. Nor are their lives taken up in imitating their social superiors or in doing what they tell them to do. They have other sides to their lives which deeply affect their relations with their superiors. This, in part, is why leadership takes so many different forms. There are, as Rousseau admits—Rousseau to whom critics of democracy trace back so many of the grosser illusions about it—leaders and followers even in the most popular of governments, in the most equalitarian of societies.

We must put ourselves to the trouble of distinguishing with some care between different kinds of leadership before we can decide what conditions must hold if leaders are to be responsible to their followers. But Pareto, though he does distinguish between elites and between the ways in which they rise to the top, never does so with a view to discovering how far leaders can be responsible to their followers. He just takes it for granted that they are not responsible.

Kinds of leadership

I suggest that one reason why Mosca and Pareto are able to speak as they do about political classes dominating the people is that they take little notice of different kinds of leadership. To be sure, they make distinctions between classes and between elites, and these distinctions are often fresh and interesting. Pareto in particular has much to say about social and cultural conditions that bring some types of elite rather than others to the top. He not only, in his very large treatise, makes more distinctions than Mosca does; he also speaks of a circulation of elites, and distinguishes between two types of leaders, whom he calls lions and foxes. The lions are tough, loyal and uncompromising, while the foxes are clever and resourceful, getting their way by bargains and intrigues rather than by force of character. When new communities are formed or old ones transformed, it is the lions that predominate among the leaders; but later they give way to the foxes, and the elite degenerates and maintains itself only until another arises strong enough to take its place. In parliamentary regimes, as you might expect, it is the foxes who are to the fore.

All this is interesting, though some of it, no doubt, is open to criticism. But my complaint against Pareto is a political theorist's, not a sociologist's, complaint. I do not suggest that, in general, he is undiscriminating when he distinguishes between elites and the conditions of their emergence and decay. He does not speak as if the lions or the foxes of one epoch or society were the same as those of another; he points merely to similarities of temperament and attitude that can go along with equally important differences. My complaint is not that he fails to make interesting and suggestive (and sometimes also new) distinctions between elites and the conditions in which they flourish and decline; it is that, though he says boldly that democracy is an illusion, he tells us nothing about elites and their relations to the masses that substantiates this claim. The distinctions he makes between lions and foxes and between types of elite are simply irrelevant when it comes to trying to decide what the conditions of political responsibility are. To distinguish between types of elite or between the economic, social and cultural conditions of their emergence is still not to distinguish between types of leadership, between the kinds of activities that leaders engage in when they lead or followers when they follow. But it is these activities that we must look at if our purpose is to decide what it is for leaders to be responsible to those they lead.

No distinction is more often made by writers about democracy than the one between an *active* minority of leaders and a *passive* majority of mere subjects or citizens. No doubt, these writers do not mean literally what they say, and would always, if challenged, admit that being led involves being active. Clearly, the passive are not the inactive; they are not moved without also being movers. This is so obvious that nobody seriously denies it. The passive majority are politically active in a variety of ways. What, then, is the point of calling them 'passive'? And how does this passiveness of theirs make democracy a sham? These are questions that cannot be answered unless we look at the activities we call 'leading' and 'being led', and take into account distinctions that writers who dismiss representative democracy as an illusion often fail to notice.

I want, therefore, without going at all deeply into the matter, to point to different types of activity, all of them forms of leadership, with which everybody is familiar. To speak of them is to remind people of the obvious, but such reminders are sometimes useful.

But first, before I try to distinguish between these activities, let me make a simple point which again seems obvious enough, though political scientists often pass it over. Followers are not the more *passive* the more authoritarian the organization they belong to. An army is, generally speaking, much more authoritarian than a political party is, and yet, though we often say that the rank and file of a party are passive, we hardly ever speak in this way of other ranks in an army. Nor, ordinarily, when a party is undemocratic, do we expect to find the bulk of its members politically less active than they would be if the party were democratic. There would seem to be no obvious correlation in large organizations between the degree to which leaders are responsible to those they lead and activity among members who are not leaders. We cannot say: the more authoritarian an organization, the less the call for intelligence and initiative in the rank and file.

Consider for a moment military leadership. The military leader controls his men as no ruler, not even the tyrant, leads his subjects. He directs their movements from day to day, and also sees that their wants are attended to, that they are properly fed, clothed and equipped. His authority over them is immense and he is responsible for how he exercises it, not to them, but to his superiors; and yet he must rely on their willing and intelligent cooperation. They may not challenge his decisions, but they must use their judgment in carrying them out, and sometimes, when they have lost contact with him, may justly disregard his orders on the ground that, if he had still been in touch with them and had known how they were situated, he would have given them different orders. Though military discipline is unusually severe, and orders may not be questioned, the military leader relies heavily on the judgment and initiative of his subordinates, especially on the battlefield when the quality of his leadership is put to the severest tests.

If we compare an army with, say, a large factory, we see that in the factory discipline is much less severe and orders are more often questioned or disobeyed with impunity. Also, often, not much judgment or initiative is required of the mass of workers, who do much the same things, deal with much the same situations, from day to day. They are more passive, if passivity consists of exercising little judgment or initiative, than soldiers are at war, if not in peacetime. Yet a factory is rather more democratic than an army, not because discipline is laxer, but because the workers are organized to present collective demands to the managers. They have shop-stewards and local trade union officials to speak for them. Their spokesmen, though they take no direct part in managing the factory, exert great influence on the managers.

There are three activities, all of them leadership in the broad sense of the word, which are important in the sphere of government and politics, though of course not exclusive to it. I shall call one *management*, another *government*, and the third *leadership*, in a narrower though still common sense of the word.

Managers and managed belong to the same organization; they work together or in fairly close touch with one another. They are engaged in the same business, on the same enterprises; the managers direct the labours of others, of whom some may be subordinate managers. Though management is not a peculiarly political activity, there is clearly plenty of it in the sphere of government and politics, in administrative departments and in parties and pressure groups.

Government, as distinct from management, consists, not in directing the labours of others, but in making rules for their guidance and applying those rules to them. Managers are, of course, quite often governors as well; they not only direct the labours of others but also make rules for them and apply the rules to them. They do this in industry, in the army and in other organizations that are not political, or not primarily political, as much as in the political sphere. Nevertheless, there is an important difference between management and government, especially in the political sphere. If we call the people whose labours a manager directs his subordinates, and the people for whom a governor makes rules his subjects, we can then say that, whereas in the economic and military spheres, a man's subjects are ordinarily also his subordinates, this is much less often so in the political sphere. Ordinary citizens are the subjects but not the subordinates of their rulers. Rulers and subjects belong to the same political community but not ordinarily to the same organization; they do not, in the same sense as managers and subordinates do, work together and are not engaged in the same business. Though government, even in the political sphere, involves a great deal of what I have called management, it does so only within the hierarchy of public officials or inside such organizations as parties and pressure groups. Thus, ordinary citizens do not stand to public officials as lesser officials do to higher ones, or as workers do to managers in industry, or as other ranks do to officers in our army. They are not the lowest rank in a hierarchy, the bottom people in the business; they do not belong to the hierarchy and are not in the business. Except when the political community is a direct democracy, ordinary citizens take no part in governing as, say, ordinary workers do in production or private soldiers in war.

No doubt citizens in a representative democracy are politically active in ways they would not be in an authoritarian state. Yet these activities of theirs differ in kind from government or administration. When a man acquires the right to vote, he is not raised, as it were, from the bottom of the political hierarchy to some higher place inside it; he remains as much outside the hierarchy as he was before. We can perhaps, in a direct democracy, assign the 'highest' place in the structure of government to the people taken collectively, but to assign a high or a low place, as summit or pedestal, to ordinary citizens in a representative democracy is surely absurd.

If being politically active means taking part in government, mere citizens are not politically active in a representative democracy, but if it means taking part in activities designed to influence those who govern, they may be highly active politically. But then so too, in this sense, may the citizens of an authoritarian state. It is the character and effects of this activity rather than the amount of it that determines whether or not the state is democratic.

The third activity, distinct from management and government though often carried on by the same persons, is leadership in the narrower sense of the term. It consists in promoting or defining some cause that the people or a section of them share, or that the promoter hopes to get them to share. The leader, in this sense, has followers who share his beliefs or aims rather than subjects or subordinates; he is (or aspires to be) their spokesman and not their ruler or the director of their labours. Though the man who is a leader in this sense may also be a ruler or a manager, or may want to become one, this kind of leadership consists, not in ruling or managing others, but in speaking for them.

To exercise this kind of leadership is to act, or to aspire or claim to act, as a representative. And yet I hesitate to call this kind of leader the representative of his followers, for that might suggest that he is responsible to them for what he does. This he need not be; as for example, Charles I was not responsible to his Royalist followers though, to the extent that they were genuine supporters of his cause, he did speak for them. Speaking for people, in the sense relevant here, does not mean merely giving expression to their aims, beliefs and feelings; it means also, and above all, giving expression to aims, beliefs and feelings that they are willing to endorse, though they may never have thought about them until they were adopted by some trusted leader.

Leaders have, no doubt, a much larger say than mere followers have in defining and deciding how to promote the aims they share or are supposed to share. That, after all, is what leaders are for. Not only does any one leader have a much larger say than any one follower, but the leaders taken together have a larger say than the followers taken together. But to say this is merely to utter a tautology. For to be a leader, in this third sense, is precisely to have a large say in defining aims, principles and sentiments which are, or are supposed to be, shared. It is in the discussions between leaders and by their decisions that aims and principles are not only promoted or realized but also defined. They do the talking which is the business of politics. But to assert that leaders have between them a much greater say than followers have in defining common aims or principles is not to imply that interests and needs peculiar to them count for more than the interests and needs of their followers in determining how the aims or principles are defined. We cannot pass immediately from this premise to this conclusion.

These three activities or forms of leadership are to be found in all developed political communities. The third of them, leadership in the narrower sense, has in recent times grown very greatly in importance; and has done so not only in democracies. It is not peculiar either to the large modern state or to modern democracy. And yet it has nowhere been so large a feature of political life as in the modern state that claims to be democratic.

One obvious effect of the proliferation of this kind of leadership is that the volume of political activity increases greatly; and it does so in all states that claim to be democratic, whether the claim is true or not. There is a great deal of political activity among ordinary citizens, even in the most authoritarian of states.

Nor is this political activity in authoritarian states a mere effect of compulsion; it is often willing and intelligent. It is, to a considerable extent (though the extent no doubt varies greatly from state to state) a willing cooperation of ordinary citizens with their rulers and leaders. And this cooperation does more than maintain the semblance of democracy where no democracy exists. It serves other purposes as well; for the modern state, authoritarian or not, makes large demands on its citizens, demanding of them, not only obedience, but also understanding, approval, and willing collaboration.

It needs to make these demands on them precisely because it has other purposes than just to maintain law and order; it seeks, in one way or another, to achieve aims that involve getting people to think and feel differently, to exercise new kinds of skill, to reject the past and to look forward to the future. The rulers of modern states not only govern and direct the energies of their subjects to an unprecedented extent; they also seek their support and understanding as never before. And, of course, achieving their aims involves increasing the number of active leaders of all kinds.

If to increase the proportion of the politically active among citizens and the extent to which they understand and support the aims of their rulers were to make a community more democratic, an impartial enquiry might establish that democracy has been growing faster in some of the states that we in the West call authoritarian than in many liberal states. I do not say that it would but only that it might do so, if the extent and intensity of political activity and of popular support for governmental aims were taken to be the criteria of democracy. For in that case, there could be democracy even though rulers were not responsible to their subjects. No doubt, where they are responsible to them, they are unlikely to remain long in power unless they have popular support. But the converse is not true; we cannot say that it is a condition of rulers having this support and its being genuine that they should be responsible to their subjects.

Government enjoying widespread support among politically active citizens and responsible government are not the same thing; for though you can hardly find the second without the first, you can quite often find the first without the second. If we have accommodating minds, we can, of course, speak here of two kinds of democracy. We can call the first kind people's democracies and the second liberal democracies. But if we do that, we must not expect the rulers of the people's democracies to accept our account of their political systems. We must not expect them to admit that they are not responsible to their subjects but merely enjoy widespread popular support. For they make for their systems the claim that we make for ours: that in them rulers are responsible to their subjects.

What is it that writers who are not taken in by common illusions about democracy are telling us when they say that it is the elites and the leaders who really matter and not the masses of mere followers? If to matter is to take part in the activities that constitute leadership in its various forms, the assertion is a mere tautology. But to be a follower is, or can be, an arduous business, calling at times for considerable judgment, initiative and courage. No doubt, it is the leaders who do all the leading, though sometimes, when they least expect it, they have to do some following. A radical leader during a crisis under the Second Republic in France, hearing the noise of marchers in the street below, ventured to look out of the window and then suddenly cried out: 'Je suis leur chef, il faut que je les suive!' He ran hard that day to retain his leadership.

APPENDIX

The demand for democracy and its political effects

The demand for democracy, when it first arises, comes from persons who believe (or affect to believe) that rulers are neglecting the needs and aspirations of their subjects, and that this neglect will continue for as long as they are not responsible to their subjects. These champions of democracy, sincere or insincere, either want to be leaders themselves or want the people to have leaders. For unless there are leaders whom the people, or some considerable part of them, follow, it is unlikely that the demand for democracy will be conceded. Thus, it is a condition of democracy's being achieved that there should be a popular demand for it, which there cannot be unless there is leadership of the kind I have tried to distinguish from government and management. Wherever there is democracy there is plenty of leadership of this kind.

The demand for democracy, even where it does not bring democracy, usually has profound political effects; it usually brings into existence a political system calling for much more leadership than the system it supersedes. This, I suggest, is what has happened in our century in Russia and in China. The Tsars of Russia and their high functionaries were much less political leaders of the people than are its present rulers, and the same is true of the Chinese Emperors if we compare them with their successors. Or, to take an example from the West, Napoleon was much more a political leader of the French people than was Louis XIV. But Napoleon, though he was more a leader, was no less a ruler and manager, than his Bourbon predecessors. Indeed, the French people were considerably more *governed* under him than they had been earlier; the governmental hierarchy was larger and its members busier, more managing and managed, than ever before. There was more government, more management, and more leadership. But it is the leadership that concerns us here, for that, if anything, was the truly popular element in the Napoleonic system. Napoleon wanted, and needed, popular support and sympathy as no French ruler before him had done. The need was not just peculiar to him. It was not just that he, as a one-time jacobin and admirer of Rousseau, needed to feel that the French people understood and approved of what he was doing. It was rather that the country could not be governed effectively, in the ways and for the purposes for which he and his subordinates governed it, unless those purposes were widely understood and approved. Though he was no more responsible to the people for how he governed them than was Louis XIV, he required from them greater and more varied responses to his initiatives. That is why Napoleon, who was as much an autocrat as anyone who ever ruled France, resorted from time to time to plebiscites and had a popularly elected chamber in his legislature.

What was true of Napoleon's France is perhaps even more true of Russia since the October Revolution and of China since Mao-Tse-tung took power. I am now only repeating what others have said, and you do not have to agree that these particular illustrations are well chosen to take the point I am making. Rulers can come to have much closer relations with their subjects, can ask more of them and affect them more deeply, without becoming politically responsible to them. But they cannot do this and leave their subjects politically as passive as they were before. They must try to convert them from being mere subjects into being subjects who are also followers; they must try to enlist their willing and active support, and not just their acquiescence and applause, and to some considerable extent must succeed in their efforts. Which is not to say that they cannot be just as oppressive, and perhaps even more oppressive, than their predecessors were. It makes perfectly good sense to say of Soviet Russia, that its rulers have been both more oppressive and more popular than the Tsars ever were, without being a whit more democratic, if by democracy we mean government responsible to the people. The assertion may or may not be true to the facts, but it is not self-contradictory. If it does not apply to the Soviet Union, its equivalent could apply to some other country.

Whether or not the Soviet Union is a democracy is perhaps open to dispute. At least it is still disputed. But no one can reasonably deny that the rulers of that country say that it is a democracy, which is more than the Tsars ever said of Russia while they ruled it. Notice that the Soviet rulers do more than claim that their rule is popular and is carried on in the real interests of the people; for the Tsars claimed that much for their rule. No less than the rulers of America or Britain, they claim that they are responsible to the people. They may also make other claims, whose implications, once they are clearly drawn, turn out to be incompatible with this claim. Nonetheless, they do make this claim also; and they make it, I suggest, not just because they have not yet got around to discarding an ideology no longer relevant to their methods and aims, but because they need to make it to help them achieve those aims. The Tsars were concerned above all to keep the peace and to preserve existing institutions, allowing little more change than they thought was needed to prevent major disturbances and to enable Russia to sustain her role as one of the Great Powers. Their successors since 1917 have wanted to refashion her economy and her social order from top to bottom. They could not achieve their purposes without requiring from their subjects greater sacrifices and more understanding than the Tsars could make do with. They have had to bring, if not the whole people, then at least considerable sections of them, into partnership with themselves, to make of them intelligent and devoted sharers in their purposes. This they could do without setting up a genuine democracy. Indeed, it could be argued that, at the time they took power, it was impossible to establish democracy in Russia, and that, had they tried to establish it, they would quickly have lost power. But it could also be argued that, in order to preserve this power and to induce the people to make the intelligent and disciplined efforts needed to achieve their purposes, they had to speak the language of democracy. They had to speak it as if they meant it, which they could hardly have done unless, to some extent, they had meant it.

I am not out now to compare the rulers of the Soviet Union unfavourably with the rulers of other countries which seem to me closer to being democracies. There is a good deal of deception and self-deception involved in all government, and I am not suggesting that there is necessarily more of it where rulers are not democratic than where they are. I am not even suggesting that there is more of it where rulers who are not democratic need to believe and to have others believe that they are. I am suggesting, for the moment, no more than this: conditions may be such that democracy is impossible and yet governments not be able to achieve their purposes unless they speak the language of democracy, and to some extent mean it. Where such conditions hold, the people, though they may be in some ways much oppressed, are also much involved in the purposes of their rulers, not as mere blind instruments, but as persons continually urged to share the purposes. They are not politically indifferent or passive. They are not mere subjects. They are also followers; or at least many of them are. Their rulers are also to a large extent their leaders, and could not achieve their purposes, nor even retain power, unless they were. They must be leaders or else pretend to be; they must speak and act as if they were popular, as if their subjects were also their followers and partners. Their rule is impossible without this myth, and the myth, to be effective, must be partly true.

Let me set against this situation another very different from it. In the European provinces of the Ottoman Empire, the Christian peasants, the *raia*, the exploited and oppressed class, often had little contact with the Turks, officials or landlords. The officials stayed in the towns and so too, at least in some of the provinces, did the landlords. The peasants collected the taxes and other payments, in kind or in money, due to the Turks, who left them alone provided they were given what they thought was owing to them. If they did not get it, they sent punitive expeditions into the villages, and also, from time to time, just to show who were the masters, indulged in quite arbitrary pillage and violence. They were oppressors of the Christians much more than rulers over them, and were hardly at all their leaders or managers. Turks and Christians scarcely formed one community together, but rather two communities juxtaposed, the one feeding on the other. The Christians, if you like, were politically passive in relation to the Turks; they expected nothing from them and for long periods were without hope of getting rid of them or changing their ways. They were politically passive and yet not docile; they kept away from their oppressors, the Turkish 'elite', or tricked and cheated them, or resorted to murder. Yet this invasion, trickery and murder could hardly, while it was sporadic and inspired mostly by a desire for revenge, be called *political* action.

PART TWO Democratic Theory Revised

Chapter 4

Schumpeter and Free Competition for Power

The attacks on older theories, as I have tried to show, were misdirected in several ways. To see why this is so is already to make considerable progress towards a more realistic explanation of representative democracy. The attacks I have examined were made, for the most part, by men who thought of democracy, or at least of 'bourgeois democracy', as an illusion. These men produced no theories of democracy of their own to replace the theories they attacked. Believing that representative democracy on a large scale is unrealizable, either in principle or in society as they knew it, they no doubt felt themselves dispensed from offering to improve on what they demolished. They did not trouble to define the conditions in which genuine democracy might be realized, nor did they explain at all systematically the political systems whose claim to be democratic they denied.

To be sure, Mosca did point to what he took to be important advantages in the parliamentary regimes whose pretensions to democracy he rejected, and some of these advantages are pretty much the same as some of the features that later writers were to point to as distinctive of modern democracies. Mosca is to some extent a precursor of Schumpeter, some of the differences between them being more verbal than real. Though Mosca denied that a regime in which the legislature consists of men who have had to compete for the people's votes in order to get office was democratic, he thought nevertheless that there was a good deal to be said for it. The writers whose arguments I want to examine in the next three chapters are all believers in democracy. That is to say, they all believe that representative democracy on a large scale is possible. No doubt they also believe that where it is possible it is desirable; that peoples capable of this kind of democracy are better off with it than without it. But they are not much concerned to make this last point, and are, most of them, keener to explain what this democracy amounts to than to argue in its favour. Sometimes they too feel the need to attack older theories as a preliminary to putting forward their own: to remove misconceptions that might stand in the way of the reader's seeing the point of their explanations. This is particularly true of Schumpeter, whose arguments I shall discuss in this chapter.

Schumpeter's scepticism about the will of the people

(a) HIS VERSION OF 'THE CLASSICAL THEORY OF DEMOCRACY'

It is a pity that Schumpeter ever took it on himself to attack what he called 'the classical theory of democracy', for his attack is ignorant and inept, and is worth discussing only because it has been taken seriously. It is uncertain whom he is attacking, and even what beliefs he is ascribing to them. There are, he says, two ideas at the heart of the classical theory, *the common good* and *the will of the people*, both of which are unrealistic, though the first is so, apparently, even more than the second.

Schumpeter's attack on the idea of the common good is entirely misconceived, for no writer on democracy has ever subscribed to it in the sense he defines. In attacking it, he attacks, not a dead horse, but one that was never alive, at least not in the stable of democratic theory. 'There is', says Schumpeter, 'no such thing as a uniquely determined common good that all people could agree on or be made to agree on by rational argument.'[1] But nobody who speaks of the common good thinks of it as 'uniquely determined'. People who, for example, say that justice is the common good do not deny that promoting justice means taking many decisions that differ greatly according to circumstances, and that it is absurd to expect everyone to agree that every such decision is just. They use the term 'common good' to refer, not to one single end pursued incessantly, but to any object of a law or broad decision of policy which they believe to be just, given the circumstances at the time of the persons for whose welfare those who make the law or take the decisions are responsible.

Did any theorist of democracy ever assert what Schumpeter here denies? Certainly not Rousseau, though he has been accused of doing so. As much as anyone, he was given to speaking of the common good, but he did not think of it as some one end which is the supreme goal of policy, in the sense that it is always to be preferred to any end incompatible with it. He used the term in such a way as to imply that, given any matter to be decided by a group or community, there is always one (and only one) just decision, one decision in the common interest, which they would all recognize for such, if they had the relevant information and reasoned correctly.

[1] Joseph Schumpeter, *Capitalism, Socialism and Democracy*, Chapters xxi, and xxii, p. 251.

It is doubtful whether there is always (or even very often) a uniquely just decision in the sense implied by Rousseau, but that is not a matter to be argued here. Rousseau was concerned with direct and not representative government, so that neither what he says about the common good or the general will is relevant when we are discussing the kind of democracy that we and Schumpeter are concerned with.

Though most students of democratic theory associate the term, *the common good*, with Rousseau (or with later thinkers, such as T. H. Green, influenced by him) and not with the Utilitarians, Schumpeter does the opposite.[1] Perhaps he had in mind the formula, *the greatest happiness of the greatest number*, which Bentham used to refer to what he sometimes called the supreme end of policy. But this formula defines a principle and not a state of affairs. It is, for Bentham, equivalent to the rule: so act that your action brings as much pleasure and as little pain as possible to the people likely to be affected by it. Actions that conform to this principle have different ends, and so too do policies that conform to it.

Besides, this principle, though it has a unique status in Bentham's theory of morals, is not one that he expects makers of law and policy actually to use. Rather, he assumes that everyone tries to maximize his own happiness, and then argues that the proper business of government is to ensure, as far as it can, that its subjects do not impede one another in their pursuit of happiness. What Bentham in his political theory is above all concerned to do is to formulate the rules and describe the procedures which, he thinks, will ensure that government does this business as effectively as possible.

Bentham's greatest happiness principle has been much criticized, and so too has his account of what government ought to do and how it should do it. But there is not to be found in his writings nor (so far as I know) in those of any other of the Utilitarians, anything like the doctrine of the common good as Schumpeter formulates it. Neither Bentham nor any other Utilitarian denies that reasonable and well informed people could differ considerably about how principles should be applied to particular cases or even categories of cases; and they ordinarily assume that the well-informed are a minority. The idea of the uniquely just or uniquely reasonable end of policy is, I suggest, not to be found in utilitarian political theory.

Schumpeter's attack on the idea of 'the will of the people' is both more to the point and clearer. People who believe in democracy do quite often speak as if, even in large political communities, there was

[1] Long before Rousseau, philosophers and political writers had spoken of 'the common good', using the term in several different senses; but they were not democrats. Rousseau was perhaps the first to use the term in constructing a case for popular government.

always to be found some such will that governments ought, on pain of forfeiting their right to be considered democratic, to look for and put into effect. Schumpeter does not say that there never is such a will; he says that there is one only on rare and special occasions, and that these occasions are not confined to democracies. It is therefore unrealistic to the point of absurdity to define democracy as government in accordance with the people's will.

This is a reasonable, and by this time, familiar, objection to a certain idea of democracy, or rather way of speaking about it. But it is astonishing that Schumpeter should attribute this idea to the Utilitarians, of all people. For they were not only among the first to attack the idea as an absurdity, along with other ideas brought into fashion by the French revolution; they also (the radicals among them) made a case for democracy which is in some ways remarkably like the case made by Schumpeter. Democracy, in their eyes, is desirable, not because it ensures that the people's will is put into effect but because it makes it the interest of rulers to take account of the interests of their subjects. It does so by making the rulers (or the supreme law and policy makers among them) responsible to the people. The Utilitarians who favour democracy do not assume that the citizen has views about public matters that rulers ought to take into account; they assume rather that he is the best judge of his own interests, and therefore also a good judge of whom he can trust to look after them effectively. To ensure that makers of law and policy have powerful motives for looking after the interests of the people, Bentham (in his last democratic stage) was willing to go further than most of his disciples; he advocated universal suffrage, annual parliaments, the secret ballot and the abolition of the House of Lords. That aspirants to office should compete for the votes of citizens seemed to him as to Schumpeter an excellent principle.

Some of Bentham's arguments for democracy are unconvincing. It is not obvious that every man is the best judge of his own interests. Indeed, it is not even clear what is meant by saying that he is. Even if we allow (what is very doubtful) that men are the best judges of what makes for their happiness, it does not follow that they are good at choosing representatives to promote policies that put happiness more within their reach. But these assumptions that Bentham and other Utilitarians make, questionable though they are, have nothing to do with the doctrine that there is a collective will of the people that democratic governments ought to give effect to.

If we take the most influential of Utilitarian democrats, John Stuart Mill, we find him qualifying in several ways Bentham's postulate that every man is to be accounted the best judge of his own interest, and we also find him attributing a large role in democracy to the politically experienced and the well informed. Not only are makers of law and policy drawn mostly from their ranks, but it is also with them that most of the demands made on behalf of the people originate. That the politically active are a minority was as clear to John Stuart Mill as to any political scientist of the twentieth century.

It does not greatly matter that an economist venturing on to unfamiliar ground should make some rather obvious mistakes; and yet it is a pity that Schumpeter should (though in all innocence) have chosen the Utilitarians as the target of his attack, for they (more than any other political theorists of the nineteenth century) come close to thinking about democracy on a large scale in the way that he does. I suspect that Schumpeter, without meaning to do so, has helped to create in American universities the fashion that Robert Dahl speaks of: which is to suggest that 'everything believed about democracy prior to World War I, and perhaps World War II, was nonsense'. I suspect that not a few American political scientists, immersed in their studies of political behaviour in the largest of the Western democracies, gladly took his word for it that the theories of the past, which they were too busy to read, were so unrealistic as not to be worth reading. *Capitalism, Socialism and Democracy* first appeared in 1942, and anything believed about democracy before the Second World War was believed before Schumpeter published his views about democracy.

(b) THE IDEA OF A COLLECTIVE WILL

Long before Schumpeter, critics of democracy or of popular misconceptions about it had denied that voters first make up their minds what they want done and then choose representatives to do it for them. There was nothing new thirty years ago about the denial that there is, except on rare occasions, a collective will of the people; and the denial was not confined to people who said that democracy is an illusion. But Schumpeter's reasons for coming to a conclusion that others had come to before him were not quite the same as theirs, and are worth looking at.

He, too, as he examines critically this idea of the will of the people, has a good deal to say about the lack of reason in human behaviour. But he does not contrast a rational minority with an irrational majority, nor does he speak of elites and masses. Rather, he distinguishes two spheres of action, the political and the non-political, and argues that the ordinary citizen is much less rational in the first of these spheres than in the second. As he puts it, a man's more rational decisions are apt to be 'the decisions of daily life that lie within the little field which . . . [his] mind encompasses with a full sense of its reality'.[1]

[1] *Capitalism, Socialism and Democracy*, p. 258.

This field consists of 'the things under his personal observation, the things which are familiar to him independently of what his newspaper tells him, which he can directly influence or manage and for which he develops the kind of responsibility that is induced by a direct relation to the favourable or unfavourable effects of a course of action.'[1]

Schumpeter is speaking here of the ordinary citizen, the mere voter. He is not, of course, suggesting that there is anything peculiarly small-minded about him, that he, unlike his leaders, is fit to take only the small decisions that he does take. After all, some of his decisions may be very difficult, and also very important to him or to his family, colleagues or friends. If they are small decisions, they are so only in the sense that they affect a small number of persons; they need not be so in the sense that it calls for only a little intelligence or a little courage to take them. The ordinary citizen does not have to take the large decisions taken by his rulers, and the decision he takes when he votes is of little and uncertain effect, being only one among thousands. As Schumpeter puts it:

> The great political questions take their place in the psychic economy of the typical citizen with those leisure-hour interests that have not attained the rank of hobbies, and with the subjects of irresponsible conversation. These things seem so far off; they are not like a business proposition.

Or, on the next page,

> The typical citizen drops down to a lower level of mental performance as soon as he enters the political field. He argues and analyses in a way which he would readily recognize as infantile within the sphere of his real interests. He becomes a primitive again. His thinking becomes associative and effective.[2]

I should go some way in agreeing with Schumpeter here but by no means the whole way. There is something important that he is saying here, though its importance is obscured by irrelevancies. There is a distinction worth making between two spheres of action, in one of which the individual is more likely to act and think rationally than in the other. Part of what Schumpeter says here is that in the domain of politics the citizen has no well-defined role, other than to cast votes at elections. He does not have a governmental or political occupation in which he takes frequent decisions for which he is responsible (whether to superiors or electors) and whose consequences are brought home to him. In other words, government and politics are not his business in the sense that they are the business of professionals.

But this distinction between, if I may so put it, occupational and

[1] *Ibid.*, p. 259.
[2] *Ibid.*, pp. 261, 262.

responsible activity on the one hand, and occasional and non-responsible activity on the other, does not apply to the ordinary citizen, the mere voter, alone. It applies also to holders of public offices and to bosses in parties, to pressure groups and other bodies close to government. Though their occupations are, in the broad sense of the word, *political*, they too are concerned, most of them, with only a small part of government and politics. The responsibility and special competence of political leaders, or of all but a few of them, are also confined; and they too, as soon as they turn their minds to what happens outside the sphere of their competence, are situated much as the ordinary citizen, the mere voter, is. Schumpeter says that 'the typical citizen drops down to a lower level of mental performance as soon as he enters the political field'; and I should add 'and so too does the typical political leader as soon as he moves out of his own corner (often a very small one) of that field'. The citizen, if he is merely a citizen and not a leader as well, acquires no political skills, but that is not to say that, *in general*, his political judgment is any worse. Whether or not it is good depends on his natural intelligence, his education, and the extent of his interest in politics, and the same is true of the political leader.

What Schumpeter says about 'infantilism', and 'associative' and 'affective' thinking is not, I suggest, much to the purpose. I doubt whether the mere citizen, merely because political questions are more remote and less intelligible to him than the questions he has to settle at his business or in his home, is more childish or more a prey to passion and prejudice when he acts or thinks as a citizen than when he does so in some other capacity. I dare say that 'childish' behaviour among adults is more to be found in the family and the home than in either business or politics. I suggest that the mere citizen, when he 'enters the political field', becomes bewildered and confused rather than 'primitive', if by primitive is meant a prey to passion and prejudice. No doubt, in a crowd he is sometimes moved by passion and prejudice, but in the polling booth, where what he does matters most, he is ordinarily alone and calm.

Nor is it true that the less people understand what is at issue, the more excited and prejudiced they are apt to be. The typical citizen seldom gets more excited and primitive than when he is watching a football match, and he usually understands well enough what the game is about. I doubt whether it is the remoteness of political issues that makes him apt to think emotionally about politics. Bentham, whose writings seem not to have interested Schumpeter much, said that it is one of the advantages of representative over direct democracy that it is less apt to stimulate strong passions in the citizen. He was probably right. Politics in Athens were probably more like a football game than

in Britain or the United States, with the ordinary citizen understanding much better what was at issue and getting more excited. The
Athenian citizen was, presumably, a spectator rather than a player;
he seldom had a chance of speaking in the Ecclesia. But he could listen
to the speakers and applaud or express anger or dismay. Schumpeter
is much nearer being right when he says of the citizen today that in
his mind 'the great political questions' take their place with 'leisure-
hour interests that have not attained the rank of hobbies' than when
he says that in the political field 'he becomes a primitive again' and
'argues and analyses' more childishly than he does in the sphere of
'his real interests'.

Though Schumpeter speaks persuasively of 'the little field' outside
the sphere of politics which is all that the 'typical citizen's mind
encompasses with a full sense of its reality', he fails to notice that
what the mind of the typical leader or officeholder encompasses is
also a little enough field, even though it is part of the political sphere.

There is, of course, a minority of leaders and officeholders whose
minds 'encompass' the whole sphere of politics, or large sections of it,
though not presumably in great detail. These few who take the big
decisions know only a small proportion of the relevant facts, and therefore have to rely heavily on advisers, who often rely in their turn on other
advisers. Thus, though there are some persons in the community much
better placed than others to see the large issues in perspective and to
get the information and advice required to deal with them effectively,
they are dependent on thousands of others, as much to supply them
with the information and advice they need to be able to take their
decisions, as to carry them out when taken. To do what is expected
of them they need to be much better informed and advised than either
the generality of citizens or the holders of lesser posts of authority.

On one essential point, Schumpeter is right. We must expect people
to act the more rationally, the greater their opportunities and the
stronger their motives for doing so. The opportunities vary with the
information and advice at their command, and the strength of their
motives with the extent to which they can predict the consequences of
what they do or are responsible for their actions. Their opportunities
are perhaps greatest when they are at their business, whether that
business is political or not; and there are very few people whose business is to take political decisions of major importance.

Though Schumpeter attributes only a modest dose of political
wisdom to the ordinary citizen, assuming that his opportunities for
thinking realistically about the larger public issues are small, he does
not enquire how far this reduces his competence as a voter. Does the
citizen need to understand these issues better than he does, if he is
to cast his vote rationally? This is an important question that Schum-

peter does not raise, though others have raised it since he wrote his book.

But he does say that, even if ordinary citizens understood these issues much better than they in fact do, even if they had clear preferences, not just for one party or candidate or leader over others, but for some policies over others, it would still be the case that the larger decisions of policy taken in a democracy would scarcely ever give effect to anything that could properly be called the will of the people. As Schumpeter puts it:

> It is not only conceivable but, whenever individual wills are much divided, very likely that the political decisions produced will not conform to 'what people really want'. Nor can it be replied that, if not exactly what they want, they will get a 'fair compromise'. This may be so. The chances for this to happen are greatest with those issues which are quantitative in nature or admit of gradation, such as the question how much is to be spent on unemployment relief provided everybody favours some expenditure for that purpose. But with qualitative issues, such as the question whether to persecute heretics or to enter upon a war, the result may well . . . be equally distasteful to all the people whereas the decision imposed by a nondemocratic agency might prove much more acceptable to them.[1]

To illustrate his meaning, Schumpeter takes the religious settlement, the Concordat, that Napoleon, while he was First Consul, made with the Pope. This settlement, he says, satisfied the French people about as well as any settlement could have done, although it could not have been reached if France had been a democracy. The groups in France having strong opinions about the Church and its relations to the State would not have agreed to make the necessary concessions, and the Pope, encouraged by their dissensions, would have been less conciliatory. Schumpeter suggests here that groups unwilling to make concessions of their own accord will sometimes accept with relief an imposed settlement which they could not have reached without making the concessions. If they had had to bargain with one another, the terms of the settlement would have seemed unacceptable to them. Schumpeter then comes to this conclusion: 'If results that prove in the long run satisfactory to the people at large are made the test of government for the people, then government by the people . . . would often fail to meet it.'[2]

Schumpeter's point is well taken and important. Anyone who wants either to explain democracy realistically or to justify it must take account of it. It may quite often happen that the settlement which most people find acceptable is one that neither they nor their elected

[1] *Ibid.*, pp. 254–5.
[2] *Ibid.*, p. 256.

representatives could have reached; and it is the more likely to happen the more bitterly divided they are.

Schumpeter says that the chances of 'a fair compromise' are greatest when what people differ about is the distribution or allocation of something measurable. I doubt whether this is true. We know from experience that disputes about economic policy or about increases in wages and other benefits are no more easily settled than other disputes. The reason for this is simple enough: all disputes, or all serious disputes, are concerned with more than is measurable, even when they are concerned with the measurable as well. It is never, or hardly ever, a mere question of doing sums; it is also a question of deciding what it is proper to take into account when doing them.

Schumpeter says, and almost everyone agrees, that democracy is not a matter of putting a sort of collective will, the people's will, into effect. And yet democracies are, or are supposed to be, responsive to the wishes of the people, and it is often claimed for them that democratic governments are more concerned than others to reach fair compromises between the demands made on them by groups of citizens or their spokesmen. Again, it is widely claimed that a democratic government, though it does not (except rarely) give effect to the will of the people, governs in some sense with their consent and is responsible to them.

Therefore, before passing to other matters, let me consider two questions: What is to count as a fair compromise? and, When are decisions taken on behalf of a group to be reckoned expressions of their collective will? For, though the whole body of citizens hardly ever have a collective will, smaller groups of them may quite often do so, and may put pressure on governments and officials.

Let us imagine a small group of only six persons. There is some matter that concerns them all, and they put forward incompatible proposals as to what should be done about it, though they agree that a decision must be taken without too much delay. They can do either of two things: they can choose some seventh person, whom they all trust, and say: 'Here are our six proposals, please take a decision that takes account of all six of them and also of the realities of the situation.' Let us assume that this arbiter chosen by them is impartial and better informed, or better placed to get relevant information, than they are. Having made his decision, the arbiter may explain to the six men why he made it, or they may accept the decision on trust.

Alternatively, the six men may resolve to settle the matter themselves, each of them stating his case, and may then reach a compromise decision. In the first case, no less than in the second, the decision is a compromise. It is not a high Platonic act of justice by a wise man who knows better than other men do what is good for them. The arbiter, in reaching his decision, takes into account the wishes of the men to be affected by it as well as the realities of the situation. And this is precisely what the six men do when they reach their compromise decision. Yet the two decisions may differ considerably, though each is as much a fair compromise as the other.

We can, however, imagine two other decisions affecting these six men, one taken by an arbiter and the other by the men themselves, neither of which is a fair compromise. The arbiter may be ill-informed or partial, and two of the men may have good reasons for believing that they have been hard done by. Yet they may think it prudent to accept the decision on the ground that to challenge it would do them more harm than good. So, too, if the six men take the decision together, two of them may think that their preferences have been taken very little into account and may have good reasons for thinking so. Yet they too may think it prudent not to challenge the decision. These two decisions, like the first two, may differ considerably from one another.

Here, then, we have four compromise decisions, two of them taken directly by the group and two by their representative. How many of these decisions, if any, can be said to express a collective will, the will of the group? If the will of the group consists of decisions which conform to what everyone 'really wants' (that is to say, if it consists of decisions of which each is preferred by everyone to any alternative to it), then none of these four decisions need express that will. At the best, two of them *may*. The two which may, but need not, are, of course, the two fair compromises. It is possible, after all, that each of the six men, having listened to the arbiter's explanation of how he reached his decision, should say, 'This is what I now want done rather than what I proposed in the first place'. So, too, it is possible that each of them, having stated his case and listened to the others stating theirs, should say it of the compromise they reach together. But they need not say it of either decision in order to agree unanimously that it is a fair compromise. Faced by the decision, some or all of them may say, 'I still prefer my own proposal but I agree, that, in these circumstances, this is a fair compromise'. If, then, the will of the group consists of decisions which the six men unanimously agree are fair compromises, two of these decisions express that will and two do not.

We have here two different senses of the expression 'the will of the group', two different kinds of collective will. The first sense, which equates the popular or collective will with some proposal that everyone prefers to any alternative to it, is important in theory but not in practice. It is important in theory because political theorists have attached importance to it. It is unimportant in practice because in the real world there are few examples of it. It seldom happens that all the members of a group or community who take a decision prefer the proposal finally adopted to any other put forward; and when it does happen, it nearly always does so in very small groups, in professional bodies or associations or committees whose members do not constitute what we ordinarily call a people. For we think of a people, however few, as forming some kind of community.

The second sense, which equates the collective will with decisions that every member of the group agrees are fair compromises, is important in both practice and theory. For, though the kind of unanimity it envisages is also rare, it is much less rare than the first kind. It happens considerably more often that everyone agrees that there has been a fair compromise than that everyone prefers the proposal finally adopted to any alternative to it. More important still, this second sense defines a limit which, if seldom attained, is often aimed at. People who pride themselves on being democrats are pleased when a decision is reached which everyone who takes part in reaching it, or—better still—everyone affected by it and whose wishes have been taken into account, agrees is a fair compromise.

There is yet another, a third, sense in which we speak of a collective will. Even the two unfair compromises among the four decisions we have considered may be said, not improperly, to give effect to the wishes of our six men. If they all agree to refer their proposals to an arbiter and to abide by his decision, they commit themselves to accepting his decision. So, too, if they all agree to discuss their proposals with the intention of reaching a compromise and to accept the decision of the majority. The term 'the popular or collective will' is often used to cover just such cases as these. And there is, I think, a point to so using it. For in these two cases the men affected by the decision have actually made proposals, have expressed preferences. Even when the decision was made by an arbiter, their proposals were considered in the making of it. The arbiter was not asked to make the decision which, in his opinion, was in the best interests of the six men; he was asked to make the decision which seemed to him a fair compromise between their proposals, taking the realities of the situation into account. And the six men agreed to abide by his decision. So, too, when the men took the decision themselves, each was free to argue his case, and they agreed beforehand to accept the decision of the majority.

But in the case from real life taken by Schumpeter (Napoleon's Concordat with Pope Pius VII), the agreement reached was not an expression of the people's will, no matter how popular it turned out to be, because it was not a compromise between proposals made by the French people reached by someone commissioned to reach it. Indeed, it was not even a compromise between a variety of wishes, for Napoleon's purpose was not to give each interested group as much as he could of what they wanted, taking into account the wishes of other groups and what was feasible in the circumstances; his purpose, rather, was to reach an agreement which would pacify them by laying to rest their fears, an agreement which they would come *in time* to accept as wise and just.

Schumpeter is not alone in suggesting that Napoleon, when he made the Concordat, was giving effect to the will of the French people. Several historians have done the same; and it would be pedantic to object to their doing so. But the political theorist, surely, ought not here to follow the example of the historians; for it is his business to make distinctions they need not make. No decision, however popular and widely understood by the people or by any group of them, gives effect to the people's will or the will of the group, unless the people or the group have been consulted and have expressed their wishes, and the maker of the decision has reached what seems to them a fair compromise.

Democracy has been called 'government by consent of the governed', 'government responsible to the governed', and 'government that gives effect to the will of the people'. These expressions are not synonymous, and each is used in more than one sense. The first two are closer to one another in meaning than either is to the third; and would also seem to apply much better than the third does to the great democracies of our time. Not that we expect to find any government that claims to be democratic governing with the entire consent of its subjects or completely responsible to them, but we do expect it to come closer to doing this than to giving effect to the people's will. As political theorists we are trying to get our ideas about democracy as clear as we can; we are not looking for an account of it which commits us to saying either that no government ever has been democratic or that all governments popular with their subjects are so.

If the six men in our illustration, instead of making proposals or expressing preferences for some courses of action over others, were, without more ado, to appoint a seventh man to take decisions in their interest and binding upon them, this man's decisions would not be expressions of their will. Their choosing the man to take the decisions would not be enough to make his decisions expressions of their will. The man, in taking the decisions, may well take into account what he believes to be their wishes, but he is not required to do this; he is required to take decisions on their behalf and in their interest. No doubt the more he knows about their wishes, the better he is able to do what they require of him; but still, what they require is only that he should take decisions on their behalf and in their interest. If, in reaching his decisions, he were to make the sort of calculations that Napoleon made when he negotiated the *Concordat*, he would still be doing what they require of him. To take decisions in people's interest, taking as much account as you think proper of what you believe to be their wishes, is not to take decisions that express their will, in any of the three senses I tried to distinguish. This is so, whether or not you have been elected to take them. Even a governess may take account of the wishes of the children in her care. Indeed, if she is wise and conscientious, she often will do so. After all, no rulers, democratic or undemocratic, beneficent or oppressive, can afford not to take considerable account of the wishes of their subjects.

Napoleon got power by force, whereas our six men choose a seventh man to take decisions on their behalf. The seventh man is their representative in a sense that Napoleon was not the representative of the French people. He acts with their consent; he has the right to do what he does only because they have appointed him to do it, and they can withdraw the authority they gave him. But a man who makes a decision with the consent of the persons affected by it does not therefore make a decision which expresses their will. Democracy, when it is representative and not direct, is much more government by consent of the governed than it is government giving expression to their will.

Government by consent is again something different from government by rulers who are much admired or loved or respected by their subjects. No doubt rulers who govern by consent of the governed are quite often admired and respected, and sometimes even loved, by many of their subjects, though I suspect that the most admired and best loved (as well as most hated) rulers have been autocrats. Democracy not only encourages scepticism and irreverence but also thrives on them, and in any case can tolerate much larger doses of them than other forms of government can. There are, as political psychologists like to remind us, people who need to admire and even to love those in authority over them, but such people are not perhaps the best citizens in a democracy.

Clearly, then, if democracy is defined as government which gives effect to the will of the people, there is precious little of it even in the countries that most of us, at least in the West, agree to call democracies. But this does not mean that it is not important in a democracy that citizens should take a keen interest in public affairs. They cannot, of course, take an interest in all such affairs; their interest must be selective. Nevertheless, it does matter that there should be groups of citizens keenly interested in every public issue, even though no citizen or group can be interested in them all. It matters, too, that they should combine in order to discuss these issues and to express opinions that they share, or at least are ready to support. In other words, though there may scarcely ever be a collective will of the whole people on any public issue, even a major one, it may still matter greatly that there should be among the people many collective wills on such issues. If we concede that there is rarely any such thing as a will of the people, we are not bound to agree that political apathy is no bad thing or even that it presents no danger to democracy.

There are two reasons why it matters that citizens should not be politically apathetic, that they should combine, not merely to define and to push shared interests, but also to express opinions about matters of policy that do not affect them directly. One reason is not peculiar to democracies but applies to all political systems in large, literate and economically advanced societies. In such societies, no government can achieve its aims unless it keeps in close touch with its subjects, and with diverse groups and categories of them, and it cannot in practice keep in touch with them unless it allows them some latitude in expressing their wishes. To be efficient, a modern government cannot in practice confine itself to indoctrinating its subjects and telling them what to do; it must also be responsive to their wishes, which it cannot be unless it allows them some scope to express those wishes.

The second reason applies to democracies. If government is to remain democratic, or if it is to come as close to being democratic as conditions allow, it must be subjected to continuous, relevant, independent and well-informed criticism, and criticism is not likely to be relevant and well informed, as well as independent, unless citizens are able and willing to define and to push their interests and opinions, and to associate for that purpose. Though democracy is essentially government by consent of the governed, or government responsible to them, and not government that gives effect to the people's will, it cannot long survive unless there is plenty of collective willing among the people.

Some democrats, and even political scientists who write about democracy, say or imply that a government is the more democratic, the closer its policies come to meeting the demands made by the people, or rather by groups of them organized to make such demands. Robert Dahl sometimes speaks in this way, and so do other modern theorists of democracy. Democratic governments do not, to be sure (except very rarely), give effect to the will of the people, but they are the more democratic the closer their policy decisions come to striking a balance between the demands made on them.

This is, I think, a mistake. Not only because it is extraordinarily difficult (not to say impossible) to lay down principles for striking such a balance, nor even because there are always some groups whose interests or opinions are involved or relevant that are not organized to make demands, but because this is not really what people want their governments to do. To be sure, they want them to take notice of their demands, to take them into account whenever they are relevant, but they do not conceive of the business of government, even democratic government, as merely (or even primarily) a balancing of demands, a devising of policies that go as far as available resources allow to meeting them, giving due weight to the size of the groups that support the demands and the importance they attach to them. This essentially utilitarian conception of government is not only (for reasons I hope to discuss later) unrealistic; it is also, I suggest, an invention of political theorists and scientists and does not express a widely shared attitude to democracy.

There is nothing inconsistent—so at least it seems to me—about deploring political apathy and wanting citizens to be active in making and pressing demands on the government, on the one hand, and on the other, denying that a government is the more democratic, the more its policies are designed to meet those demands as fully as they can be met. A government is democratic to the extent that it is responsible to its subjects, and the criteria of responsibility may be such that they are never, or hardly ever, completely met; they may be such as to oblige us to admit that every government claiming to be democratic is considerably less so than it claims to be. This we can concede, and yet deny that the extent to which a government meets the demands made on it is a measure of its responsibility. As political writers have so often observed, responsibility and responsiveness, though connected, are not the same thing. To say that responsible government is unlikely to survive for long unless governments are exposed to many, diverse and continuous pressures from their subjects is one thing; it is quite another to say that government is the more democratic, the more responsive it is to these pressures. The second assertion is, I suggest, mistaken, and would still be mistaken even if it were possible (as it is not) to measure responsiveness over the whole field of policy-making, and not only within this or that part of it.

If democracy is government responsible to the people, then a government can be democratic even though it refuses to meet widespread popular demands which it could meet with the resources at its disposal. A government may not only do this without ceasing to be democratic; it may be its duty to do it, and not the less so because it is democratic. A democrat can, without inconsistency, argue in favour of the kind of relation that Burke, in his famous speech to the electors of Bristol, said ought to hold between a member of Parliament and his constituents. Burke, of course, was very far from being a democrat, but there is, so far as I can see, nothing undemocratic about his conception of proper relations between members of Parliament and their constituents.

According to Burke, the prime duty of a member to his constituents (and to his country) is to give the best of his mind to the business they have sent him to do; which is to discuss and vote on proposals of law and declarations of policy affecting not only his constituents but the people generally. He has also a more particular and secondary duty to his constituents alone: to watch over their interests. Neither of these duties carries with it the obligation to do what his constituents tell him to do or to work out a compromise between their various demands and use it as a guide to action in Parliament. The member ought, of course, to take notice of his constituents' opinions and wishes, just as he ought of other opinions and wishes which seem to him relevant and which may help him to reach sounder conclusions. He is not a solitary thinker; he is a practical man doing business with other such men, and cannot but rely heavily on others for information and advice. Burke's position, put in a few words and generalized, comes down to this: though makers of law or policy acquire their right to make them by being elected to their offices, it is not their duty to make the laws or policies which come closest to the wishes (where they have any) of the electors; rather it is their duty to do what, in their judgment, is in the best interest of the community.

This doctrine of Burke's about the obligations of elected legislators and makers of policy to their electors is not now widely held, in the form he gave to it, in any Western democracy. In his day, England was an aristocracy, and the doctrine, as he put it, now looks undemocratic to many democrats. And yet it is quite compatible with government by consent of the governed. If we hold, as many people do, that no government can give effect, except on rare occasions, to anything that deserves to be called the will of the people, that it ought not to try to do so but ought to lose power if it does not retain their confidence, we come close to holding Burke's doctrine. That government, even in a democracy, ought not to defer too much to public opinion, is a respectable belief.

For public opinion is not the will of the people. Most people have no opinions about most public issues, and it is often the opinions of small minorities that are the most widely and loudly publicized. Opinion polls are deceptive, even when they put as simple a question as: *Would you vote the government out of power, if you had the chance?* The man who says he would quite often votes for the government, when eventually he gets the chance. No government can govern effectively unless it can rely on a considerable period of power and can act with considerable independence. It may be true that, on the rare occasions when there is a will of the people, a democratic government is more likely than an undemocratic one to give effect to it, but what makes a government democratic is not its giving effect to that will.

It may help us to get clearer ideas about democratic government and 'the will of the people', if we consider how holders of public authority are influenced by the persons over whom they exercise it; or, to use more old-fashioned but simpler language, how rulers are influenced by their subjects. This influence is of three kinds. Rulers in taking their decisions are influenced by how they expect their subjects to react to the decisions or to their effects, by the demands their subjects make for specific benefits, and by the preferences they express for some policies over others. Clearly, to the extent that rulers are influenced by anticipated reactions—whether what they fear is a riot or a defeat at the polls or what they hope for is good will and applause or victory at the next elections—their decisions do not give effect to anything that can properly be called 'the will of the people'. Shepherds are influenced by the anticipated reactions of their sheep. But sheep, it might be said, do not try to influence shepherds, and merely react to what shepherds do, whereas the reactions of subjects are often intended to affect the further decisions of their rulers in some particular way. But then, so too, in the Western desert, were the reactions of Montgomery to the decisions of Rommel, and vice versa. Each of these commanders sometimes produced an intended effect on the decisions of the other, yet neither gave effect to the will of the other; at least not in the sense that an agent or representative is supposed to give effect to his principal's will.

Rulers, to the extent that they feel obliged, when they take a decision, to prefer one course of action to another on the ground that it enables them to meet demands for specific benefits or is more in keeping with what they have reason to believe their subjects, or some considerable section of them, wish them to do, may be said to be *influenced* by the wishes of the people, or of part of the people. Only on those rare occasions when there are good grounds for believing that a majority of the people (or of the electors) have expressed a clear preference for some course of action, and the rulers take that course because there is a popular or electoral majority in favour of it, may they be said to give effect to the will of the people.

I suggest that this is how we should use the term 'the will of the people' when we seek to explain what democracy is and to distinguish it from other forms of government. This is not, of course, how democratic politicians use it, nor yet how we use it in ordinary political conversation; and I am not suggesting that either they or we should abandon our usual practices. It is only when, as students of politics, we aim at a precision of language unnecessary, and sometimes even intolerable, on other occasions, that we have anything to gain by the uses I suggest.

If we use the term in this way, we can concede that no government, even the most democratic, gives effect to the people's will all the time, or even much of the time, and yet argue that democracy, much more than other forms of government, encourages people to have and to express opinions as to what their rulers should do and encourages the rulers to give effect to them. We can also admit that rulers who are not democratic sometimes give effect to the will of the people. They may do so, for example, by holding a plebiscite or referendum, encouraging their subjects to choose freely between several courses of action, ensuring that they do so without intimidation or fear of reprisal, and then taking the course of action preferred by the majority. An autocrat could do this, if he chose, and it would be absurd to deny that he was giving effect to the will of the people merely because he was an autocrat. Equally, it would be absurd to insist that he was a democratic ruler and not an autocrat merely because, occasionally and at his own discretion, he chose to consult his subjects. Democratic rulers are (in a sense still to be defined) politically responsible to their subjects. Just as rulers can be politically responsible to their subjects without giving effect to their will, so they can sometimes give effect to their will without being politically responsible to them.

I suggested earlier that students of politics ought not to say of Bonaparte's Concordat with Pius VII that it gave effect to the will of the French people, even though many a historian says just this about it. The student of politics or political scientist (call him what you will) ought not to follow the historian's example, for his business is different. He would do well to deny that the Concordat did this, if the most that can be said for it is that it allayed widespread fears and was eventually recognized by most Frenchmen as a wise and fair settlement, given the circumstances.

The political scientist ought also, again in the interest of clear thinking, to deny that a ruler, merely because he takes a decision that enables his subjects to get what they want, is giving effect to their will, even though he takes the decision with precisely this intention. For his subjects may never have wished him to take the decision, and may never even have considered the possibility that he might take it. Or they may have been opposed to his taking it, because they did not realize that it would help rather than hinder them in their endeavours to satisfy their wants.

If a grown-up person, a parent or a teacher, were to do something with the sole intention of enabling the children in his charge to get what they wanted, we would not say that, in doing it, he was giving effect to their will; unless, of course, they had asked him to do it or had indicated in some other way that they wanted him to do it, and he was doing it because they had asked or otherwise expressed their wishes. We would not even say that he was acting with their consent. Children, especially when they are very young, are much less capable than adults are of understanding the decisions that others take for their benefit, or of understanding after the event how they have been affected by them. This presumably is one reason among others why they cannot be governed by their consent. Indeed, they cannot even, for some considerable time after they have learned to make demands on others, be governed by rules; they have to be told what to do on every occasion when it is dangerous, or for some other reason undesirable, to let them do what they please. But this difference between children and adults in relation to those in authority over them, though relevant in other connections, is not to the point here. The point is essentially a simple one. To give effect to another person's will, in the sense relevant here, is to do what he wants you to do because he wants you to do it. It is not to do what makes it easier for him to satisfy his wants; not even when your reason for doing it is to make this easier for him.

The Utilitarian holds that what is ultimately desirable is that people should get what they want in the order of their own preferences. Yet the Utilitarian can, without inconsistency, be in favour of compelling people to do what they do not want to do and giving them what they would rather not have. He need not stop at preventing people doing harm to one another; he can also prevent them doing harm to themselves, if he has good reason to believe that by so doing he will ensure that in the long run more of their wants are satisfied. The Utilitarian believes in educating children; and this often involves giving them what they do not want because they cannot yet appreciate its usefulness. To be true to his own assumptions, the Utilitarian must distinguish between situations in which doing what other people want him to do increases the chance that their wants will be satisfied and situations in which it does not. He must make this distinction even when he is discharging the duties of an office to which he has been democratically elected.

To be responsible *for* looking after other people is one thing, to be responsible *to* them for how you look after them is another, and to give effect to their wishes is still another. About the first responsibility there is nothing democratic though there is about the second; and yet you can be responsible *to* people without being required to give effect to their wishes just as you can be responsible *for* them. What is required of you is that you should carry out the duties of your office. Those duties may, of course, be so defined as to require you, within broader or narrower limits, to give effect to, or at least to consult, the wishes of the persons for whom you are responsible, who are to benefit from your carrying out your duties. But this may be so, as much when you are appointed to your office by someone who is not to benefit from your services, as when you are elected to it by the beneficiaries. A man who employs a governess to look after his children may require her to accede to their wishes as far as she can do so without harming them, and may believe that she can go a long way in doing so. In a democracy, persons elected to public offices may be allowed a great latitude. Though the citizens who vote for them no doubt wish them to exercise the duties of their offices, these duties may not require them to take the decisions the electors want them to take.

I have said that rulers can give effect to the people's will without being politically responsible to them. I would now add that they cannot give effect to it unless the people owe obedience to them. When we say of someone that he gives effect to the people's will, we assume that he has authority over them. General de Gaulle probably knew that there were many people in Britain who did not want their country to join the Common Market, and that some of them not only expected but hoped for his veto. They could not rely on Macmillan or Wilson to keep Britain out but they could rely on him. Yet the General, reliable though he was, was not, when he pronounced his veto, giving effect to their will, even though he did what they wanted him to do. He was not acting on their behalf; they were not members of a group or community in his charge or under his authority. I do not say that he was not giving effect to their will in any allowable sense of those words, but merely that he was not doing so in the sense that concerns us here.

Schumpeter's account of democracy

According to the classical theory (as Schumpeter interprets it), it is the people, the electors, who decide the political issues and who then choose representatives to see to it that their decisions are carried out. Thus the people's choice of representatives or rulers is treated as a means to an end. The people choose their rulers in order that they should give effect to their will. This, says Schumpeter, is the wrong way to go about explaining democracy. What distinguishes democracy from other forms of government is not what rulers are supposed to do but how they come to be rulers. The crux of the matter is the selection of the supreme makers of law and policy.

Schumpeter does not deny that democratic governments do have aims in important respects different from those of other governments, and that their priorities among their aims are also different. People who prefer democracy to other forms of government do so, no doubt, largely because they want governments to pursue certain aims. Nevertheless, what makes a government democratic is not, according to Schumpeter, the type of aim it pursues. As we have seen already, undemocratic governments as well as democratic ones sometimes give effect to the will of the people, and all governments (except direct democracies) do so only very rarely. Schumpeter does not even think it worth while enquiring to what extent it is possible or desirable to give effect to such a will, or what methods a democracy might use to elicit such a will more frequently. Indeed, he does not even distinguish between giving effect to the people's will (at best a rare occurrence) and taking account of the political demands of the various groups that constitute the people (a never ending business in all democracies). He devotes only three chapters of his book to discussing democracy, and uses one of them to dispel what he thinks are widespread illusions about it. But he does, as a social theorist, make a plea for one principle of analysis in preference to another: it is better to distinguish forms of government by their institutions, and especially by their methods of appointing and dismissing the supreme makers of law and policy, than by their aims. It is better because it provides us with criteria more easily applied.

As Schumpeter puts it, 'the role of the people [in a democracy] is to produce a government or else an intermediate body which in turn will produce a national executive or government'.[1] Having made his essential point, he then puts forward his well-known definition: 'The democratic method is that institutional arrangement for arriving at political decisions in which individuals acquire the power to decide by means of a competitive struggle for the people's vote.'[2] I doubt whether any definition of democracy (or of 'the democratic method', whatever that may mean) has been as much quoted by students and teachers of politics in English-speaking universities as this one. It is worth considering for a moment how it is worded.

Though what Schumpeter wants to say is perhaps clear enough, it is so largely because the reader does not take him at his word. For example, he speaks of 'political decisions'. But a vote is a political decision, and yet the voter does not acquire the power to vote by competing for votes. Schumpeter, clearly, does not mean political decisions of any kind; he means the kinds that governments take. Why, then, does he not use the word 'government' or 'govern'? Again, he speaks of *the democratic method* when he might have spoken, more simply, of *democracy*, and of the *power to decide* when he might have spoken, more correctly, of the *right*. Suppose that he had confined himself to saying, 'In a democracy those who govern acquire the right to do so by competing for the people's vote'. Would he have left anything important unsaid which he put into his definition? I do not see that he would. He would have used eighteen words instead of thirty. But it is not so much this economy that I would bring to your notice; for every writer knows that

[1] *Capitalism, Socialism and Democracy*, p. 269.
[2] *Ibid.*

it often takes longer to say something in ten words than in twenty. What I would have you notice is merely this: if Schumpeter had put his meaning into these eighteen words, few of his readers would have supposed that he was saying anything new. He would have made a simpler, clearer and much less often quoted statement. His contribution to democratic theory consists, not in this now famous definition of democracy, which points to nothing about it not long familiar to political writers, and says clumsily what could be said simply, but in the reasons he gives for preferring some criteria to others in distinguishing democracy from other forms of government.

It is easier, according to Schumpeter, to discover whether rulers get their authority by competing for the people's vote than to discover whether they use it to give effect to the people's will. The competition must, he says, be 'free competition for a free vote'.[1] Though he makes no attempt to define either *free competition* or a *free vote*, he is not to be criticized for failing to do so. His discussion of democracy is only a relatively small part of a big book. It is brief and summary. His intention is not to give a full explanation of democracy but to suggest that it is more useful to go about the business of explaining it in one way rather than in others. Even if Schumpeter's definition were simpler and shorter than it is (which it could be without loss of meaning), it would still be only a beginning. Not every kind of competing for votes is compatible with democracy. Nevertheless, the man who tells us to attend first to this competition rather than to anything else, when we try to explain democracy, is saying something important not often said at the time that Schumpeter said it. To say that the competition must be free and must be for a free vote is only to make a beginning. But then when you set about constructing a theory, it matters greatly how you begin, what your first moves are. It matter greatly, no matter what your purpose is, whether it is merely to explain or to approve and condemn. It is no accident that in the West we like to say that in a democracy those who aspire to govern compete freely for a free vote, whereas in certain other parts of the world, they prefer to say that in a democracy those who govern give effect to the will of the people—or even promote their real interests.

Another reason, according to Schumpeter, for preferring his way of looking at democracy to older ways is that it allows us to recognize just how important leadership is. Schumpeter is here using the word 'leadership' in the broad sense, and not in the narrower sense which I tried to distinguish from government and management. Organized groups and communities 'act' through their leaders. What Schumpeter calls 'the classical theory' did not, he thinks, recognize the importance of leadership; 'It attributed to the electorate an altogether unrealistic

[1] *Ibid.*, p. 271.

degree of initiative which practically amounted to ignoring leadership.'[1]

I have already given my reasons for doubting that there was ever a
classical theory of democracy. But there was, and still is, a democratic
rhetoric which may, if we allow ourselves to take it seriously, mislead
us in some of the ways that Schumpeter suggests. Most of the earlier
writers about democracy had little that was specific to say about the
role of leaders in it. But this, I suggest, was not because, in their
simplemindedness, they did not understand that all government, even
the most democratic, involves leadership; it was because they were
arguing in favour of a political system which did not yet exist, and
were not explaining how it works. They were arguing to such conclusions as these: 'No man has the right to govern other men unless
they have consented to his doing so', or 'Governments should, as far
as possible, do what the people want them to', or 'Governments should
promote the happiness of their subjects and are most likely to do so
when they are popularly elected'. They were arguing for some general
principle or other and were not explaining the machinery of democratic government, the political roles involved in it. Or, rather,
they were doing the first of these things much more than the
second.

To be a leader or a plain citizen is to play a political role. Neither
leadership nor citizenship can be discussed to much purpose except in
relation to a political system. Now, we could as truly say of these early
champions of democracy that they neglected the citizen as that they
neglected the leader. If we take, for example, such advocates of popular government as Tom Paine or James Mill, we find that they have
as little to say about the citizen as they have about the leader—that
they come no nearer to giving a full and realistic account of his political
role. They say so little that is specific about any of the roles that constitute the political system that we can hardly accuse them of attributing too great an initiative either to the plain citizen or to the leader.
They do not consider in any detail how 'the people' act. They speak
vaguely of 'the will of the people' or 'the general interest' without
troubling to enquire how either the one or the other comes to be
formulated—what the citizens or their leaders contribute to making
or to achieving it.

As soon as we find a champion of representative democracy taking
much account of the machinery of government—as, for example, John
Stuart Mill—we find him very much concerned with the role of leaders.
In his book on *Representative Government*, though he does not discuss
leadership in the sort of terms that political scientists do today, he is
very much aware that the initiative in politics does not belong to the

[1] *Ibid.*, p. 270.

ordinary citizen. That large numbers of people can act only through leaders was as obvious to him as it is to us. Like Tocqueville, he believed that democracy would in time spread everywhere in the West, and he deplored some of the effects of the growing passion for equality. But he did not attribute to citizens a greater initiative than they were capable of. On the contrary, he wanted them to take a keener interest in public affairs.

The first modern champions of democracy were, as a matter of fact, much more afraid of irresponsible leadership than inclined to overrate the energy and enterprise of the people. Rousseau produced an early version of what Michels was to call the iron law of oligarchy, and was the first to suggest that the political role of the elector, who is just that and nothing more, is virtually insignificant. And Bentham, so keen to be lucid and so often misunderstood, came in the end to favour democracy because he believed that rulers are apt to be too powerful for their subjects' good. They must be kept in check, he argued, by making it a condition of their getting and retaining power that they should win the people's votes at periodic elections. And if he preferred representative to direct democracy, it was because he thought it more likely that law and policy would be in the general interest if they were made by persons elected by the people rather than by the people themselves. What he wanted was government by leaders whose power depended on their getting or retaining the people's confidence, expressed annually at free elections. It is, *pace* Schumpeter, much more distrust of leaders than excessive faith in the people which is prominent in the writings of the early champions of democracy.

Since Schumpeter wrote his book, political scientists, especially in America, have done what earlier writers about democracy did not do and perhaps could not do: they have put forward systematic explanations of the functions of parties and pressure groups and have distinguished between types of leaders. They have done what Schumpeter had no time to do in the few pages of his book which treat of democracy.

It is true (and it may be this that Schumpeter had in mind when he spoke of the neglect of leadership) that, until quite recent times, political theorists have been more concerned with rulers and holders of public offices than with other types of leaders. But this is true of all political theorists and not only of theorists of democracy. They have discussed, above all, three problems: the nature of public authority and of the state, the limits of political obligation, and the distribution of authority best suited to promoting whatever they took to be the proper ends of government. They enquired how the state was or should be organized, how holders of public authority were or should be related to their subjects or to one another. The leader who holds no public office, who mobilizes and organizes sections of the people to help candidates get elected to public office or to put pressure on the government, interested them much less. But this neglect, not of leadership in general but of a certain type of it, diminished with the spread of democracy and the proliferation of theories about it.

This type of leader, the persuader and spokesman who tries to draw people together to achieve aims which involve putting pressure on government or getting control of it, was neglected only by political philosophers who constructed general theories about government; it was not neglected by historians. Nor was it neglected by writers who tried to explain how government functions in this or that country. If you look at books about how Britain or France or the United States was governed, books written during the last quarter of the nineteenth century, when for the first time in history there were several great democracies in the world, you will not find them neglecting parties and pressure groups and other efforts to mobilize and direct public opinion to some purpose. What is lacking in these books is not attention to such obvious facts of political life; it is rather clear and coherent ideas about the roles of leaders, parties and pressure groups in large democracies. It is only in the last thirty years that political scientists have attempted to construct general theories to explain how some leaders compete for power and how others compete for influence with those who have power or who stand a chance of getting it. Only if neglecting leadership means not producing general theories about it, is it true that writers about democracy have neglected it until quite recently.

And if now they have ceased to neglect it, this is not due, as Schumpeter suggests it is, to their having discarded the absurd belief that in democracies governments give effect to the people's will. For in fact very few of them ever did believe this. And, in any case, even if the belief were true (even if the will of the people, in the sense of a clear preference of a majority of them for some policy over others, were often expressed and given effect to) there would still be as great a need as ever for leadership. There would still be the need for some men to take the initiative in proposing possible courses of action, and to argue publicly for and against them; and they would be the politically active minority, and no less active perhaps than they are now. Even in a small direct democracy, there are leaders; the business of making proposals and debating them devolves on a minority. And if, in a large modern democracy, ordinary citizens were to be given the chance of voting for and against major proposals of law (if, in other words, there were many referenda), the task of organizing these frequent consultations, of deciding what proposals to submit to the people, and of putting the case for and against them in such a way that citizens could understand what was at issue, would be immense. The citizens would, no doubt, be considerably more active politically than they now are, but leaders would not be less numerous or less active, and their activities would be different from those of the citizens.

What do these writers mean who say that the great mass of citizens are politically passive? Do they mean only that they are not active in the ways that leaders are? This is a truism that nobody contests. Or do they mean that most citizens are indifferent to most public issues, even the important ones? This, no doubt, is true, but is quite compatible with most citizens having strong and definite opinions about some issues.

And is it not true also of leaders that most of them are indifferent to most public issues? It is said that they are by people better placed than I am to judge—by other leaders. 'The trouble with trade union leaders', I have sometimes heard leaders who were not trade unionists say, 'is that many of them—though mind you, not all—don't really understand or care about any but the few problems they spend their time dealing with.' And I have heard trade union officials say the same about shop stewards, who are also leaders at a different though still important level. There are, no doubt, some leaders who have strong and clear opinions about many public issues, but they are a minority among leaders. The leader who cares deeply about only a few issues and is as indifferent as the ordinary citizen to most of the others— for example, many a trade union leader or party boss or business magnate in close touch with government circles—is ordinarily very active politically. He spends much of his time, and sometimes most of it, trying to influence political decisions.

Leaders are of course politically more active than ordinary citizens are. But this does not mean that they come any closer to having a collective political will. For all their political activity and the proliferation of strongly held political opinions among them, for all the political skills and contacts they acquire, they are not in a democracy, any more than the mass of citizens are, organized to act together as one body politically.

There are other advantages that Schumpeter claims for his way of explaining democracy as compared with older ways, the ways that he calls 'the classical theory'. But I shall not consider them all, for my purpose is not to assess in general his account of democracy; rather, it is to look carefully at those of his arguments which seem to me to raise important issues for the theorist of democracy. And I am as much concerned to discuss these issues as to agree or disagree with what he says about them. In some ways, I have used his ideas as he used 'the classical theory': though, with this difference, I hope, that the ideas I attribute to him really are to be found in a book published under his name.

Schumpeter's conception of the manufactured will

Another advantage that Schumpeter claims for his way of explaining democracy is that it draws attention to something important that the older theories played down or ignored altogether. This something he calls the Manufactured Will. The classical theory, he says, either fails to notice it or else rejects it as an aberration, as something that ought not to be; whereas in his theory it comes in, as he puts it, 'on the ground floor',[1] which is its proper place in any realistic assessment of democracy. This manufactured will is 'the product and not the motive power of the political process'.[2] This will, he says, is in fact created by the leaders who, according to the classical theory, are supposed to give effect to the will of the people. They and the organizations they control are, in theory, the agents of the people; their business is to satisfy the people's demands to the extent that they can be satisfied by political action. But, in practice, it is organized groups and their leaders who, to a large extent, produce the demands. As Schumpeter puts it:

> These groups may consist of professional politicians or of exponents of an economic interest or of idealists of one kind or another or of people simply interested in staging and managing political shows. The sociology of such groups is immaterial to the argument in hand. The only point that matters here is that . . . they are able to fashion and, within very wide limits, even to create the will of the people. What we are confronted with in the analysis of political processes is largely not a genuine but a manufactured will.[3]

This argument is far from simple. Nobody comes by his political beliefs and preferences uninfluenced by others, and where there are many people to be influenced, those who want to influence them will form organizations to enable them to do so more effectively. Also, as we have seen already, no group can have a collective will, unless they are organized to give expression to it. And whatever the decision they accept in the end, it will probably differ considerably from what most of them wanted to begin with; it will be, at the best, what they agree is a fair compromise, and their leaders (if they have any, which they will have unless the group is very small) will have had a lot to do with getting them to agree. Indeed, many of them will accept their

[1] *Capitalism, Socialism and Democracy*, p. 270.
[2] *Ibid.*, p. 263.
[3] *Ibid.*, p. 263.

leaders' advice because they trust them without bothering to examine their arguments. Again, not every leader of an organized group, even one that is democratic, expresses what is in any strict sense the collective will of the group, for he may not have consulted their wishes; and yet when he makes demands or statements in their name, he may be acting with their consent and have their support. Speaking for a group of people, whether the speaker expresses their collective will or is merely authorized by them to make demands and statements that they are ready to stand by, involves a great deal of influencing people, of getting them to accept, or to feel committed to, decisions and pronouncements which do not originate with them and which they do little or nothing to formulate. This must be so, if organized groups are to be effective, especially when they are large groups.[1]

Schumpeter is not, I take it, suggesting that organized persuasion, merely as such, is 'manufacturing a will' that is not genuine. For, however reasonable and well-informed people are, they cannot act together effectively unless they are organized, and wherever there is organization, there is organized persuasion. Also, in a large community, people must always take many of the decisions of their authorized spokesmen on trust, without fully understanding them or considering the arguments for and against them. All this is obvious enough and is not, so it seems to me, what Schumpeter has in mind when he speaks of the manufactured will. This is, I think, made clear when he says: 'The weaker the logical element in the processes of the public mind and the more complete the absence of rational criticism and of the rationalizing influence of personal experience and responsibility, the greater are the opportunities for groups *with an axe to grind*.'[2] It would seem then that there is a manufactured will, not wherever there is organized persuasion, but only where there is an organized attempt to exploit ignorance and credulity.

People with 'an axe to grind' are, in this context, people who have something to gain by inducing others to hold certain beliefs or to support certain demands or policies or parties or leaders. Now, we have seen (and we have supposed that Schumpeter would agree), that, no matter how rational the voter in a large democracy, he needs the

---

[1] No one objected to organized bodies seeking to mobilize groups of citizens and to formulate their opinions more strongly than Rousseau did. But what he was afraid of, when he banned organized political groups in his ideal republic, was not anything that could be called a *manufactured* as distinct from a *genuine* or *spontaneous* will; it was rather a *sectional* as distinct from a *general* will. Citizens should come to the assembly, in which the big decisions affecting the entire community are taken, as far as possible with open minds, which they cannot do if, in organized groups outside the assembly, they commit themselves before hand to some course of action in the assembly.

[2] *Ibid.*, p. 263 (my italics).

services of organized groups of persuaders, if he is to be able to make rational political choices. It could never be enough to supply him with the relevant information and then leave him to get on with it politically. To be able to make a rational choice between candidates or policies, he needs to be presented with a limited number of each and to hear some, *but not too many*, arguments for and against them. Presumably, the makers of these arguments, the selectors of candidates and policies for his choice, even the selectors of the information to be supplied to him, often have some axe to grind; they stand to gain by persuading him and other voters that they, and not their rivals, are right and well informed. It could hardly be contrived that no one should argue publicly for any candidate or policy, or compare candidates and policies, or supply information about them, unless he had nothing to gain by doing so; and if it could be contrived, it would not be worth contriving. Because persuaders have 'an axe to grind', it does not follow that their persuasion is an exploitation of ignorance and credulity.

Clearly, then, this manufactured will of Schumpeter's cannot consist of all the political preferences that citizens would not have unless they had been exposed to organized persuasion by persuaders who hoped to gain thereby. It must consist of those preferences which they have been induced to have, not by rational persuasion, but by appeals to prejudice and passion and by exploiting their ignorance. To be sure, citizens who acquire their preferences thus irrationally sometimes gain by doing so, just as their persuaders sometimes lose by their having done so. But whoever gains or loses by citizens having them, these are the preferences that make up 'the manufactured will'.

No doubt, many citizens come by their political convictions and preferences irrationally, even in highly literate industrial societies, whether they are democratic or not. In these societies (even those that are authoritarian) there are many more political leaders, and many more organized groups intent on getting the people, or some part of them, to prefer some candidates or policies to others. In these societies, if we compare them with simpler and less literate ones, there are many more strongly held opinions about public matters. There are, for example, more of them, or a greater variety, in Britain today than there were in the days of Oliver Cromwell. Presumably, where there is a great variety of political opinions there are many opinions not rationally acquired. There is, also, presumably, a considerable 'manufactured will'; there are many, among the opinions not rationally acquired, that have been deliberately propagated. Yet everyone agrees that in a large, industrial and literate society, no matter how it is governed, there is a need for organized political persuasion on a big scale. The need is for persuasion and not just for information. There is no less a need for it in Britain and the United States than in Russia or China.

I fail to see the point of Schumpeter's claim that in his theory 'the manufactured will' comes in at 'the ground floor'. Does the claim imply that earlier theorists of democracy wanted 'the will of the people'—or, more realistically, their opinions about public matters, their political opinions—to be pure or genuine, in the sense of un-affected by organized persuasion? If it implies this, the implication is false. Even Rousseau, who wanted no parties or pressure groups in his ideal republic, did not want every citizen to make up his mind about public issues uninfluenced by organized discussion. The general will, he tells us, emerges in an assembly where proposals of law and policy are open to debate; it is not established by a referendum in which each citizen indicates his preference without consulting the others or hearing their views. As for the Utilitarian democrats, though they feared the deliberate exploitation of popular ignorance and prejudice, they welcomed organized persuasion, provided the persuaders had to compete for the people's favour. That is why they were so strongly in favour of freedom of speech and of association.

To be sure, the Utilitarians did not go deeply into the question of where legitimate persuasion ends and the exploitation of ignorance and prejudice begins, nor did they study in detail how voters come by their beliefs and preferences. But then neither does Schumpeter go into this question or engage in this study. I do not suggest that, in his few short chapters, he should or could have done so. I am merely at a loss to understand what he is claiming for his theory. Is he saying that he does not share the fears of these earlier theorists? That he does not care how much ignorance and prejudice are exploited? Or is he saying that democracy is democracy, no matter how much of this 'manu-factured will' there is? That it can tolerate any amount of it without ceasing to exist? Or, finally, is he merely saying that we must not deny that a political system is democratic merely because there is a good deal of 'manufactured will' in it? I do not pretend to know.

If he is saying that a political system does not cease to be demo-cratic merely because many of the voters' political preferences are not acquired rationally, but are products of deliberate attempts to exploit ignorance and prejudice, then, very probably, he is right. But if he is saying that a democracy can tolerate any amount of exploitation of ignorance and prejudice and still remain a democracy, then, so it seems to me, he is wrong. No doubt, if democracy is defined as a political system in which those who govern acquire the right to do so by com-peting freely for the freely given votes of the people, it does not follow logically that there is no democracy where all political preferences are 'manufactured'. The voter whose political preferences are irrationally acquired votes just as freely as the most rational voter, provided he has preferences and expresses them when he votes. Whether his vote is free or not does not depend on how he acquired his preferences; it depends on how elections are conducted and on his being aware of what he is doing when he votes—that is to say, on his actually voting and not just going through the motions of doing so. Just as the voter can vote irrationally and yet freely, so too he can vote rationally and yet not freely. Where, for example, there is only one candidate for whom he must vote whether he wants to or not, his vote expresses no preference, though he may have excellent reasons for doing what is required of him. In that case, when he casts his vote, he acts rationally; or (if we assume that to vote is necessarily to express a preference) he acts rationally in going through the motions of voting, in pretending to express a preference.[1]

But though, given Schumpeter's definition of democracy, it is not true *necessarily* that there cannot be democracy where all political preferences are 'manufactured', it is true *empirically*. It is virtually impossible that a free competition for a free vote[2] could survive in a community where there was such wholesale 'manufacture' of political preferences. It is hard to believe that 'manufacture' on this scale could be achieved if there were free competition for the vote. Long before it was achieved, some organized group or other engaged in this manufacture would be strong enough to put an end to the competition—to silence its rivals.

I have used the word *manufacture* because Schumpeter uses it, though I think it misleading to apply it (as he does) to persuaders who compete with one another. If someone were to decide to make soup, what would emerge from his efforts would be the soup pretty much as he intended it to be, provided he were a good enough cook. But if he were freely to compete with other cooks who wanted to make different soups in the same pot, what would emerge from their joint but non-cooperative efforts would not be the soup he wanted to make but something quite different, which neither he nor his competitors intended or foresaw. It would be, I presume, a manufactured soup, a soup made with hands, and yet not one of the cooks could be said to have successfully taken advantage of the emptiness of the pot to get the soup he wanted. I admit that my analogy is not perfect. Competing for influence on human beings, even the most empty-headed of them,

---

[1] A voter does sometimes express a preference when he votes, though his vote is not free in the sense of a vote cast at free elections. He may be able to choose between several candidates all nominated by the only party allowed to nominate candidates. In that case, he is free to choose between the candidates, although he has not a free vote, as that term is ordinarily understood.

[2] It is perhaps unnecessary to speak of *free* competition for a *free* vote. If the competition is free, then the vote is so too.

is not really like several cooks trying to make different soups in the same pot. It makes sense for people to compete for influence as it does not make sense for them to try to make different soups in the same pot. Still, I hope that my analogy serves to make my point, which is quite simply this: the manufacturer, the maker of material things, can shape what he works on pretty much as he pleases, but the persuader cannot. He cannot do it, even when he is the only persuader at work on particular minds, and can do it still less when he is competing with other persuaders. And yet it can be worth his while to compete with other persuaders, whereas it would be madness for craftsmen to try to make different things at the same time out of the same pieces of material.

Let us imagine two democratic communities, of which one consists of intelligent and well-informed citizens and the other of stupid and ignorant ones. In both there are leaders and organized groups competing for votes; or, to use a convenient modern term, there are political persuaders. In the first community, it pays the persuaders to appeal to reason, whereas in the second it pays them to exploit the passions and prejudices of the people. We can say therefore that there is much more of a 'manufactured will' in the second community than in the first, for this manufacture, as Schumpeter describes it, involves exploiting ignorance and prejudice. But should we expect persuaders in the community of fools to be more successful in getting what they aim at, in getting citizens to vote the way they want to? Surely, we should not! If you compete with others in persuading fools, are you more likely to get the response you want than if you competed with them in persuading wise men? Sometimes it is easier to persuade fools than wise men to do what is to your advantage but not theirs, but only while there is no one else around trying to persuade them to do something different. But we are speaking of democracies where persuaders have to compete for influence; where, as Schumpeter puts it (and we agree with him) there is a free competition for votes. If 'manufacturing a will' is getting people to do willingly what they would not want to do if they understood better the situations in which they act and the probable consequences of the courses of action open to them, then there is likely to be more of it in a democracy of fools than in a democracy of wise men. But if 'manufacturing a will' is getting people to do willingly what you want them to do, it is by no means obvious that there will be more of it in the more foolish of our two democracies.

Let me put a question here that Schumpeter does not put, though it is both relevant and important. If to 'manufacture a will' is to influence people by deliberately exploiting ignorance and prejudice, why should not the will of leaders be as much 'manufactured' as the will of ordinary citizens? We can pertinently ask this question even though ordinary citizens can do little to manufacture the will of their leaders, for they lack the more effective means of doing so. If they had the means, they would be leaders and not just ordinary citizens. They can, of course, exert influence on their leaders, and can do so deliberately. For example, they can rebel or disobey or vote for rival leaders. But deliberately to cause a leader to do from fear of rebellion or loss of support what he otherwise would not do is not to exploit his ignorance or his prejudices. This sort of exploitation is the prerogative of leaders, but they can, and do, exploit one another. Indeed, it is often more worth their while to exploit other leaders than to exploit ordinary citizens. We cannot assume that people who are well placed to practise on the credulity of others are themselves beyond the reach of such practices.

The will of the people is a myth. So we are told often and told truly. I suggest that it is equally a myth that the people, 'the masses', want what others, cleverer than they are or better placed to exert influence, decide that they shall want. It comes closer to the truth *perhaps* in what are called 'totalitarian' states than it does in democracies, or did in the oligarchies and absolute monarchies of the past, but it is pretty far from the truth even in them. I say *perhaps* because it is much easier to find out whether people are *doing* what they are required to do than whether they are *wanting* what they are required to want. Even in totalitarian states, there is competition among leaders for influence, both over ordinary citizens and over other leaders. The competition, of course, is not a *free* competition for votes. But it is competition nonetheless; fierce competition, sometimes dangerous to the competitors and to the uncompeting masses. The collective will of the leaders is also something of a myth, though less so than the collective will of the people. So too is the 'monolithic party'.

I am not suggesting that Schumpeter believed in a collective will of the leaders. I am merely following up some of the implications of what he says about 'the manufactured will' and also going beyond them. Since *Capitalism, Socialism and Democracy* was published, other writers in America have gone much further than Schumpeter in discussing how political leaders in a democracy compete for influence over the voters, and have also (as he did not) considered how this competition for votes affects and is affected by another kind of competition—the competition of pressure groups for influence over elected holders of public office. These writers are about as far from believing in a collective will of the leaders as they are from believing in a collective will of the people. I have in mind both the more theoretical of them, such men as Dahl, Lindblom and Downs, and the more empirical, of whom V. O. Key and David Truman are good examples. It is, of course, the more theoretical writers who try to draw general and yet precise conclusions from the many empirical studies made in the United States—or, perhaps I should say, who try to construct theories to accommodate the many conclusions reached by the makers of these studies. I shall be considering later some aspects of some of their theories, which all make large use of the idea of free competition for office and influence—the idea which, according to Schumpeter, is central to any realistic theory of modern democracy. I mention these writers now only to observe that they have relatively little to say about 'the manufactured will': they certainly do not bring it in at 'the ground floor' of their theories. They do not draw from it any important theoretical conclusions beyond pointing to it as evidence that there is no such thing as a will of the people, except on rare occasions. But this they could have established without pointing to it, for it has nothing to do with the matter. If ever there were to be a more than ephemeral collective will of the people, it could only be an effect of indoctrination; it could only be a manufactured will.

Chapter 5

The Spoiling
of American Democracy

C. Wright Mills, whose account of American democracy in the twentieth century I shall discuss in this chapter, is not to be reckoned among the sceptics who believe that representative democracy on a large scale is not possible. As he makes clear in the later chapters of his book *The Power Elite* (1956), he believed that the United States was a democracy in the nineteenth century, or came close to being one, although it was already at that time a vast country with a large population. Nor did he believe that the United States a hundred years ago was more democratic than it is now merely because the smaller communities, whose rulers are closer to their subjects and supposedly better known to them, were then relatively more powerful; he spoke of a community of 'publics', as distinct from a community of 'masses', to whom all leaders, whether at the federal level or lower down, were responsible in a way that they are not now. The simple proposition, that where there are leaders who do much more than just carry out the will of their followers there is no genuine democracy, is not one to which Wright Mills subscribes. American democracy in the twentieth century falls, in his opinion, far short of what it was in the nineteenth, not because political leaders have a great influence over the people, but because they are less responsible to them than they used to be and make decisions less intelligible to them. There has arisen in the United States what Mills calls a 'power elite'. But by a power elite he does not mean any minority of the politically active; he means a minority of leaders or policy makers so related to one another that they cease to be responsible to the people or to their representatives for the major decisions of policy they take.

As I shall try to show, Wright Mills's conception of a power elite is not clear.[1] But what is clear is that it differs considerably from Mosca's conception of a ruling class, which, if it applies at all, applies just as

---

[1] Most of the time, Mills uses the term 'power elite' in such a way as to imply that, where there is a power elite, there is no genuine democracy. But in the thirteenth chapter of his book he distinguishes between a power elite compatible with genuine democracy and one not so compatible.

readily to nineteenth as to twentieth century America. The general argument of *The Power Elite*, confused though it is, is not just a later version of the theses of Mosca, Pareto or Michels.

We have seen that Schumpeter, though he speaks of a *manufactured will* in the Western democracies, does not attribute to political leaders in them any kind of collective will of their own, setting them apart from the citizens generally and reducing to little or nothing their supposed responsibility to the people. Merely to say that leaders often exploit the ignorance and prejudices of ordinary folk to induce them to want what it suits the leaders that they should want is not in itself to imply that democracy is a sham, that the competition of leaders for freely given votes is not genuine. It is not to imply that there is a power elite in the sense of a group of leaders whose shared interests or preferences determine the general lines of policy, or of some important aspects of policy, and whose power depends only to a slight extent on competition for popular support. Nor is it to suggest that the leaders whose power does depend on this competition do not make the really important decisions, or take only a small part in making them.

Wright Mills seems to have been at times considerably influenced by Marxist ideas. Whether or not he would, at any time, have called himself a Marxist, I do not know. But, whatever the label that he or others might have been inclined to attach to him, it is clear that his attack on American 'democracy' (which, in any case, is much less severe in the later than in the earlier chapters of his book, as if he had suddenly been afflicted by doubts about the solidity of his arguments) differs greatly from the Marxist attack on bourgeois democracy. It is, despite the confusions of thought that spoil it, more sophisticated and realistic. The members of his 'power elite' do not form a social class in the Marxist sense of the word, even though many of them are recruited from wealthy families. They do not promote class interests and are not responsible to any social class. They are the people who hold the top positions in three great hierarchies, the government, big business, and the armed forces. Given Mills's conception of a power elite, there could be one as easily in the Soviet Union as in the United States.

Mills does not say that the power elite have common policies; he therefore does not attribute to them anything that could fairly be called a collective will, in the sense in which Schumpeter denies that the people, except very rarely, can have one. Rather, he attributes to them something that he calls an *ethos*; though, unfortunately, he fails to make it clear what he understands by this term. It is, presumably, a political ethos that he has in mind, a set of beliefs or assumptions, often tacit, about how policy should be made at the top level and what general ends it should pursue. This agreement about ends allows, apparently, quite big differences of opinion about policy and does not exclude some quite fierce competition for power and influence, but it also keeps these differences and this competition within bounds. Part of what Mills has in mind, when he speaks of this ethos, is not unlike what American political writers understand by the word *consensus*; it is a set of attitudes, assumptions and standards that hold a group (usually a political community) together in spite of the conflicts inside it. Only the consensus that Mills has in mind holds together, not a political community, but a ruling minority inside it.

I have tried to put Mills's meaning succinctly in my own words, and I may have failed to do full justice to him. My purpose is not to follow him through all the intricacies of his argument but rather to use some of his ideas about American democracy to illustrate a way of looking at the large democracies of the West. I want to examine the idea of a power elite as he presents it in his book rather than to agree or disagree with him that there is such an elite in the United States. Though his book is about just one country, it contains ideas that could apply to any large state that claims to be a democracy.

Mills does not, and for his purpose need not, deny that, apart from this ethos confined to the elite, there is another political ethos, shared by the elite with the American people. This other ethos I shall call the democratic ethos. The elite, to act and think and feel as Mills says they do, do not need to pay mere lip-service to beliefs which other Americans hold more sincerely than they do. They can be as much attached as anyone to the political system and to the political rights that all citizens enjoy. The way they do business at the top levels does not require that they should act unconstitutionally or in disregard of popular rights. They are not cynical exploiters of the democratic ethos; they are sharers in it who have also another ethos of their own.

Mills does not say that the elite all work together according to plan, not yet that the rest of the people have little or no influence on policy. They expect many kinds of services from the Federal Government, and their anticipated reactions as well as the demands made on their behalf by organized groups count for a great deal when decisions are taken at the top level about these services. But there are large and growing spheres of policy-making at the national level—for example, the conduct of foreign affairs—in which the elite are much less restricted by demands coming from outside their own circles. And even in the spheres where such demands count for more, the elite have a considerable latitude in the making of policy. They are restricted, not so much by the preferences of citizens for some general policies over others, by their beliefs about what government should do in the best interests of all whose interests are at stake, as by the demands made on the government by a wide variety of pressure groups in their own group interests.

Mills rejects emphatically a theory about democracy, and more particularly about the American political system, which some political scientists in America have put forward. This theory likens the political system to a market economy as conceived by the *laissez-faire* economists. It assumes a wide scatter of organized groups independent of one another making demands on elected holders of office whose interest it is, if they are to avoid unpopularity and retain their offices at the next election, to meet as many of these demands as they can. According to this theory, the holders of office make policy, but in making it do not impose their wishes on the people. Their policies are solutions to problems set for them by the groups making demands on them. To the best of their ability, they try to ensure that the resources at their disposal are used to meet as many demands as possible. This they do because they stand to gain by doing so. They want the authority or prestige attached to the offices they hold or seek to hold.

This does not ensure that whoever is elected to public office or aspires to election considers impartially the demands made by the groups that come his way. His concern is not to be impartial but to get as much support as he can. He does not hope for the support of all groups he comes into contact with; he knows that he can get the support of some only by forgoing that of others. And yet it is in the interest of everyone in office or aspiring to it to antagonize as few groups as possible. Thus every group organized to make demands on government will find some leaders who are in office, or aspire to be, keen to get its support. Democracy encourages citizens with interests in common to form organizations to promote them, and provides everyone who aspires to be elected or re-elected to public office with a motive for doing whatever he can afford to do politically for any organized group expecting political services from him.

Mills makes, I think, two objections to this theory. I say 'I think' because I am not sure that he sees that they are different objections. The first is the more obvious of the two and perhaps also the less damaging to the theory he attacks. He denies that there is politically a free market, and does so on the ground that some of the groups exerting pressure on policy dominate the market. Mills means, I take it, that makers of policy take much larger notice of some groups than their relative size would warrant. The top men in the giant corporations are, he says, in close touch with the executive branch of the Federal Government, and some of them are inside it. These corporations may employ vast armies of workers, but the men at the top are concerned with the interests of the stockholders rather than with those of the workers.

This is a variation on a familiar theme, and I shall not stop to consider it—even though there is a good deal of truth to it—because the political scientists that Mills attacks themselves take notice of it. They merely give less weight to it than he does. Besides, some of them claim to be constructing a theoretical model of democracy. They do not say that the United States or any other country comes very close to the model; they say only that the nearer a political system comes to it, the more democratic it is.

More interesting and less familiar than this objection is another, which Mills puts less clearly than the first, almost as if it were supplementary to it, though in fact it is nothing of the kind. He suggests that the groups constituting the power elite subvert democracy even when they are not concerned to push special interests of their own. They have their own views, confined mostly to their own circles, about national policy—views which deeply affect that policy even when they do not favour interests peculiar to them. For example, the 'top brass' in the American Armed Forces have views about American foreign policy which have a large influence on it and yet do not favour their own interests—nor even, more generally, the interests of the officers and men who have made a career of military service. Views very different from theirs might entail just as large a military expenditure.

We can admit that professional (and other similar) *interests* have some influence on national policy, and yet say that it has been greatly exaggerated by Marxists and by others who think like them. We can say that professional *attitudes* and *opinions* often have a much greater influence on national policy, especially some aspects of it, than do professional *interests*. Mills does not say this outright but he does suggest it in the course of his argument, and he suggests also that it is undemocratic. Whenever the groups having the largest say in the making of policy are in close touch with one another, taking much greater notice of each other's opinions than of the opinions of outsiders, they constitute what Wright Mills calls a power elite. What makes them a power elite is not their using power to promote their own interests (though they may do that also); it is their making a whole range of important policy decisions, with too little notice taken of what is thought and said outside their own circle. Or if notice is taken it is rather to appease or divert the outsiders than to give effect to their wishes, except when the wishes are in line with those of the elite.

Mills does not deny that in the United States the interests of groups outside the power elite have a considerable influence on policy, both at the federal and at lower levels. Though the makers of policy at the highest level belong to the executive branch or to groups in close touch with it, they have to placate Congress where these sectional interests are paramount; they have, in making their policies, to take account of the demands that Congressmen support in response to the pressures put on them. The theory he criticizes has, Mills concedes, a substantial measure of truth to it. The activities of pressure groups and the hopes and fears that centre on the next elections are politically important. And yet it is misleading, he thinks, to speak of the makers of policy at the federal level as if they were little more than political brokers for the people; as if their policies were designed primarily to solve the recurrent problem of satisfying, as far as resources permit, a wide variety of sectional demands. Policy at the federal level may have been that, rather than anything else, two or three generations ago, when Congress was much stronger than it now is in relation to the executive, when the Armed Forces were much smaller, when there were few giant corporations or none.

I sympathize with Wright Mills in his attack on the idea that in the United States makers of national policy are concerned above all to satisfy sectional demands. I only wish he had gone on to say that, even if this were their principal business, it would not suffice to make America a democracy. No doubt, in America, as in all large industrial countries, this is part of the business of government, and a considerable part. It may well be—it probably is—a larger part of it in democratic than in authoritarian states. Liberal democracy does encourage the proliferation of organized groups making demands on government, and does provide governments with unusually strong incentives for taking notice of the demands and doing something about them. But there is much more to government and to the making of policy, even in a democracy, than satisfying these demands. There is also a pursuit of aims, national and ideal, that cannot be treated as means to the fuller satisfaction of sectional demands.

This is obvious enough in an authoritarian state, especially when it is 'revolutionary' and its rulers claim to be transforming society. Their policies are then designed rather to change popular demands than to satisfy them. Though the rulers have some support among the people, and their policies are to some extent in line with existing group interests, their aim is to refashion the social order so that people's wants and standards cease to be what they were. The demands that the rulers, as they carry out their policies, make on the people are not responses to demands made on them in the first place by the people. Nor do their supporters among the people constitute a group whose common interests determine official policies, for these supporters may have little more in common beyond the fact that they support the rulers and some of their aims.

What is true of revolutionary or 'progressive' authoritarian states is true also, though in a lesser degree, of democratic states. The policies of a democratic government are only to some extent designed to meet the demands made on it by organized groups; and the policies that are the least so have to do with defence and foreign affairs.

Wright Mills's argument, as I see it, is essentially this: the less policy decisions are affected by the need to satisfy specific demands made on behalf of organized groups, the more free the power elite are to take what decisions seem good to them, influenced by one another's arguments and guided by their own *ethos* but paying little attention to outside opinion. Of course, to show that there is a sphere of policy-making in which makers of policy are largely independent of outside opinion is not to show that they are a power elite. What makes them a power elite is that they share an 'ethos' which largely determines their policy decisions within that sphere. So Wright Mills, if he is to make his case, must do two things: he must show that there is this 'independent' sphere of policy-making, and that the persons who make policy within it share an 'ethos' which powerfully influences their decisions. And the point of his speaking of an ethos rather than of *interests* shared by the elite is that he is willing to concede that the elite may to a large extent be public-spirited. No doubt, they do look after their own interests, but they need not be out to feather their own nests, nor much concerned to look after the interests of the classes and professions from which they are drawn. They may have ambitions for their country, and even other ideals, which affect their policy decisions more than their personal ambitions and group interests do. It is above all to their insulation from outside influences, their irresponsibility, within a large and important sphere of government, rather than to their sacrificing the national interest to interests of their own, that Wright Mills points when he argues that their increasing power is a threat to democracy.

Before I try to assess Mills's argument, let me consider for a moment the kinds of influence that citizens exert on makers of policy. Sometimes they exert influence for the benefit of groups to which they themselves belong (e.g. trade union leaders); sometimes for the benefit of groups or categories to which they do not belong (e.g. people who run charitable organizations); and sometimes in order to promote policies not intended to benefit any particular group.

In the great democracies of the West, the first kind of influence is exercised on behalf of groups who between them cover almost the whole population, though some sections are much better served than others. The persons who exert this influence, who formulate and press the demands of which it largely consists, are (or are reckoned to be) spokesmen of the groups who stand to benefit if the demands are met. It is, as we have seen, the great merit of Western democracy, in the eyes of some of its presentday academic champions, that it encourages the making of these self-regarding demands by organized groups and produces governments with strong incentives to meet them. There is, so it would seem, something peculiarly democratic about these demands. They are made, as it were, *by* the people and not just *for* their benefit. To meet these demands, if it is not to give effect to the will of the people in the sense dismissed as nonsense by Bentham and by Schumpeter, is at least to satisfy to some considerable extent the wishes of diverse sections of the people.

The men and women who actually formulate and push these demands, who exert the influence that I have called self-regarding (though the persons exerting it may be devoted and unselfish), are only a minority of the people. Yet the groups they speak for include the whole people, and they (the spokesmen) are responsible to the groups. Their responsibility is all the more genuine because the demands they make are limited and concrete, and are therefore intelligible to the people on whose behalf they are made.

The second kind of influence, the kind that people exert for specific groups or categories to which they do not themselves belong, is mostly philanthropic. There is nothing specifically democratic about it, even though the persons benefiting from it in one way or another may include a large proportion of the people. Yet this influence, too, takes the form of making and pushing fairly precise demands for the benefit of well-defined categories or groups. A society to assist and protect the unmarried mother and her child may well have no unmarried mothers or children in it. But the demands it makes on the government or on the general public are precise and readily intelligible.

It is when we pass from the first and second kinds of influence to the third that we move to a sphere in which aims and arguments are much less clearly defined and understood. It is the sphere of what I shall call, for want of a better word, general policy. There are, outside government circles, farmers or doctors or teachers who understand agricultural or medical or educational problems just as well as, if not better than, anyone within those circles. These men, if they create pressure groups or come to prominence inside them, can argue realistically and to good purpose with civil servants and legislative committees. Widely trusted and also understood (though perhaps less widely) within their own trade or profession, their status and competence are acknowledged. They are formidable critics of government policy looked at from the point of view of whatever group they speak for. But they are not competent to give advice about either of two kinds of important decisions: policy decisions that aim at striking a balance between the demands on government made by different groups, and policy decisions that are not a matter of striking such balances.

Or, rather, they have no special competence to give advice about these policy decisions.

There are, no doubt, outside government circles, people competent to advise about these more general decisions, but they are seldom spokesmen for powerful organized groups. A government can therefore often afford to disregard their advice, for it can do so without losing popular support. And, in any case, advice in these spheres is not easily assessed. The people who give it are not only less representative but also less widely understood than the spokesmen for special group interests. They may be formidable intellectually without being so politically. On the other hand, the politically formidable critics of general policy proposals are often not well-informed; they are often either leaders of rival parties or spokesmen for special interests with inadequate or mistaken ideas about how general policy affects those interests. They are formidable because they enjoy wide support, but this support they owe, not to the soundness of their views about general policy, but to other things. Though the government feels the need to placate them, it can often do so by making concessions that are more apparent than real. The critics are either ill-informed and cover up their ignorance and lack of understanding by the vagueness of their criticisms, and so are easily appeased or fooled, or else they hope later to step into the shoes of the men they criticize and do not wish to commit themselves in advance to definite policies which they may come later to regret. It has been argued, for such reasons as these, that public discussion of what I have called general policy is often little more than shadow-boxing, and that makers of policy and their advisers are less inhibited in making it than they are when they take decisions that affect directly the interests of organized groups.

I would agree that in some spheres makers of policy are much less inhibited than in others both by public opinion and by pressures exerted for the benefit of specific groups, and I would agree also that these spheres have increased considerably in most of the Western democracies, and in none more so than the United States, which has assumed enormous responsibilities all over the world. American foreign and defence policies are vastly more important than they used to be, and have large domestic repercussions, most of them difficult to assess. 'Public opinion' as it relates to these spheres is often so ill-informed and vague that it can have little influence on policy. But, as I shall argue later, it does not follow from this that makers of policy within these spheres take no notice of well-informed and well-argued opinions from outside their own official circles. For some spheres of policy the effective public, the unofficial circles whose opinions carry weight, may be so small that we do not call their views public

opinion; which does not prevent their being independent and influential. And if these circles really are independent as well as influential,
we must not include them in the power elite merely because they are
small.

Before I say any more about 'public opinion' and its influence on
policy, I want first to look more closely at this 'ethos' that makers
of policy and their official advisers must have if they are to constitute
what Mills calls a power elite. Clearly, the mere fact that they make
policy or give advice to those that make it is not in itself enough to
make a power elite of them. For even if America were to live up to
her democratic ideals, policy-makers at the top level and their official
advisers would still be a small group within the nation. To be a power
elite, in the sense intended by Wright Mills, the group must either
have common interests or they must have an ethos affecting the policy
decisions they take and making them less amenable to influences from
outside. But, as we have seen, it is their 'ethos' rather than their group
interests that Mills points to when he calls them a power elite.

The first thing to notice is that this 'ethos', if it is to have the
effects that Mills ascribes to it, must be something different from a
merely professional or business 'ethic'; that is to say, from a set of
attitudes and standards that make it easier for people engaged in the
same kind of business to do business together. Every profession and
every organization that endures for any length of time acquires such
an ethic. But this ethic may affect only how they do business together
and may have little effect on the aims they pursue, and may even serve
to make them more amenable to external influences.

Congressmen in the United States have a professional ethic; they
have conventions and attitudes which, though they might be hard put
to it to define them, deeply affect their way of doing the business
peculiar to them, as much when they seek to oppose one another as
when they work together for some common purpose. These attitudes
and conventions do not shut them off from external influences. In
learning to do what they are elected, or at least expected, to do, Congressmen, no less than trade union bosses and other leaders acting in a
representative capacity, acquire attitudes, habits and values which they
do not share with the people they represent. Persons who engage in
the same line of business, even when they are rivals who try to frustrate and to get the better of each other, have also to be able to rely
on one another in ways in which they do not have to rely on outsiders; they need and soon acquire an 'ethic' or 'ethos' peculiar to
themselves. They do so as much when their business is to act in some
representative or public capacity as when it is anything else. Congressmen, far from ceasing to represent their electors when they acquire the
ethic peculiar to them, need to acquire it if they are to represent them

effectively. Their acquiring it may not ensure that they do represent them effectively but it is at least one condition among others of their doing so.

Wright Mills would not, presumably, deny that Congressmen have an ethic of the kind I have described, and yet he nowhere suggests that they form a power elite. Clearly, then, this kind of ethic, even though the men who share it hold public office and have a great deal of power, is not enough to make a power elite of them.

Far from treating Congressmen as a power elite (even a small one included in a larger one), Mills excludes all but a few of them from his power elite. He excludes them and yet admits that they affect policy, that the elite who make the really important decisions take notice of what they say. But their influence, considerable though it is, is indirect. They make on behalf of a wide variety of groups demands that the policy-makers in reaching their decisions take into account; but they take no direct part in making the decisions. They are not consulted but appeased. According to Mills only a few Congressmen (the chairmen of some of the important committees) exercise a direct and considerable influence on the making of general policy; and he promptly includes them in the power elite.

His power elite is therefore quite a mixed bag; it is drawn from several professions and clearly has no professional ethic peculiar to it. What is most obviously common to its members is that they all take part in making the policy decisions that really matter within spheres that are of great and growing importance. They are a small minority, not just of the American people, but of the leaders of that people. And yet Mills, though he attributes an 'ethos' to them, never explains what that ethos is, nor does he show how it affects their policy and decisions and makes them less amenable to outside influences. He merely asserts, again and again, that they have an ethos which has these effects.

He does not see that, to establish his thesis, he must do more than just point to a number of groups that take a direct part in making general policy, and distinguish between making policy and having the sort of indirect influence on policy decisions that Congressmen and other leaders have when they ask for benefits for specific groups. He does not see that he must show that the groups who make up his elite share attitudes and ideals peculiar to them which largely determine what policy decisions they make and serve to insulate them from outside influences—not, of course, completely but to a considerable extent.

All that he in fact does is to show that the important policy decisions, especially in certain spheres whose relative importance is growing fast, are taken by a small number of persons drawn entirely from a few professional groups and largely from the wealthier classes, and that these persons are in close and constant touch with one another. He shows that, in reaching their decisions, they have to take one another's opinions and arguments seriously, to defer to one another continually. They are, he thinks, the persons who 'count' and who recognize one another as 'counting'; for their influence on each other differs both in urgency and quality from the influence of 'outsiders' on them. They consult and make concessions to each other much more than they consult and make concessions to persons outside their circle. But all this, though Mills gives great weight to it, is not enough to show that they are a power elite, either in the more familiar sense (which Mills occasionally, in his 'Marxist' moods, has in mind) that they push the interests of the groups they belong to at the expense of other groups, or in the sense (which is more peculiarly his own) that they have an ethos which largely determines their policy decisions and makes them less persuadable by outsiders than they would otherwise be.

We must expect to find in a developed industrial society important policy decisions affecting millions of people taken by a very small number of persons in close touch with one another. These persons, the ones who actually take the decisions and the advisers who work with them, necessarily consult and listen to each other more than they consult and listen to 'outsiders'. Unless this were so, they could not do their work effectively. In the discussions that lead up to the decisions which it is their business to make, they cannot, and ought not to be, as accessible to outsiders as they are to one another. The information and points of view that come to them must be 'processed' on the way, if they are to be able to make intelligent use of them or take them into account. Everyone within the 'inner circle' has informants and advisers outside it, and these outside influences reach the others within the circle through him. This, no doubt, may not ensure that all important and relevant information and advice reaches the inner circle, nor yet that every group with a reasonable claim to be heard in fact gets a hearing. We all know that it can (and often does) happen that the few men who make important decisions are 'out of touch' with the community or group on whose behalf they act, and yet we should be hard put to it to define at all precisely criteria to be used to decide whether or not they are 'out of touch'. Yet, clearly, we cannot argue, as Mills seems to do, that they are out of touch because, when dealing with matters which it is their business to deal with, they are in much closer touch with one another than with outsiders.

Nor, so far as I can see, does Mills give good reasons for holding that the inner circle (or circles) of policy-makers and their advisers are in general more influenced by demands for concessions and benefits made on behalf of special groups than by outside opinions about general policy. Not only does he fail to provide sufficient evidence that this is so in the United States; he also fails to explain what sort of evidence could support such a conclusion. To be sure, he assumes, as other American political scientists have done, that most citizens have no opinions about most issues of general policy or have opinions so vague that there is no telling what practical decisions they point to; and he also assumes that they care less about these issues than about the demands made for the benefit of the groups they belong to. But, even if we grant the truth of both these assumptions (which may well be true), it still does not follow that public opinion about these issues has little influence on general policy. Public opinion does not cease to be influential because on most issues it is confined to a minority of the people. What makes it *public* as distinct from *official* opinion is not its being shared by most citizens but its being held and propagated by persons outside official circles. People were already speaking of *public* opinion in contrast to governmental or official opinion, and attributing great importance to it, long before most Western countries had become democratic and literate. Public opinion has nearly always been, and still is, very largely minority opinion.

The public—that is to say, the citizens who have and express definite opinions about issues of general policy—are not all of one mind about every issue. They are more agreed about some issues than about others. Also, there is for some issues a much larger public (a much larger number of people who have opinions of some kind or other about it) than for others. The public having opinions about issues that arise in any one sphere of policy, even when they are a small public and have to be exceptionally well informed if their opinions are to carry weight, are not (or need not be) a power elite, in Mills's sense of the word. They often have no interests and no *ethos* peculiar to them. Nor are the small minority, the small public, of the 'politically minded', who have strong and definite opinions about a variety of major issues, an elite in this sense. And yet makers of policy do often take their opinions seriously, either because they find them enlightening or disturbing or because they believe that the men who hold them are influential.

Makers of policy and their close advisers ordinarily differ in their opinions about what policy should be less than the public does—or, perhaps I should say, less than the publics do. Official opinion is often, though by no means always, less divided than public opinion. But this, surely, is as it ought to be; it is desirable that makers of policy should be broadly united and should not start on their discussions from widely divergent positions, just as it is desirable that their policies should be criticized from very different points of view. Policy makers often have better access to relevant information than other people do and therefore see more clearly that some of the courses of action finding support among these publics are unrealistic. Yet differences in official circles, though less wide ranging, do sometimes go deep. When they do, the official supporters of one policy as against another draw comfort and inspiration from people outside their own circles who think as they do. The fact that they have to make compromise decisions with officials who support different policies does not make them less susceptible to influence from outside official circles.

Let me make myself clear on two points. I am not saying that in a liberal democracy of the Western type there could not be a power elite of the sort that Wright Mills describes. Nor am I saying that, as long as there is none, there is nothing seriously wrong. I am saying only that what Wright Mills points to as evidence that there is such an elite in the United States is not good evidence. All people who do business together, no less when they make policy than when they do something else, have to consult one another and defer to each other continually. They have to do it even when their business is to dispute with one another publicly, as advocates do in a court of law or political parties in a legislature. The forms that the consultation and deference take vary with the nature of the business. They vary even from legislature to legislature, for the business of one legislature, its functions within the political system, can differ considerably from the business of another. The business of the House of Commons in Westminster differs from that of the House of Representatives in Washington, and so too does its ethos. Frequent consultation and deference, and the sharing of attitudes and standards peculiar to them, are not enough to make a power elite of a group of men who do important business together. Not unless the attitudes and standards deeply affect the decisions they take and make them less amenable to influences from outside their own circles. Wright Mills does not show that the *ethos* he speaks of has these effects. Indeed, he does not seriously enquire what kind of ethos it is and how it affects policy decisions. For all that he has to say about it, it might be just a business or professional ethic, or, in other words, no more than respect for the rules of the game, the rules (spoken and unspoken) which anyone must respect if he is to play that particular game effectively.

In the thirteenth chapter of his book, Mills abruptly shifts his ground, as if he had suddenly had doubts about this own conception of a power elite. He describes in the abstract two types of society, of which one is a democracy as it ought to be and the other is not. In both there is a 'power elite'; there is a small number of persons in close touch with one another who take the really important policy decisions. In the genuine democracy, the power elite are 'truly responsible to' . . .

'a community of publics'; whereas in the other type of society, which is 'a society of masses', the power elite 'carries a very different meaning'. So now, at last, we are told that there is nothing undemocratic about having a small number of persons in close touch with one another taking the really important decisions; and presumably nothing wrong with their having an ethos (standards and attitudes peculiar to them) provided the ethos does not cut them off from the community of publics.

In this thirteenth chapter, Mills takes back a good deal that he said or implied earlier about the United States; he goes out of his way to admit that a power elite of the objectionable kind is not yet firmly established in his own country.[1] The United States is neither altogether 'a community of publics' nor altogether 'a society of masses', though it is becoming, as time passes, less of the first and more of the second. Wright Mills's book is a kind of Dunning's motion passed on this elite, whose power, he thinks, has increased, is increasing, and ought to be diminished.

In 'a community of publics', there is plenty of discussion of important issues, not only among ordinary citizens but also between them and their leaders. Opinions that emerge from this discussion have a powerful influence on policy. Citizens are not exposed to the mass media; they are not mere listeners to what their leaders or those who control the mass media have to say. In 'a society of masses', the opposite holds. Citizens generally take their opinions about public matters from a small minority of opinion-makers. If they discuss these matters among themselves, it is the uninformed talking to the uninformed, and the discussions are of almost no consequence politically. No doubt, in the Western democracies opinion-makers, using the mass media, do put divergent views to the people; but this does little to stimulate reflection, partly because citizens listen only to the views they want to hear and partly because what they are offered are mostly the set phrases and shallow arguments that prevent thought more than they provoke it. People may be more educated now than they used to be in the last century but not (so Mills thinks) in ways which make them better able to assess critically the political arguments put to them by the opinion-makers. A great deal of modern education is vocational; it imparts information and skills which are accepted marks of competence in particular trades and professions. It is more akin to indoctrination than to teaching people to think critically. In the big cities, more and more people have merely impersonal, formal, business relations with one another. This isolation, this failure of people to say what they really think and feel, inhibits reflection; it makes for fantasy and thinking in stereotypes.

[1] C. Wright Mills, *The Power Elite*, Galaxy Book edition, p. 302.

This is a not unfamiliar indictment of the urban and industrial societies of our day. I do not find myself rejecting it so much as wondering what political conclusions can be drawn from it. No doubt the United States—and Britain too—is much nearer today to being 'a society of masses' than it was a hundred years ago. But was it any nearer, a hundred years ago, to being a 'community of publics'? Did the American citizen in the 1860s, any more than the British subject, give much thought to public matters? Did he come any nearer than he does now to looking critically either at the arguments put before him by politicians competing for his vote or at what he read in the papers? True, he was not exposed to the 'mass media', for they did not then exist. But was his thinking about larger than local or professional issues less stereotyped *then* than it is now?

Wright Mills takes it for granted that the more a large democracy is 'a society of masses' the less it is a 'community of publics'. But could it not be *more of the one and the other* than it used to be? Surely, it is possible for a country to acquire both a larger proportion of citizens who listen intelligently and critically to what political leaders have to say and a larger proportion who take their opinions uncritically from 'the mass media'. It may be that the United States is such a country. I do not say that it is. I forbear from contradicting an American sociologist when he speaks of his own country. I merely say that it may be so, because I have failed to see in Wright Mills's book any evidence that it is not so.

In a vast democracy, most citizens cannot hope to discuss public matters with those who make policy at the highest level. Only one citizen in thousands can hope to speak his mind to any of the top men. The most that the others can hope for is sometimes to listen to some of them, to read their published words, to hear or to read what others have to say about them. But there are, after all, tens of thousands of leaders. There is plenty of argument about public matters, though most citizens take only a small part in it, and the top men take no part in most of it, for it occurs outside the circles in which they move. It is extraordinarily difficult to assess the impact of this argument on either the makers of national policy or on ordinary citizens. But, difficult though it is, it is not more so than to assess the influence of what are called 'the mass media'. How can Wright Mills (or anyone else) be so sure that serious argument, the give and take of genuine discussion, has much less influence than the mass media do on the political opinions of most citizens?

There are perhaps many people who, even in the most favourable conditions, cannot be taught to be thoughtful and critical about matters that do not affect them directly and obviously. These people, if they have political opinions, take them readymade from others, and it may well be that—to avoid bewilderment and the need to compare and to choose—they take them always from the same sources. But they need not take them more from the radio and the popular press than from friends and neighbours. Nor do I see why, when they do take them from the mass media rather than from other sources, their opinions should be any more rigid, empty or mistaken than they might otherwise be. And if we take the thoughtful and intelligent, I do not see how, intellectually, they are the worse off for living in an urban and industrial society wealthy enough to educate all its children, provided that the society is liberal. In a poorer, more primitive and less literate society, they would lack the ideas and discussions that rouse the mind to fresh and sustained thought about impersonal matters. In an authoritarian society they would be inhibited in other ways. But in a wealthy, literate and liberal society, the naturally intelligent, the intellectually bold, have as good a chance as anywhere to acquire their skills and indulge their tastes.

In an industrial and literate society which is authoritarian the mass media are used to get people to act, and as far as possible to think, as it suits their rulers that they should. In a liberal society of the same type they are used for this purpose very much less. This is not to say that they do much to stimulate intelligent and independent thought about political issues—or, indeed, about anything else. They may or they may not. But, however shallow or dull they are, they need not prevent us getting something better than they have to offer, whether it is more reliable information or more sophisticated discussion. We are free to look and to listen elsewhere. It is not obvious that they convert 'a community of publics' into a 'society of masses'. Wright Mills certainly makes no attempt to explain how they do so, for all his insistence that America (where these media flourish as never before) is changing from 'a community of publics' into 'a society of masses'.

Nor is it clear why a country which is becoming more 'a society of masses' than it used to be—and let us concede that, say, Britain, Germany and Japan are doing so no less than the United States—should also be acquiring a closed or remote power elite of the kind that Wright Mills condemns because it is undemocratic. He is right in thinking such an elite undemocratic. In a democracy, the men who have the last word in making policy, who decide what advice to take and to reject when it is made, must be exposed to independent, varied and effective criticism. Critics must not owe the status and prestige that give weight to their criticisms to the favour of these supreme makers of policy or of their rivals for power or to organizations controlled by them or controlling them. Their criticism must be effective; it must be such that makers of policy and their rivals for power need to take frequent and serious account of it, or risk losing the public confidence on which their power or chances of getting it ultimately depend.

In all that I have said, I have been concerned only to consider certain types of argument, the assumptions they rest on, and the conclusions drawn from them. I doubt whether there is a power elite in the United States, but I have not been concerned to argue that there is not. I do not doubt that in America, as much as in Britain and perhaps more, there are enormous inequalities of power and influence. Some of them are inevitable in any large industrial society, even in the most democratic, while others are not. Wright Mills's indictment of American democracy does not, so it seems to me, help us to decide what kinds of inequality are inevitable in so large a political community, if it is to be effectively governed, and what kinds are not; what kinds are inherent in democracies that have millions and tens of millions of citizens, and in which many of the most important decisions have to be taken at the centre because these democracies are also advanced industrial societies.

How many of the frustrations and injustices that afflict the individual or the small group or community would remain, if these inequalities were greatly reduced and power were as little centralized as is compatible with the efficient government of a vast industrial society? I do not know the answer to this question. Indeed, though I have often heard it said that these frustrations and injustices are getting worse as the scale of industry and commerce and the business of central government grow in these societies, I have come across little evidence that it is so. No doubt, the greater the proportion of important decisions taken at the centre, the greater the chance that citizens will be frustrated or unjustly affected by such decisions. But then the greater too the chance that such decisions will create new opportunities for them and ensure that they are more justly treated. If power is decentralized and a larger proportion of important decisions are taken by local authorities, it is not obvious that they will be, on the whole, less frustrating and more just, or more intelligible to the persons affected by them, or that the legislatures and officials who take them will be more closely responsible to the communities they govern. Have there been studies made of democracy operating on a large and on a small scale to suggest that when it operates on a small scale it is more likely to live up to the standards it professes? I know of none.

Chapter 6

Neo-Utilitarian Theories
of Democracy

Several of the theories I have been discussing have a utilitarian bias. They take large notice of groups and their interests, and take it for granted that democracy encourages people having interests in common to associate the better to define and push them and provides governments with strong motives for acceding to their demands. Even Wright Mills, when he criticizes some political writers for what they say about American government and politics, accuses them, not so much of misconceiving democracy, as of exaggerating the extent to which the American system is democratic.

They describe the system, he says, as one in which leaders compete for power and popular support and organized groups of citizens compete for public funds and political concessions in ways that ensure that popular demands on government are met as fully as possible. But this description is not true, or is much less so than these writers suggest.

Mills's criticism implies that, if the description were true, America would be a democracy; it suggests that his conception of democracy is at bottom much like that of the writers he criticizes. And so, a good deal of the time, it is; for he both shares their idea of it and half rejects it, without providing a clear alternative. He also exaggerates the extent to which, in the eyes of these political scientists, America comes close to being a democracy, in their sense of the term. These American writers make quite modest claims for their country; for the most part (and especially the more theoretical among them) they are concerned to define the criteria that a political system must meet to count as a democracy rather than to claim for any particular country, even their own, that it comes close to meeting them. Though, of course, they do not look on these criteria as defining standards peculiar to themselves as students of politics; they see them rather as implicit in common ways of speaking about democracy in the West, or of assessing institutions and political behaviour in the Western 'democracies'.

I shall not discuss any theory as a whole, nor even all the utilitarian aspects of any theory. I shall select a number of arguments and examine them critically to help me explain why, in my opinion, it is not possible to give a realistic utilitarian account of democracy or to make a valid utilitarian case for it. I do not deny that utilitarian arguments have a large and important place in social and political theory, and I admit that the writers I am going to criticize use some good arguments of this type. My purpose is limited but, I believe, important for social theory. I wish to argue to this conclusion: Though we can often produce a realistic utilitarian explanation or justification of some practice or policy within a social or political system, we cannot produce such an explanation or justification of the system taken as a whole. Or, in other words, such explanations or justifications, when they are sound, always presuppose a form of society or government or economy not to be explained or justified on utilitarian assumptions.

The arguments I select for criticism all come from two books, Downs's *An Economic Theory of Democracy* and Dahl and Lindblom's *Politics, Economics and Welfare*, both of them among the best books of their kind. They are full of good ideas that throw light on many aspects of what political scientists like to call 'the democratic process', and I have learnt a great deal from them. I say this the more readily because I disagree strongly with some of their assumptions and aims.

Downs's book is about as utilitarian an explanation of democracy as you can find; and though Dahl and Lindblom's is considerably less so, it has a strong utilitarian bias. These writers do not call themselves Utilitarians, but I call them so to draw attention to what they have in common with Bentham and his disciples. Unlike the English Utilitarians of the last century they are not hedonists, but like them they wish to explain political institutions and practices as serving to maximize the satisfaction of wants or wish to consider the extent to which they do so. Their conceptions of what constitutes rational political action and of what makes a political system rational are, at bottom, very much like Bentham's.

Rational action and self-interest

Rational action, says Downs, 'is efficiently designed to achieve the consciously selected political and economic ends of an actor'.[1] Dahl and Lindblom vary the formula slightly: 'An action is rational to the extent that it is "correctly" designed to maximize goal achievement. . . . Given more than one goal (the usual human situation), an action is rational to the extent that it is correctly designed to maxi-

[1] Anthony Downs, *An Economic Theory of Democracy*, p. 20.

mize net goal achievement.'[1] Unlike Bentham—and this is an important difference—they admit that the concept of the rational, as they define it, applies only to some kinds of characteristically human behaviour. There are other kinds of behaviour, no less distinctively human than the kinds they are concerned to explain, of which it would be pointless to enquire whether or not they are rational, in the sense they give to the word. And yet these kinds of behaviour are also peculiar to intelligent and moral beings, and are of the utmost importance to them. Friends and lovers, in their dealings with one another, are not out to maximize goal-achievement, and their actions are not efficiently designed to achieve a variety of consciously selected ends. These latterday Utilitarians are better aware than Bentham was that rationality, *as they define it*, applies not to all but only to some spheres of peculiarly human behaviour. They quite deliberately select a sense of the word *rational* which suits their limited purposes, and do not claim that it is the only proper sense of the word.

Economic and political behaviour is not, of course, always rational in this sense, but it is meant to be so. The manufacturer, the trader, the housewife spending the family income to provide for recurrent wants, the political leader, the civil servant, the judge and the voter all think they are, or wish they were, rational in this sense. In these spheres of action (which are the ones that the economist or the political scientist seeks to explain or assess) the agent is, or aspires to be, some kind of maximizer, acting so as to get as much as he can of what he wants. Therefore (so it seems reasonable to conclude) we can explain these sides of human behaviour as the behaviour of would-be rational agents, and we can also criticize the behaviour of these agents on the ground that it falls short of being what they themselves want it to be.

In their books, Downs and Dahl and Lindblom consider how far, and under what conditions, certain kinds of institutions or certain principles or rules either help individuals to achieve their aims (or goals, as Dahl and Lindblom prefer to call them) or else hinder them from doing so. They take these aims or goals for granted. They do not, as for example Rousseau and Marx (to take two conspicuously non-utilitarian thinkers) do, enquire how men acquire their aims or goals, and how their accepting some values rather than others, or having some institutions rather than others, effects their aims. They neither deny that men's values and institutions affect their aims nor enquire how they do so. Indeed, they are not even much interested in the nature of the aims or goals whose achievement political action is to maximize; they have little enough to say about them. When aims are

[1] R. A. Dahl and C. E. Lindblom, *Politics, Economics and Welfare* (1953) Harper Torchbook edition, p. 38.

political, they describe them; leaders want to get votes or to propagate beliefs, candidates aspire to offices, voters want the parties they favour to win elections. But such aims as are not political, though political action is designed to achieve them, they take more or less in the abstract: they refer to them simply as the aims (or goals) for whose sake such action is taken.

Rational action, according to Dahl and Lindblom, involves calculation and control. To *calculate* is to consider what means are best adapted to achieving your goals, and to *control* is to affect the behaviour of others. Sometimes (and oddly, considering normal linguistic usage) they use the word 'control' to refer even to unintended effects, but more often (and more properly) they mean by it the deliberate and at least partly successful attempt to get other people to do what you want them to do. They distinguish *prime goals*, which vary greatly from person to person and society to society, from *instrumental* goals, shared by most or many people because their achievement contributes, or is believed to contribute, to the achievement of prime goals. Prime goals, presumably, are things that someone wants for himself or for others close to him or known to him personally (such things as a good income or good health or a congenial occupation); whereas instrumental goals are, for the most part, institutions or organizations or social rules and standards that people either want to preserve or to establish. Though Dahl and Lindblom, in at least one place, say that prime goals are desired for their own sakes, their way of speaking of them more often suggests that they need not be. Prime goals can be desired as means, and instrumental goals can come to be valued for their own sake. I can desire good health for what it enables me to do, and I can value freedom or equality for what it is. Dahl and Lindblom do not deny this; and I suspect that the distinction they have in mind would be more clearly made if *prime* goals were called *private* or *personal* and instrumental goals were called *social* or *public*. But of this more later.

Dahl and Lindblom assure the reader that they do not intend to argue in favour of any goals, prime or instrumental, but only to show how they are connected. They make no case for some *values* as against others. Values, as they conceive of them, are a type of instrumental goals; they are rules or standards that are generally accepted in some community or group because people have come to believe that their general acceptance conduces to the achievement of prime goals. Dahl and Lindblom do not consider how such beliefs arise, but they are, presumably, born of experience and reflection. This does not mean that the beliefs cannot be mistaken. Still less does it mean that everyone who accepts a rule or standard must have satisfied himself that it conduces to this achievement. Rules and standards are taught to children long before they are capable of assessing their usefulness. And the teaching, at least in its early stages, does not take the form of persuading them that what they are taught is useful. Children are *trained* before they are *enlightened*. Nevertheless, teaching them to be rational does involve getting them to see that the rules they are required to obey are in their own and the general interest. They then desire that the rules should be generally obeyed; and this general obedience becomes a goal they share with others. It becomes what Dahl and Lindblom call an *instrumental* goal, or rather a set of such goals.

A political system is democratic, as they explain democracy, to the extent that it achieves certain of these instrumental goals. No system can achieve them completely; and in that sense democracy is more an ideal to be aimed at than a reality. Nevertheless, where the goals are generally accepted and are pursued with considerable success, we have what is ordinarily called a democracy; though Dahl and Lindblom sometimes prefer to call it a *polyarchy*.

I can see little advantage in confining the name democracy in this way to an ideal condition and inventing another name for systems that approximate to the ideal. We often use a word in several closely related senses without confusion of thought, relying on the context to make our meaning clear. It makes perfectly good sense to say that democracy always falls short of its ideals, and yet would not be democracy unless it took those ideals seriously; which involves both understanding them and striving to achieve them. Though the ideals or instrumental goals that Dahl and Lindblom speak of are not confined to the political sphere, they can quite properly be called *democratic*; for wherever people accept them and set great store by them, they either have a democratic political system or aspire to have one.

Political democracy is only one theme among several in Dahl and Lindblom's book; it is the entire subject of Downs's. Downs recognizes that 'adjustment in primary groups' (especially the family) matters more to most people than do economic and political considerations, and he does not suggest that his type of analysis is well suited to explaining behaviour in primary groups. He does not regret that nobody has yet constructed an economic theory of the family and admits that his methods are suited to explaining only some spheres of human activity. Yet he does claim—for the claim is implicit in his whole enterprise—that they are suited to explaining not just certain kinds of political activities but entire political systems. He uses them to explain Western democracy; he constructs what he calls a theoretical model. His purpose is both to throw light on how the large democracies of the West operate, and to expose some of their defects. He makes a number of assumptions about people's aims and the conditions in which they seek to achieve them, and he judges the defects in the light of the aims. The defects are defects only because they prevent rational action; that is to say, action efficiently designed to achieve these aims. The assumptions about aims and conditions, if they are to throw light on how Western democracies work, must of course be realistic.

If we are to be fair to Downs, we must recognize that such a theory as his cannot, and is not meant to, explain how a certain type of system came into the world, nor to prove it superior to other systems, nor to show how it differs from them. His model does not, and is not intended to, include what is common to all the Western democracies, not even the larger ones. No Western democracy conforms in all respects to Downs's model; there is lacking in each of them some feature or other that he puts into that model. But that, in itself, would not make the model of little use in explaining how Western democracies function, any more than the model of a *laissez-faire* economy was of little use in explaining how the British economy functioned a hundred years ago. I am not objecting to Downs's model on the ground that it is too abstract to be useful. Theoretical models can be just as useful to the political scientist as they are to the economist. At least I see no reason for holding that they cannot. Yet Downs's model, admirable though it is in some ways as an intellectual exercise, is, so it seems to me, of limited use. It is much less useful that Downs meant it to be. What makes it of such limited use is precisely that it is an economist's model and therefore utilitarian. A theoretical model of another kind might be much more useful. The economist or the Utilitarian thinks in terms of measurable costs and benefits, and also finds it convenient to assume that every agent (whether a natural person or a corporate body) is concerned wholly with costs and benefits to himself or itself. The firm is out to maximize its own profits, and not those of some other firm or profits in general. What Bentham called the 'self-preference principle' is an assumption widely made by social theorists who are Utilitarians.

Downs makes it in his book. He admits that in the real world people are not self-regarding in every sphere of their lives, but he assumes that in their political behaviour they are. He speaks of his model's 'basic reliance on the self-interest axiom'. But, so far as I can see, this axiom is quite superfluous. Downs need not assert it to reach any conclusion which he thinks important. There is no need whatever for behaviour that is rational (as he defines that word) to be also self-regarding; it can be 'efficiently designed to achieve consciously selected political and economic ends', even though the ends are benefits to others. Indeed, it can be rational even though the ends are not benefits to anybody in particular or to categories of persons but are merely states of affairs that the agent desires for their own sake. Whether a man wants benefits for himself or for others or for nobody, he is equally rational provided he knows what he wants and his actions are efficiently designed to achieve it. Nor need we suppose that his actions are not likely to be efficiently designed to achieve their aims unless those aims are benefits to himself. For the purposes of his model, Downs needs to assume only that in their economic and political roles men have fairly well-defined aims and stable orders of preference among them. So, too, given his purposes, it is enough for him to assume that political parties seek to maximize the votes cast for them; he need not add that party leaders act always with the intention of furthering their private ambitions. Indeed, why mention private·ambitions at all? No doubt, public men do have such ambitions. Men acting in an official capacity have private as well as official intentions, and it is sometimes important to distinguish between them. But given that Downs wants to explain what it is rational for party leaders to do when they compete for votes, he has nothing to gain by making assumptions about their private ambitions. Even if the private ambitions of public men were in fact always self-regarding, Downs would gain nothing for his model by assuming that they were.

This predilection of hardheaded social scientists for Bentham's 'self-preference principle' (renamed by Downs the 'self-interest axiom') is odd, and calls for some comment. Downs says:

> From the point of view of society . . . the object of each man's action is the discharge of his social function. But from his own point of view, he acts to attain his private ends. . . . Every economist recognizes this state of affairs when he is talking about private economic agents. He does not advise monopolistic corporations to increase social welfare by cutting prices . . . he does not suggest that the men involved stop being selfish. . . . Economists apply this reasoning to private economic agents not because they are private but because they are agents. In short, they are human, and the realities of human nature must be accounted for by any economic analysis . . . the same type of reasoning must be applied to every institution run by men, i.e. to every agency in the division of labour.[1]

Downs is here (so it seems to me) running together two distinctions that need to be kept separate. He begins by distinguishing a man's social function from his *private* ends, and then goes on to speak of *private* economic agents and of the absurdity (recognized by economists) of expecting them to stop being selfish. But the economic agents he has in mind include monopolistic corporations, and when he calls them *private* he is using that word in a quite different sense from the sense in which he uses it when he contrasts *private* ends with *social*

[1] Downs, *An Economic Theory of Democracy*, p. 283.

functions. The men who run a business are acting as heads of an organization, and we can distinguish their aims as managers of the business from their private aims. Their aims as managers are, as contrasted with their private aims, *official*: that is to say, they are aims they have by virtue of the position or office they hold in some organization. That organization may, of course, be *private*; it may not be owned or controlled by the state or some public authority. But a *private* firm or corporation is not private in the same sense as private ends or ambitions are so. The absurdity of expecting a monopolistic corporation to increase social welfare by cutting prices has nothing whatever to do with the absurdity of expecting people to sacrifice their private ends to their official aims.

The distinction between *self-regarding* and *other-regarding* aims is different from the distinction between *private* and *official* aims, though Downs, in the passage I have quoted, seems to run the two together. And it is, I suggest, the second of these distinctions, and not the first, which is important to the political theorist. That is to say, what he needs to know is much more often whether someone is acting in a private or in a representative or official capacity than whether his actions are self-regarding or other-regarding. As I shall argue later, it is ordinarily much easier to discover whether official or representative actions are rational, in the utilitarian sense of that word, than whether private actions are so; for official aims are ordinarily more clearly defined than private aims are, and (more important still) are much more often placed in a definite order of preference. By official action I mean here the actions of anyone acting as an officeholder, whether or not he exercises political authority.

There is another distinction that the political theorist (and, indeed, the social theorist generally) should bear in mind: between *personal* and *social* aims. A *personal* aim consists of what a man seeks for himself or for others known to him personally; and a *social* aim consists of what he seeks for anyone belonging to a given category, or else for some group or community as a whole, regardless of what individuals stand to gain or to lose by it. Examples of social aims are such things as higher pensions for widows or milder punishment of law-breakers, or (and here we have a different kind of object, important in real life, though it does not lend itself easily to cost-benefit analysis) a rise in the prestige or morale of some group or community, or a change of attitude or belief inside it or towards it. For though many citizens, when their country's prestige is enhanced, stand to gain thereby, the man who seeks to enhance it may care little or nothing about that.

Private aims can be either personal or social, and so too can official aims. A man acting in a private capacity can try to obtain something

for himself or for others whom he knows personally, or he can seek
to benefit (or hurt) anyone to whom a certain social description
applies, or he can strive for something that accrues to a group or a
community as a whole but not to its members severally; and so too
can a man acting in an official capacity.

Downs, in the passage I quoted, does not even distinguish *self-
regarding* from *selfish* aims; or, rather, he calls aims selfish when
what he really means is that they are self-regarding, for he does not
call them selfish in order to condemn them. The economist, he says,
'does not advise monopolistic corporations to increase social welfare
by cutting prices . . . he does not suggest that the men involved stop
being selfish'. But when he says this, Downs does not really mean that
'the men involved' ought to be doing something that they are not
doing but which it is a waste of time to invite them to do because
they are too selfish to respond. Their duty, as directors or managers,
is to look after the interests of the corporations they manage. In
looking after these interests they may be quite unselfish; and yet,
when we think of their actions as actions of the corporations they
run, we often call them 'self-regarding', meaning thereby that they
aim exclusively or primarily at getting benefits for the corporation or
for its members or owners. Official actions can, in that sense, be self-
regarding.

But actions that are self-regarding, whether they are private or
official, are not also selfish, unless those who take them ought to have
taken account of interests other than their own or those of the
organization or community on whose behalf they act.

Aims that are official from one point of view are often called
private when looked at from another. The decisions taken by the
directors of a corporate body which is not an organ of the state define
the official aims of that body. Provided they are decisions taken in the
prescribed manner, everyone in the organization, including the
directors, recognizes that they are official decisions. If their official
character is not challenged inside the organization, it is ordinarily not
challenged outside it. And yet to government officials, or to anyone
who considers them from the government's point of view, the decisions
are taken by a private body and are therefore private decisions taken
in the pursuit of private aims. The men who take the decisions may
be personally unselfish; they may be loyal servants of the organization
who do not sacrifice its interests to their own.

When we call the actions of such men *selfish*, we may mean either
of two things. We may be passing a moral judgment on them; we may
be saying, for example, that they are neglecting their obligations to
the wider community or some corporation for which they are responsible. Or we may pass no moral judgment on them, nor even imply

that they ought to have acted differently; we may mean only that their activities ought to be controlled in a larger interest by the government or by someone else whose business is to look after the larger interest.

Though for ordinary purposes we need not trouble to distinguish the action or aim that is merely self-regarding from the one that is also selfish, the social and political theorist ought to bear the distinction in mind. He ought not to call selfish what he believes to be justifiably self-regarding, whether he has in mind private or official action. Business firms are ordinarily self-regarding, and Downs probably thinks it a good thing that they should be. What he finds absurd or misguided is not really expecting businessmen to be unselfish; it is expecting them to sacrifice the interests of the firms they run to larger interests which it is not their business to look after. And he assumes that what applies to the businessman applies also to actors in the game of politics. Just as you do not expect the directors of a firm to sacrifice the firm's interest to some wider interest, so you should not expect the leader of a party or pressure group to sacrifice the party's or the group's interest to something wider, at least not when he acts in an official capacity. This, with some qualifications, is perhaps acceptable; though, of course, it does not apply to the mere voter, who does not act for an organized body and is nobody's representative.

I suggest that Downs should have substituted for his *self-interest axiom* another assumption which is both more realistic and more relevant, which I venture to call the *minding one's own business axiom*. This axiom has nothing whatever to do with the ineradicable or even predominant egoism of man, even economic or political man.

Psychological egoism (the doctrine that men are always, or nearly always, concerned for their own good, and for the good of others as a means to their own) is an invention of the philosophers; and it is a delusive doctrine, plausible largely because it exploits certain ambiguities in the use of language. But that is not to the point here, for what I am now suggesting is merely this: the doctrine (even in its qualified forms which confine egoism to certain spheres of human behaviour) is quite simply irrelevant. The social theorist need not worry his head as to whether man, take him all round or only in some of his social roles, is completely or predominantly egoistic, in the sense of the philosophers who have said that he is. Enough for the theorist to take note of the fact that men do often set greater store by their private aims (which may or may not be egoistic) than by the official aims of the organizations or communities they belong to, when the two kinds of aims conflict, *except when they are themselves acting in an official capacity*. There is plenty of evidence that this is so;

and the social theorist does well to assume that it is so. So, too, does the official; he does well to assume, not only that ordinary citizens set greater store by private than by official aims, but that officials set greater store by their own official aims than by the aims of other officials. This assumption applies, to use Downs's own words, 'to every agency in the division of labour'. We live in a world in which there is an immense division of labour, an immense variety of business, and we assume that most men most of the time set greater store by aims which it is their recognized business to pursue than by aims which it is not.

At this point, an objector might say, 'Is not Downs's *self-interest axiom* much the same as your *minding one's own business axiom?* After all, he nowhere says that men always act in hope of benefit to themselves.' True, he does not say it; but he does assume that people who act in an official capacity pursue official aims as a means to achieving their private aims. He wants to construct a theoretical model to throw light on how democracy works, and he thinks he can achieve his purpose better by making this assumption. Indeed, he speaks of his 'self-interest axiom' as if any political theory, to be realistic, ought to include it. The axiom helps, he thinks, to explain all political behaviour, democratic or not, as well as economic behaviour. So devoted is Downs to his axiom that he holds fast to it even when he himself puts forward opinions which make it look doubtful. For example, though he admits, time and again, that the voter often cannot know what he stands to gain or to lose *personally* from the policies of the parties and candidates soliciting his vote, he still holds to his assumption that the voter, when he prefers some policies to others, does so because he believes that he stands to gain more from their being put into practice. He will not have it that the voter often has strong preferences for some policies over others, even though he neither has, nor believes that he has, more to gain (or less to lose) by their adoption. In the light of his model, a voter who had such preferences would be irrational. But if we put aside the 'self-interest axiom' and assume instead that citizens ordinarily prefer private to official aims except when they are themselves acting in an official capacity, we can admit that they often strongly prefer some official policies to others, though they do not believe that the policies they prefer further their private aims. We can also admit that they are being rational when they take action to ensure that these policies are put into practice.

I am not concerned here to defend human nature from the 'cynical' imputations of Utilitarians and professors of economics and political science. If to be selfish is to act in conformity with Bentham's self-preference principle or Downs's self-interest axiom, then some of the vilest actions are not selfish. And many selfish actions, though not exactly noble, are both prudent and harmless to others (or even beneficial to them), and are therefore to be encouraged. My concern here is only for relevance and realism in social and political theory.

In Downs's model there are, on the one hand, the political parties competing for votes in the hope of getting power; and on the other, the citizens, each of them trying to use his vote to ensure that the party or combination of parties most likely to benefit him gets power. Parties put forward policies designed by the leaders to attract the most votes, and both leaders and voters are out to maximize the benefits coming to them as a result of what governments and their agents do. To be able to act rationally, both leaders and voters need relevant information; but this information is costly, and some people (leaders and the rich) are better placed than the others to get it, or stand to gain more by getting it. These are the broad assumptions of the model, and I shall confine myself to them; for I want to examine a type of theory rather than any one example of it.

In confining myself in this way, I pass over the refinements of Downs's model, though some of them are ingenious and original. I also pass over some of the most suggestive arguments of Dahl and Lindblom. Explanations of the type they like to give apply more to the actions of leaders than to those of ordinary citizens, just as, in the sphere of economics, they apply more to the producer or middleman than to the consumer. In a democracy political leaders do want to win as many votes as possible, and when they devise party programmes to attract votes they often make calculations of the kind that American political scientists (and especially Downs) excel at explaining. There is plenty of scope in the study of politics for explanations that are utilitarian, and these explanations, especially in the United States, are often highly sophisticated without ceasing to be realistic. But my concern, at the moment, is not with these explanations in the limited, though numerous and important, spheres in which they apply; it is rather with attempts to apply them where they do not apply.

Private aims and social means to their achievement

Nothing is more striking about utilitarian theorists than the little interest they take in the ultimate ends to which they point to explain or justify the practices or principles that interest them. Their concern is much more with proximate than with ultimate ends, and their arguments are ordinarily of this type: 'Given these conditions, certain practices or the general observance of certain principles will ensure that, on the whole, people are better placed to maximize their happiness or the satisfaction of their wants. Therefore, in these conditions, these practices or the observance of these principles are to be desired.' They then devote their energies to showing that the conditions exist or are coming into existence, and to considering how to establish the practices or observances they think desirable, without bothering to explain how in these conditions they help people to maximize happiness or the satisfaction of wants.

For example, Bentham believed that it would make for greater happiness (as he conceived of happiness) that justice should be done expeditiously as well as impartially and thoroughly. He therefore undertook to show how courts of law should conduct their business to achieve this end; and he went about this business carefully, ingeniously and judiciously, to the considerable enlightenment of later students of judicial procedure. What he never did, what he never seriously attempted, was to show how the realization of his principle (that justice be done expeditiously as well as impartially and thoroughly) served to maximize happiness; he merely took it for granted that it must do so. So too, John Stuart Mill, in the most impressive and the most widely read of his essays, *On Liberty*, took it for granted that truth makes for happiness, and then went on to argue that certain kinds of liberty favour the discovery and propagation of true beliefs, or at least of beliefs supported by the best available evidence; but he never stopped to consider how far and in what circumstances truth does make for happiness.

This type of argument has a long tradition behind it in social and political theory, and can be formulated in abstract terms: 'Everyone or nearly everyone wants X, and is on the whole better placed to get it if he admits that others have as much right to pursue it as he has. X is therefore desirable. But Y favours the pursuit of X, and Z is a means to Y.' This formula in the abstract is sound enough. But, too often, the theorist who applies it just takes it for granted that Y does favour the pursuit of X, and confines himself to showing that Z is a means to Y.

Dahl and Lindblom and Downs are all in this tradition. They do not speak, as Bentham and Mill do, of pleasure or happiness; they speak of prime goals or private ends. It is their achievement that is to be maximized. Nor do they speak, as Bentham sometimes and most unwisely does, of a general sum of achievements; there is nothing in their thinking that corresponds to Bentham's greatest happiness of the greatest number. They speak rather of each individual trying to achieve as many as possible of his prime goals or private ends in the order of his own preferences, and they admit that this trying does not cover all he does. They assume that it covers only his economic and political activities, to which alone they apply their concept of rationality. They make rather different assumptions from Bentham's and are more careful to qualify them. Nevertheless, having made them, they proceed much as he did: they assume that, in a certain type of society, certain practices or principles serve to ensure that individuals generally, or else some category or other of them, are more successful than they would otherwise be in achieving their 'prime goals' or 'private ends'. They make no attempt to show that these practices or principles really do ensure this, or even that they are generally accepted because they are believed to do so.

Dahl and Lindblom put forward seven *instrumental* goals, as they call them, typical of advanced industrial societies of the Western type, and suggest that, the more they are achieved, the better placed the individual to achieve his *prime* goals. Among these seven goals, they put a principle that I want to look at more closely in a moment, and they call it *political equality* or *democracy*. This principle is, they think, one by which Western peoples set great store, and they take it for granted that they do so because experience has taught them that its observance helps the individual to achieve his prime goals more fully. How it does so, or why it should be thought to do so, they do not enquire.

About these prime goals Dahl and Lindblom have little to say. Indeed, it is not clear, from the way they speak of them, what the point is of calling them *prime*. Do prime goals in societies of the Western type differ greatly from prime goals in other types of society? Do the means (and especially the political means) to achieving them differ from one type of society to another because these goals differ or because social conditions differ? Most of Dahl and Lindblom's instrumental goals are either moral or political principles. What do they want their readers to understand? That people in the West come to value these principles because their general observance helps them to achieve their personal aims (to get what they want for themselves or for other persons they care about)? Or would they admit that even personal aims are determined, at least to a considerable extent, by the principles (not excluding these instrumental goals) that people accept?

Dahl and Lindblom do not put such questions as these. They merely assume that, under certain conditions which they call Western without explaining what they are, the more these principles (with *political equality* or *democracy* prominent among them) are observed, the more fully the individual can achieve his private and personal goals; and that is why they call the principles *instrumental* goals.

Again, though they admit that no man is or ought to be rational (as they define rationality) in every sphere of his life, they do not enquire how far we can sensibly speak of a man's maximizing the achievement of his goals. They do not deny that in principle it makes sense to speak of his doing so only when he acts in certain capacities over limited periods of time, but they do not explain in what capacities and within what limits. For all their talk of prime goals, they tell us very little indeed about what they are and how their achievement is to be maximized. As far as I can see, they make no attempt to show how political equality contributes to the achievement of prime goals in societies of the Western type; they confine themselves to explaining what political equality is and how it is to be achieved.

Much the same is true of Downs. He assumes that the voter, when he prefers some policies to others, does so because he believes that their implementation will bring him greater benefits; or, as Downs puts it, will increase 'the streams of utility' he derives from what government does. The voter casts his vote for the party whose policies are most likely to benefit him; or, if that party has no chance of getting power, he gives his vote to that one among the parties with a chance of getting it (or a share of it) which he thinks is most likely to use power to his benefit. This, we are told, is what the rational voter does. But Downs, when he shows us the rational voter actually at work, exercising his reason, never shows him deciding that some policies or parties are to be preferred to others because they are likely to bring him greater benefits. He always shows him deciding to vote one way rather than another so as to help some party or coalition to get power or to increase the chances that some policy will be put into practice. The calculations of the rational voter, as Downs describes them, have to do only with the chances of parties getting power and policies being carried out; they have nothing to do with deciding what policies are likely to confer greater benefits on the calculator or to contribute more to his achieving his private ends.

Whatever, in the explanations of Dahl and Lindblom or the model of Downs, throws light on how Western democracy functions, whatever is clearly stated and carefully argued, whatever is a genuine contribution to political theory, gains nothing at all from their perfunctory and loose references to *prime goals* or *private ends* or *streams of utility* accruing to the voter. Their explanations are least informative where they are most utilitarian; where the citizen or voter is assimilated to the consumer in economic theory, and is treated as a subject of wants seeking to satisfy as many as possible of them in the order of his preferences.

Though today every social theorist admits that it makes no sense to speak, in the manner of Bentham, of sums of pleasure or of the maximizing of happiness, there are still some, and perhaps even many, who hold that it makes sense to speak of maximizing the satisfaction of wants or (as they sometimes prefer to put it) 'goal-achievement'. It makes sense, they admit, only within limits; and then, having made the admission, they either forget to define the limits, or else define them much too broadly. It makes sense, they say, within the spheres of political and economic behaviour. But to say this without further qualification is not enough, for it suggests that it makes sense to speak in this way of either of these spheres taken as a whole.

I agree that it often makes sense to speak in this way, and nowhere more often so than within the political and economic spheres. But it always, so it seems to me, makes sense within limits so narrow that we cannot say of one political system or type of economy as compared with another that it ensures that wants or goals are more fully satisfied or achieved.

Within what limits, then, can we speak sensibly of maximizing the satisfaction of wants? We can do so, I suggest, wherever in some sphere of action (which is always much smaller than the economy or the political system taken as a whole) we can distinguish wants from one another because their objects are readily identified, and the wants are predictable because they recur regularly in certain circumstances, and everyone whose wants we are considering has a stable order of preferences among them, so that we can ask about some rule or practice that regulates action within that sphere, or of some policy likely to affect it, whether or not it helps (or will help) people to satisfy their wants more fully. If we take men in some fairly well-defined part of their lives, in a profession or trade or in some other social role, we can quite often distinguish between their predictable wants and discover that they have stable orders of preference among them over periods of time long enough to be worth taking account of.

Their predictable wants are not, of course, all their wants, even in that part of their lives, for they may have wants which they do not avow or are only dimly aware of. What is more, their avowed (and even their conscious) preferences among their predictable wants may not correspond to the strength of their desires; for our preferences are often responses to what others expect of us. Or, in other words, avowed and predictable wants and stable orders of preference are to a large extent conventional. They can be deeply frustrating to the persons who have them: which is one reason among others why conspicuous success in maximizing the satisfaction of wants or 'goal-achievement' is compatible with great unhappiness. 'I want to be happy' and 'I want to maximize the satisfaction of my wants' are not equivalent expressions, and there is, so far as I know, no good reason for believing that, the more successful I am in maximizing the satisfaction of my wants within the limits in which success is possible, the more happy I am likely to be.

If we take every part of a man's life, the entire range of his activities, it makes no sense to speak of his maximizing the satisfaction of his wants. No man has a stable order of preferences among even his predictable wants, and many of his wants are unpredictable or so vague that their objects cannot be defined. Many wants are unconventional, and not obviously connected with a man's profession or trade or any definite social role. Even predictable wants are apt to be so for only a limited time, because a man's social roles and his ideas about them often change in ways that neither he nor others can foretell.

Of two or more policies affecting people in some occupation or other well-defined aspect of their lives, it is often (though by no means always) possible to say that one will do more than the others to enable the people it affects to satisfy the wants typical of that occupation or aspect of life. But governments are concerned with many different occupations and aspects of life, and we cannot say, if we compare any two governments, that the policies of one have in general done more than those of the other to enable their subjects to maximize the satisfaction of their wants. We cannot say it when the governments are of the same type, and still less when they are not. Where forms of government differ greatly, so too do other institutions; and so also do the values and beliefs of the people concerned. The wants of the individual, even the predictable and conventional wants, differ considerably from one type of political community to another.

We cannot justify democracy, or indeed any form of government, on the ground that, where certain conditions hold, it does more than would some other form to ensure that people can maximize the satisfaction of their wants. Nor can we explain what makes it acceptable to the peoples that practise it by saying that this is what it does. A man's personal as distinct from his social or impersonal aims, what he wants for himself and for those close to him for whom he cares personally (what Dahl and Lindblom call his *prime goals* and Downs his *private ends*) are affected by his beliefs about justice and freedom, and about what is honourable or respectable or generally useful. The principles and standards he accepts, the social and political order to which he is attached, do not stand to his aims as means to ends. His aims, personal or impersonal, have no meaning outside a social context, real or imaginary. They are the aims of a social and moral being, who could not have aims or orders of preference among them, unless he were such a being. Even those of his aims that cannot be realized within the social and political order as it is are the aims of a being who has acquired his aims in the process of learning to sustain a variety of roles within a social order and of assimilating a culture and reacting to it, often in ways peculiar to himself. This learning and assimilation include the acquiring of standards and principles which greatly affect his aims, even the more idiosyncratic among them.

I am not now suggesting that a man takes his values, his standards and principles, exactly as he finds them in society. For one thing, values differ considerably from group to group in society, and everyone belongs to many groups during the course of his life; and for another, no one is an altogether passive recipient of group values. I am saying only that a man acquires his aims, personal and social, as he acquires his values. If then, in a liberal democracy, people have aims that differ considerably from those of citizens in an authoritarian state, this is largely because their values differ; because they are liberals. They do not accept liberal values because they believe that their general acceptance helps people to achieve aims standing to those values as ends to means.

As I said earlier, it is important, in the interests of clear thinking, to distinguish personal from social aims (benefits or burdens that we want for particular persons from principles and practices that we want to see applied to categories of persons or situations) just as it is important to distinguish private from official aims. No doubt, to the extent that a man's personal and social aims are compatible with one another, the achievement of his social aims contributes to the achievement of his personal ones, and vice versa. Either kind of aim can be a means to the other. If a man aims at increasing equality of opportunity, he may, if he succeeds, make it easier for his own children to get what they want in life, and his ambition for his children (a personal aim) may have moved him in the first place to fight hard for greater equality (a social aim); but his ambitions for his children and theirs for themselves might be quite different if he and they did not live in a society where certain principles are widely accepted, even though not understood by everyone in the same way. Personal aims no more deserve to be called *prime* goals (or goals desired for their own sake) than do social aims, and social aims no more deserve to be called *instrumental goals* (or goals desired as means to the achievement of other goals) than do personal aims. Jones may want Robinson to become a judge because he wants the quality of justice improved and believes that Robinson will improve it. Indeed, he may even want to be a judge himself for that reason.

Though everyone has both personal and social aims, the theorist who wants to explain social rules and practices as means to satisfying wants or achieving goals seems always to have personal aims in mind. What has to be maximized is always their achievement. And yet, in the world as we find it, people not only have both social and personal aims; they also quite often choose between them, sometimes preferring social to personal aims, and sometimes the other way about. From their behaviour, we cannot infer that it is always, or even predominantly, their personal aims that matter to them in themselves, their social aims being only means to ends.

Why, then, does the social theorist so often take it for granted that it is the achievement of personal aims that is to be maximized? Not, I suggest, because there is anything about them that makes it more plausible to speak of maximizing their achievement, but because the theorist, with his utilitarian bias, has already decided that the proper way of explaining (and even justifying) social rules and practices is to show how they serve to maximize the achievement of personal aims. Though the theorist usually fails in his utilitarian purpose, he easily persuades himself that he has succeeded. What he actually does is to show how the practice or rule he wants to explain (or justify) realizes some principle or furthers some social end, taking it for granted that to realize the principle or further the end is to make it easier for people to achieve their personal aims. This is what Bentham and James Mill did in their day, and what so many social and political theorists, especially in the English-speaking countries, still do in ours. This is what makes their explanations all of the same utilitarian type, though the later theorists say nothing of pleasure or happiness and keep Bentham's name out of their books.

I said that it makes sense only within fairly narrow limits to speak of maximizing the achievement of aims. I would add now that it ordinarily makes better sense to speak in this way of social than of personal aims; and, above all, of official than of private aims. Social aims are usually more widely shared than personal aims, and official aims than private ones; while official aims are the most clearly defined and ordered. It is persons who act in an official or representative capacity who are most apt to pursue definite aims and to have stable orders of preference among them. I do not say that all, or even nearly all, their aims are well defined, but many are so. There are often set procedures for defining official aims and establishing priorities among them, and official aims, though they can be personal, are more often social. Or, rather, they are primarily social. Though the decision to give Mrs Smith a widow's pension aims 'at benefiting a particular person, it is taken in conformity with a rule requiring that any person within a given category shall receive that benefit. It is the manager of a business, the director of a government department, the organizer of any complicated set of activities in which several persons or groups take well-defined parts, the allocator of labour and other resources to diverse purposes, who is *par excellence* the maximizer of 'want satisfactions' or 'goal achievement'. The housewife spending a family income to meet the diverse needs of her family is also, to a considerable though smaller extent, a maximizer.

The manager, the director, the organizer, has his personal aims; he wants things for himself or for others for whom he is personally concerned. These aims may be as important to him, or even more important, than the official aims of the organization he runs or helps to run. Nevertheless, he is ordinarily much more a *maximizer* of 'goal achievement', an allocator of resources to purposes ranged in an order of preferences, in the pursuit of his official than of his other aims. And his official aims are mostly, or at least primarily, 'impersonal'; they are directed to categories of persons, and to this or that person as a member of a category, or else they are such things as outselling rivals, building a larger fleet, raising the country's prestige, raising the national income. I am not saying that in general people set greater store by social than by personal aims, or by official than by other aims; I am saying only that it is above all in the pursuit of official aims, which are mostly or primarily impersonal, that they are maximizers.

The housewife, spending the family income, has personal aims; she aims at satisfying the wants of particular persons. She often has some order of preferences among her aims, and tries to make her money go as far as possible in achieving them. Indeed, every spender of a regular income does so to some extent, though there are many personal wants that cannot be satisfied with what money can buy. And yet, even in the sphere of personal wants, it is the spender who has to look after others (the father or mother of a family, or the head of a household) who comes closest to being a rational provider, a maximizer of satisfactions; though he is often as much concerned to give those in his care what he thinks they need as what they ask for or desire. Thus, even when it is a question of maximizing the achievement of personal aims, the maximizer is often someone in authority. The aims are personal because the wants or needs are those of specific persons, but they are also, in a sense, official. They are parental or tutelary.

At this point the reader may be tempted to say, What of it? Granted that the theorists I call utilitarian mistakenly believe that democracy (or any other political or social system) can be explained or justified as serving to help people to maximize the achievement of their personal aims, and treat social aims as means to personal ones, do they not also in practice—by my own admission—have much more to say about maximizing social aims than personal ones? So, mistaken though they may be about what they are doing, they are nevertheless doing something well worth doing; they are throwing light on certain kinds of social activities—on those that are managerial or official, especially when the manager or officeholder has to use measurable resources to achieve a diversity of clearly defined aims. So why not leave it at that?

For two reasons. The first is that these theorists claim that by their methods they can explain (or justify), not just this or that managerial or official activity, but an entire system of such activities: Western democracy or capitalism or socialism. They make this claim, even though they admit that there are important spheres of human action that cannot be explained (or justified) by their methods. One such sphere, they sometimes admit, is the family; though the family as we know it in the West, the so-called 'nuclear' family, is a spender of money as no earlier type of family has been. Its domestic economy is more flexible, and its spending of money and labour less rigidly fixed by custom. A larger part of its activities are *rational* in the utilitarian sense of that word. And yet no sociologist, as far as I know, has argued that the nuclear family arose to enable personal wants to be more fully satisfied, or personal aims more fully achieved; or has suggested that to understand how it operates (the relations and modes of behaviour of which it consists), we must assume that this is its function. What is true of the family is true also of larger communities; there is no utilitarian explanation of them, and no utilitarian case for one kind of social or political order as against another.

The second reason for objecting to these methods of explaining democracy or any other political or social order is that they turn our minds away from what really matters. For example, a utilitarian explanation of Western democracy diverts attention from what that kind of democracy means to those who care for it and to those who dislike it, from what is thought good about it and from what is thought bad. Neither its champions nor its critics are concerned with maximizing the satisfaction of wants or the achievement of goals. They favour it because it gives men certain rights and opportunities; or they reject it because it does not. But these rights and opportunities are not valued because they make it easier for people to maximize the satisfaction of their wants. Dahl and Lindblom, and Downs also, raise a number of issues which they think are important though in fact they are irrelevant, and they do so because their methods of explaining Western democracy impel them to it. Let me give two examples, which I choose because they illustrate (so it seems to me) how far theorists who aim at being precise and realistic can fail of their purpose. The first example is Dahl and Lindblom's discussion of *political equality*, and the second is Downs's paradox that it is (or may be) irrational for the voter to be well-informed.

Irrelevancies and false issues

(a) POLITICAL EQUALITY

Among the *instrumental goals* highly valued in the West there is one that Dahl and Lindblom call *democracy* or *political equality*.

It consists of a condition to be attained and a principle guiding the procedure for attaining it. The condition is political equality, which we define as follows: *Control over governmental decisions is shared so that the preferences of no citizen are weighted more heavily than the preferences of any other citizen.* The principle is majority rule, which we define as follows: *Governmental decisions should be controlled by the greater number expressing their preferences in the last say.*[1]

The point of this sharing of control and weighting of preferences is to ensure that, as far as possible, governmental decisions make it easier for citizens to maximize the achievement of their prime goals.

Notice that in defining both the condition to be attained and the principle Dahl and Lindblom use the words *control* and *preferences*. These are key words in their explanations of social behaviour, especially the kind of behaviour that consists in taking decisions which lay obligations or penalties and confer rights or benefits on other people. There are usually settled procedures for taking such decisions: for putting forward proposals and choosing one in preference to the others. Political equality, which is a condition to be aimed at though it can never be fully achieved, requires that, when such decisions are taken, the preferences of no citizen (or no member of the community or group affected by the decisions) should have greater weight than those of any other. But, since these decisions, except very rarely when there is a referendum, are not taken by the citizens but by officials, the majority rule scarcely ever applies to them. That is why Dahl and Lindblom, when they formulate their majority rule, put in the words 'in the last say'. All that the citizens, except on rare occasions, decide by majority vote is who is to take official decisions; or rather (since most such decisions are not taken by *elected* officials) who the supreme makers of such decisions are to be.

Though Dahl and Lindblom are defining a condition that can never be fully attained and a principle that can never be fully adhered to, they claim to be realistic. Their definitions are meant to be operational; to use a word now fashionable among social scientists. That is to say, they are meant to be such that they can be used to assess actual conditions or to guide behaviour. Though political equality can never be fully attained, there can be progress towards it, and there are criteria for deciding whether or not progress has been made. All this talk of 'control' and 'the weighting of preferences' and 'the last say' is intended to make the explanation of democratic processes more precise and more realistic. In my opinion it does the opposite.

I shall not stop to enquire what the preferences are that the greater number of citizens express in 'the last say'. I do not deny that, given appropriate electoral rules and arrangements of public offices, it can

[1] Dahl and Lindblom: *Politics, Economics and Welfare*, Harper Torchbook edition, p. 41.

be contrived that a majority of citizens decide who is to have 'supreme' authority: who the persons are to be to whom all other holders of public office are responsible, directly or indirectly. But to contrive this would not of itself ensure that the majority had 'the last say' in deciding matters of policy, even the most general. Electors do not stand to those they elect as superior officials do to their subordinates; and to speak of 'the last say' makes much better sense when we are considering superiors in relation to their subordinates than electors in relation to their representatives. We understand far better what it is for a commanding officer to have 'the last say' than for a majority of electors to have it. Just what this expression means, as Dahl and Lindblom use it, is by no means clear. But I shall say no more about it. I shall turn at once to the question of what can be meant by saying that people have or have not *equal control* over decisions taken by others.

In most contexts in which they use the word *control* Dahl and Lindblom seem to have in mind the intended effects of some people's actions on the behaviour of others. This may not be how they define the word, but it is the sense in which they ordinarily use it. So, presumably, when a number of people try to influence a decision made by someone else, they can be said to have equal control over the decision when their attempts to influence it have equal effects upon it. But if this is equality of control, we can never know whether or not it has been achieved. Let me take an example to explain what I mean. Seven men choose an agent to act on their behalf. Each of them has one vote in choosing him, and each has the opportunity, which he takes, of letting the agent know what he wants him to do. If they express different wishes, how do we set about determining how much the agent has been influenced by each of them? Even if what he does accords more with one wish than another, it does not follow that he has been more influenced by that wish than the other.

Here we have two questions, both of them difficult to answer and often unanswerable. The first is: Where there are several opinions about what a man should do, how do we decide that what he does accords more with one opinion than with the others? And the second: Where there are several persons trying to influence someone, how do we decide what influence each of them has had? The second of these questions is, I suspect, more difficult even than the first, more often unanswerable.

In the case of our seven men, what more can we discover beyond the fact that each of them did or did not cast a vote when the agent was elected and did or did not tell him what he wanted done? What can their equal control consist in, if not in each of them voting and conveying his wishes to the agent? There is really no measuring the impact or persuasiveness of their wishes on the agent to discover whether their influence on his decision has been equal. To say that our seven men ought to have equal control (or influence) over their agent's decisions is merely to say that each ought to have a voice in choosing him and the opportunity to make his wishes known to him. It is to assert an equality of right. The equal control is not an effect of the men exercising their rights; it consists in their doing so. If we suppose it to be an effect, we can hardly know whether it has been achieved. If the question is raised: Do citizens have an equal control over the decisions of their rulers? it can be answered only by considering whether or not they have and take certain opportunities. In practice, therefore, equality of control is the taking by all who have them of certain opportunities or it is the exercise of certain rights.

Dahl and Lindblom speak as if it were possible to go beyond this exercise to some other equality which the exercise helps to achieve. They do this, so it seems to me, because of the utilitarian bias in their thinking. They assume, or they suppose that champions of democracy assume, that everyone should, as far' as possible, get what he wants. Where there is democracy, men are not ready to put up with whatever rulers they have, relying on them to use their authority in ways that make it easier for them to get what they want; as, for example, motorists leave it to traffic policemen to regulate the traffic to ensure that in general motorists get more easily and safely to destinations of their own choosing. They believe that they will be better placed to satisfy their wants if they can decide who is to have authority over them and the purposes for which the authority is to be used.

But this, for obvious reasons, they can do only to some extent: not all offices are filled by election, and opinions often differ about who should be elected and what elected officials should do. The most that democrats can aim at realistically (though they can never fully achieve it) is that every citizen's vote should count for as much as any other's at elections that decide who are to hold certain offices, especially the offices carrying 'supreme' authority, and that his wishes should count for as much in determining policy. This, so Dahl and Lindblom imply, is the political end (or, as they put it, the *instrumental goal*) distinctive of democracy. This, if I have not misunderstood them, is what they mean by political equality; this is equality of control over governmental decisions. A variety of political rights—the vote, freedom of speech, freedom of association, and so on—are, as they see it, *means* to the achievement of this goal. They imply that this goal can be defined apart from the rights whose exercise is a means to its achievement; that is to say, that the exercise of the rights by all who have them would not be in itself the achievement of the goal.

I am not denying, of course, that rights do help people to achieve their purposes, and are valued largely because they do so. This is no more to be denied than its converse: that it is as possessors of rights and obligations that people form their purposes, so that the purposes they form and their preferences among them depend largely on what rights and obligations they recognize. I am denying rather that universal suffrage, freedom of speech and of association, and in general the exercise of democratic rights, can be justified on the ground that they ensure that governments maintain conditions enabling their subjects to maximize the achievement of their aims. I am denying also that these rights are valued because it is believed that their exercise has this effect, or because it helps to ensure that the control of citizens over the decisions of their rulers is more equal. This equality of control is really only another name for the exercise of the rights whose effect it is supposed to be.

In asserting these rights, men express their sense of what is proper to their kind. The rights, of course, are not asserted everywhere, and we must not say that their exercise is involved in being properly or adequately human. They are not essential human rights in the sense that they are implicit in ideas shared by all men everywhere about how men should live or what they can properly require of one another. I do not deny that there are such ideas, but I see no reason for believing that, if there are, the liberal values of the West are implicit in them.

The historian can point to social conditions that encourage the assertion of these values, and these conditions no doubt affect men's wants as well as their values. Nobody denies that wants and values are closely bound up with one another, or that they change as social conditions do so, for they are part and parcel of those conditions. Certainly I do not deny it; I deny only that we can go far towards explaining or justifying the values that men hold by showing that they enable them to satisfy their wants more efficiently.

(b) RATIONALITY AND INFORMATION. DOWNS'S PARADOX

Anthony Downs, the most utilitarian of recent theorists of democracy, comes to several conclusions that are paradoxical. They point, he thinks, to defects inherent in democracy on a large scale. He does not claim to have been the first to notice these defects; he claims only to explain with the help of his model, how they are inherent in our sort of democracy. One of his paradoxes has attracted a good deal of notice, no doubt because it expresses forcefully misgivings widely shared.

Downs puts his paradox in these words: '(1) rational citizens want democracy to work well so as to gain its benefits, and it works well when the citizenry is well-informed; and (2) it is individually irrational to be well-informed. . . .'[1] It is not rational for the ordinary voter to be well-informed because the difference to the outcome that his vote makes, among the thousands or even millions that are cast, is small and the cost (whether in time or money) of getting the information he needs to decide what he would stand to gain or lose by one party or candidate rather than another coming to power is great. It is therefore not worth his while getting the information he needs to enable him to use his vote rationally. It is not the ordinary citizen but the man who is much better placed than he is to exert influence on others who has much to gain by being well-informed, all the more so as his being well placed to exert influence often means that he is also well placed to get relevant information. Thus, it is the powerful and the influential who can get relevant information easily and can use it effectively to achieve their aims.

This looks like a formidable argument. I would not reject it altogether but I want to qualify it in ways that change it considerably. Its force as a criticism of democracy depends largely on the assumption that everyone, when he behaves politically, is concerned primarily with what he stands to gain for himself or for his family and friends —with personal benefits. Downs, of course, makes this assumption, which (so it seems to me) is unrealistic. The citizen, whether he is a mere voter or is politically more active, is often concerned that the government should uphold certain principles, or should look after the interests of groups whose interests (in his opinion) have been neglected. Even when he wants the government to look after the interests of a group he belongs to, his conception of these interests is only to some extent determined by what he wants for himself or for others personally known to him.

The trouble with Downs's assumption, as with Utilitarianism in general, is not that it takes a low view of man; it is its lack of realism and its irrelevance. Man is not an accumulator of satisfactions; he is not that even when he is most self-centred. Everyone has many personal aims, most of them ill-defined, and he can scarcely ever decide, taking into account all of his aims likely to be affected by governmental action, what he stands to gain or to lose by one party rather than another getting power. If, to be well-informed politically, he must have the information he needs to be able to take such a decision, *then nobody is well-informed*. The powerful leader or the millionaire is, by this standard, scarcely better informed than the poorest and most ignorant citizen. Of course, if the leader or the millionaire wants specific concessions from the government or one of its organs, he knows far better than does the poor and the ignorant

<hr />

[1] *An Economic Theory of Democracy* (1965), p. 246.

man how to set about getting them. But if we make Downs's fantastic assumption that every citizen (or every rational citizen) when he acts politically is out to maximize in general the benefits that accrue to him and to those for whom he is personally concerned from governmental action, then the powerful and the rich, as well as the weak and the poor, know far less than enough to enable them to act rationally.

The political leader ordinarily knows more than the mere citizen about the intentions of other leaders, the pressures to which they are exposed, their likely reactions to events, and also about how political decisions are taken and political influence is exercised. Unless he knew much more than the mere citizen has time to discover about these things, he would not be much of a leader. If a political system is to function adequately, the chief actors in it, the leaders, must be fit to do what is expected of them, which they cannot be unless they acquire skills and information that ordinary citizens lack. Obviously, the greater a man's power and influence, the better placed he is to get other powerful and influential men to do what he wants. Yet his power and influence are circumscribed; they are considerable only within a limited sphere.

Nobody denies that the powerful are ordinarily much better informed politically than are ordinary citizens. But this, as we have seen, is of little advantage to them, if we assume (as Downs does) that all political actors (leaders and mere voters) are out to maximize the benefits that accrue to them from governmental action. On the other hand, if we reject this assumption as hopelessly unrealistic, it is not obvious that ordinary citizens know so much less than they need to know to ensure that their rulers and leaders are responsible to them that it is not worth their while trying to be better informed. No doubt rulers and leaders can (and often do) abuse their power, and they owe their power largely to being better informed than ordinary citizens can afford to be. But whether or not they abuse their power depends on whether or not they use it unconstitutionally or use it to achieve aims that are unjust or harmful or condemned by most citizens; it does not depend on whether or not they use it effectively to help citizens maximize the satisfaction of their private and personal wants.

If we want to decide whether leaders or ordinary citizens are well enough informed to be able to act rationally when they act politically, we must consider what their political functions are, what kinds of decision they have to take and what they need to know to be able to take them effectively. If we do this, we may then find that some leaders are *maximizers*, that part at least of their function is to get as much as possible of something quantifiable (e.g. votes). But in defining the functions of various types of leaders, we take into account only their official aims; and we need take account of their private aims only to the extent that they favour or impede the pursuit of their official aims. Leaders act rationally when their actions are 'efficiently designed' to achieve their official aims, which sometimes involves their making calculations of a kind that can be called maximizing and sometimes does not. And, of course, if their actions are to be 'efficiently designed', they need a good deal of information, its kind varying with their functions.

Ordinarily, the mere citizen in a large democracy votes for the candidate or party most likely to promote the policies he favours or to look after the interests of groups he belongs to or is concerned about or the one fittest (in his opinion) to carry out the public duties that devolve on whoever wins the election. It is probably, in his case, much more difficult than in the case of officeholders to decide what he must know and do to act rationally, for the criteria of rationality that apply to him cannot be defined at all precisely. But the difficulty has little or nothing to do with his inability to adapt political means to personal ends; it has to do much more with the character of his political ends. His political role is so different from that of the political leader that it is much less easy to decide in his case whether or not he performs it rationally, if to be rational is to take action correctly designed to achieve well-defined aims. And yet he must perform this role if there is to be democracy; if makers of law and policy are to be responsible to the people. The ordinary citizen, the voter, because of the nature of his political role, cannot, however intelligent and well-informed he is, come as close as the political leader (especially if the leader's role is a narrow one) to meeting Downs's criteria of rationality. But this does not entail that it does not matter how ill-informed he is.

Downs admits that it can be 'rational for a man to delegate part or all of his political decision-making, no matter how important it is that he make the correct decisions'.[1] It is rational for him to do this, apparently, when he has good reason to believe that the person or persons to whom he delegates it has or have much the same aims as he has. What, then, are these aims? They are, presumably, what I have called social aims; for the man, in choosing the delegates, is not choosing a housekeeper or nurse to look after him personally. He chooses them to promote general aims, even though he may stand to gain from their doing so; he looks to them to get benefits or concessions for anyone placed as he is. He also looks to them to promote other things he cares about, even though neither he nor anyone he is concerned for personally stands to gain thereby. Downs may say that, if he does this, he is not rational; but his not being so follows merely

[1] *Ibid.*, p. 233.

from certain quite unrealistic assumptions that Downs chooses to make.

As a matter of fact, Downs makes realistic as well as unrealistic assumptions about the rational voter, but unfortunately he speaks as if all these assumptions were logically connected with one another. For example, he often speaks of the rational voter as if he had several aims not to be achieved without the help of government, and then took political action to ensure that this help was given; which makes good enough sense. But he also takes it for granted that this limited and reasonable endeavour is part of a general attempt to maximize personal benefits resulting from governmental action. If I want A, B and C, in that order of preference, and I need governmental assistance to get them, I may well be able to take political action 'efficiently designed' to get that assistance; and the more powerful and wealthy I am, the better placed I am to take it. But if I want to maximize the benefits accruing to me from governmental action, then, since that action affects me in innumerable and unpredictable ways, it is hard to see what I can do to achieve my object, rich and powerful though I may be.

Downs admits that a man can have good reason to trust some persons rather than others to pursue aims that he favours, though he does not know what policies are most likely to achieve the aims. But if this is so, then, surely, he may need, in order to act rationally, less information than either the maker of public policy or the person well placed to bring pressure on him; he may need both less information and different information.

Nobody, no matter how powerful he is, has more than a small part of the information relevant even to the largest issues that makers of policy have to decide. Information is always widely and unequally distributed, just as power is. Unless power were unequally as well as widely distributed there could be no effective government on a large scale, responsible or irresponsible. We do not say that power is irresponsible merely because it is unequally distributed. So why should we say, when relevant information is unequally distributed, that those who need a lot of it to make their decisions cannot be responsible to others who have much less? We cannot argue that those who have least of it have little to gain by trying to get more on the ground that the most they can reasonably hope to get is far less than enough to enable them to make rational decisions of policy; for *it is not their business to make such decisions.*

If a vast political system is to work effectively, the persons whose activities constitute the system must have *between them* an immense store of information and a wide variety of skills—vastly more information and more skills than any one man can possess. Nobody in the system, no matter how important, can play his part in it unless he can rely on other people playing theirs, even though he does not know what is involved in their doing so. The information and the skills on which he must rely if he is to be able to make intelligent decisions are incomparably greater than the information and skills he uses in making the decisions. Downs does not fail to take note of this. What economist could? For, in the eyes of the economist, information and skills are resources like any others, and no man, even the most favoured, has more than a small share of them.

What the theorist of democracy has to do is to explain how relevant information must be distributed in a vast political community if makers of law and policy are to be responsible to their subjects; he must explain what kinds of information are suited to different kinds of political decisions. This Downs does not do, though he comes closer than most writers on democracy to recognizing the need to do it. He does not do it, partly because he makes unrealistic assumptions about what citizens in a democracy aim at when they vote at elections, and partly because he gives so little thought to what political responsibility is.

He aims at economy and precision of explanation, and that is a praiseworthy aim. Unfortunately, he sometimes imagines that he has attained greater precision when he has done nothing of the kind. He notices that democracy is often defined as 'government by consent of the governed'. This definition seems to him lacking in precision, for the word *consent* is used in several different senses. So he undertakes a more precise definition:

> We can further define 'government by consent of the governed' as *decision-making in which the decider makes each choice on the basis of the preferences of those affected by it and weights the preferences of each in proportion to the degree to which he is affected.* Though this complex definition is still ambiguous, it is clear enough to compare with the method of weighting preferences used by the rational government in our model.[1]

This attempt at greater precision is a move towards irrelevance. Downs's formula throws no light at all on what is ordinarily understood by government by consent. Where government is by consent of the governed, it is responsible to them, but Downs's formula makes no mention of responsibility. A benevolent despot eager to satisfy his subjects would, according to this formula, be governing with their consent, provided he made careful enquiries to ascertain their wants and preferences. Indeed, he might come closer to doing so than democratic rulers have ever done, and yet be quite irresponsible. In a

---

[1] *Ibid.*, p. 257 (my italics).

note at the bottom of the page on which he gives us his formula or definition, Downs says of it that it is incomplete, but only because, as he puts it, 'it ignores the problem of how to translate individual preferences into social choices'. The individual preferences concern, presumably, matters that the government has to decide, and the problem is to ensure that its decisions take account of these preferences to the extent that the persons having them are likely to be affected by the decisions. Now, I dare say that this kind of problem could sometimes be solved, if there were agreement about what was to count as a preference, how the effects on the individual of policy decisions were to be measured, and so on. But the agreement could be reached only by experts, and the necessary calculations made only by computer. The problem would then be solved to the satisfaction of the experts who defined it and who decided how it should be solved. But what has this to do with democracy as anyone understands it who cares for it? As even the political scientist understands it when he acts as a citizen and not as a student of politics?

People who spend their time governing or trying to influence government (directly or indirectly) are for the most part much better informed politically than the great mass of citizens. Nobody doubts that they need to be if government is to be able to do what its subjects expect of it. There must be a more active minority much better informed than the less active majority. This, in itself, neither prevents makers of policy being effectively responsible to the people nor ensures that they are so. It is compatible with both authoritarian and democratic government. There would still be a need for the services of this minority of whole-time politicians, of leaders and persuaders, even if the mass of citizens took a much greater part in government and in ancillary political activities than in fact they do. This professional minority are, and need to be, better informed politically than the unprofessional majority. Whether their being so contributes to democracy—that is to say, helps to ensure that rulers are effectively responsible to their subjects—depends on how the professionals are related to one another and to ordinary citizens. It depends not only on their having to compete for popular support in order to get power and influence; it depends also on the extent to which they compete for it in ways that make their controversies about the larger issues that governments have to decide enlightening both to themselves and to ordinary citizens.

There are not two stores of politically relevant information, a larger one *shared* by the professionals, the whole-time leaders and persuaders, and a much smaller one *shared* by ordinary citizens. No leader or persuader possesses more than a small part of the information that must be available in the community if government is to be effective and responsible; and the same is true of the ordinary citizen. What matters, if there is to be responsible government, is that this mass of information should be so distributed among professionals and ordinary citizens that competitors for power, influence and popular support are exposed to relevant and searching criticism.

Chapter 7

A Summary and Some Further Arguments

I have been criticizing other men's arguments, and it is time now that I should indicate how, in my opinion, democracy should be explained and justified. I shall not attempt a systematic account of democracy; I shall make only a number of suggestions as to how such an account might be constructed. Already, in my criticisms of some recent theories, I have argued that some ways of explaining democracy are better than others. They are more lucid and realistic; they provide us with criteria we can apply to actual systems of government to discover whether or not they are democratic. So, too, some ways of justifying democracy are sounder than others. They may not be the more convincing immediately, but they rest on assumptions that stand up better to close scrutiny.

There is no question of starting afresh from the beginning. There have been excellent books and articles written about democracy, not only since the Second World War, but also long before it. There is a large store of ideas and arguments, there are many empirical studies, for us to draw on. We do not need, if we want either to explain democracy or to justify it, to furnish ourselves with an entirely new stock of ideas; we have rather to decide what the important questions are. We may then find that they have all been put already, though perhaps not all put as clearly and simply as they might be. We may find also that they have been mixed up with logically absurd or unanswerable or irrelevant questions that spring from confusions of thought. The need, I suggest, is not so much to devote our energies to new enterprises as to distribute them more judiciously among old ones, abandoning some altogether and pressing forward more vigorously with others. But, of course, we must be able to give good reasons for what we do; we must be willing to explain why we think that some lines of enquiry should be discontinued and more time spent on others. This is what I have tried to do in the course of this book.

I want now to bring together some of the arguments I have used in my criticisms of other men's doctrines and theories. I want to make it clear how they are connected, and also to draw some further implications.

Democracy and political equality

Democracy is a matter of rights and obligations and of procedures that secure rights and ensure that obligations are, or can be, fulfilled. Whoever seeks to explain it, no matter how much his purpose is merely to explain and not also to justify, cannot avoid a kind of exercise which is more properly called philosophy than science; especially if the natural sciences are taken to be models of what science should be. To define rights and obligations and to consider what institutions are best adapted to secure and discharge them is not to establish what men do; it is not to make hypotheses about how men behave which can be tested by experience or observation. It is to define rules and principles which those who invoke them often fail to observe and are often incapable of defining; it is to explain the significance of their behaviour and the point of their own assessments of it. It is neither science nor persuasion; it is a critical examination of specifically human—of rational and moral—behaviour. It is an exercise which everyone engaged upon it was willing, until quite recently, to call political philosophy.

This exercise does, of course, involve observing what men do, for we cannot explain the significance of their behaviour and the standards implicit in their assessments of it, without observing how they behave; but it also involves something more.

Of the rights and obligations called democratic, some are political while others are not. Those that are political help to secure those that are not, and the opposite is true also. These two kinds of rights and obligations ordinarily go together, or most of them do; for a community that respects one kind generally respects the other kind also, at least to some extent. But rights of neither kind are valued only as means to the other; nor do countries that claim to be democratic set equal store by both kinds or achieve equal success in securing both. If we call *liberal* a community in which the rights and obligations that are not political are secure, and *democratic* a community in which the political rights and duties are so, we can say of a country that it comes nearer to being liberal than democratic, or nearer to being democratic than liberal; though it cannot be either to any great extent without also being to some extent the other.

Democracy can neither be explained nor justified as a political system that maximizes the satisfaction of wants (or the achievement of goals) better than other systems do. There is no utilitarian argument for democracy, not even for democracy under certain conditions; for example, under conditions peculiar to societies of the Western type. Not only because to decide what the relevant conditions are is extraordinarily difficult, but also because the wants of people living under these conditions often cannot be defined apart from the rights and duties, and the forms of social intercourse, supposed to be means to satisfying or achieving them. What is more, these wants change unpredictably as a result of what people do in the hope of satisfying them. Wants are both less stable and less definite than rights and duties. It is often much more difficult to decide whether or not wants are satisfied than to decide whether or not rights are secure or duties performed.

This is not to deny that utilitarian arguments have a large place in social and political studies. Of course they do. Not only a large but also a growing place. It is often possible to measure how often, and sometimes even how far, people get what they want. Social scientists are more ingenious and more sophisticated than they used to be in defining wants, in establishing orders of preference among them, and in measuring the frequency and degree to which they are satisfied. And if measurement is what we are after, we can also (and perhaps quite often) measure the extent to which rights are effectively exercised and duties performed. Indeed, since rights and duties are, on the whole, more stable and more easily defined than wants are, it may well be that their exercise and performance can be measured more often than can the satisfying of wants. But it is of wants and preferences rather than rights and duties that Utilitarians and quantifiers like to speak.

When I say that the exercise of rights is perhaps more susceptible to measurement than is the satisfying of wants, I do not mean to suggest that democracy could be preferable to other forms of government on the ground, that, in general, it ensures better than they do that the individual can exercise his rights. Maximizing the exercise of rights is, taken thus generally, as absurd a notion as maximizing the satisfaction of wants. The democrat is not concerned that the individual should exercise his rights, whatever they are, as fully as possible; he is concerned rather that he should have certain kinds of rights, and should be able to exercise them. Moreover, democracy, in his eyes, is not a means to people's having and exercising these rights but consists in their doing so.

I said earlier that democratic institutions cannot be described apart from the rights and duties they are intended to secure and discharge. But this does not mean that the student of democracy must first define the rights and duties and then go on to explain the institutions; for he cannot define the rights and duties adequately except by explaining the institutions, nor explain the institutions without defining the rights and duties. That is why to explain a political system, or indeed any system of social behaviour, always involves more than just observing what men do; it also involves interpreting and assessing their behaviour, which in turn involves defining their principles and ideals, though they live up to them only in part. We discover what these principles and ideals are partly by observing what they do, and partly by bringing out the implications of their comments upon, and criticisms of, their own and each other's behaviour.

I said that political equality, defined as Dahl and Lindblom define it, as the sharing of control over governmental decisions in such a way that no citizen's preferences count for more than any other's, is an empty formula. It does not apply even to the simplest case, not to speak of the complexities of ordinary political life. For example, if we have one man, taking decisions that affect three other men, we cannot contrive that the three men have an equal influence on him. Indeed, we cannot even discover, after the event, whether or not they have had an equal influence. The most we can do is to contrive that the three men make their wishes known to the fourth man, the decision-maker, and that he takes cognizance of them. We can devise rules to ensure that this is so; we can confer rights on the three men and lay obligations on the fourth. We can then say that, if the rules are obeyed, the three men are politically equal. But if we say this, we speak only of rights and duties; we define political equality in terms of rights and duties, and not in terms of something else to which they are means.[1]

The extent to which some political theorists go the wrong way about explaining democracy is brought out by the importance they attach to an argument of Kenneth Arrow in his book *Social Choice and Individual Values* (1951). Arrow there shows that, where there are several alternatives to choose from and several choosers, the orders of preference of the choosers among these alternatives may be such that there is no alternative that stands higher than the others in a collective order of preferences, none that is clearly the most popular or the least unpopular. Robert Dahl, in a footnote to page 42 of *A Preface to Democratic Theory*, describes a quite simple situation, in which there

---

[1] When we say that the decision-maker gives equal weight to the claims of the three men, we do not mean that his decisions stand to their claims as, say, the direction in which an object moves stands to three separate but equal forces acting upon it. The rules we are concerned with here are not rules for the weighting of claims or the measuring of influences; they are rules of justice that makers of claims and decisions are required to observe. Thus when we say that the makers of the claims are equal, or politically equal, we imply one or other of two things: that the rules are just or that they are accepted because they are thought to be just.

are only three choosers and three alternatives, to illustrate Kenneth Arrow's meaning.

There is nothing wrong logically with Arrow's argument; or, if there is, I am not logician enough to detect it. But why, I wonder, should a political scientist take more than passing notice of it? For politicians, democratic or otherwise, are never faced with the sort of problem which, according to Arrow, is insoluble. Such problems are of purely theoretical interest, and politicians have not heard of them. Or, if they have, it is only as students of political science, and afterwards they forget about them. Dahl does not say that democratic politicians are brought up against such insoluble problems, but he does suggest that their existence makes it impossible to achieve complete democracy. The suggestion is false. If complete democracy is out of reach, it is not for this reason.

Dahl would no doubt agree that few citizens have an order of preferences among the courses of action proposed to them by political leaders soliciting their votes. His point, I take it, is that, even if every citizen did have such an order, there could still arise situations in which no course of action could be said to be either the most popular or the least unpopular, in which no decision could be taken on strictly democratic grounds. It is this that Kenneth Arrow, according to Dahl, has proved. But he has proved it only if we accept some such account of democracy as Dahl offers; and there is no need for us to do so. Indeed, we ought not to do it, for it is a mistaken account.

To return for a moment to the simple example I used earlier. One man takes decisions that affect three other men. If his acting democratically required that he should invite these three men to choose between different courses of action and then take the course they prefer to any other, it might quite often happen that he could not act democratically. But since his acting democratically requires only that they should have elected him to act on their behalf, that they should be free to criticize his actions and to make their wishes known to him, and that his right to act on their behalf beyond a certain period should depend on their again electing him to do so, he can act democratically no matter how often there is no decision which these three men want him to take in preference to any other.

Political Responsibility

There is democracy where rulers are politically responsible to their subjects. And there is political responsibility where two conditions hold: where citizens are free to criticize their rulers and to come together to make demands on them and to win support for the policies they favour and the beliefs they hold; and where the supreme makers of law and policy are elected to their offices at free and periodic elections. The criteria for determining whether these conditions hold are not easily defined.

Everyone agrees that in a democracy citizens have the right to meet and to act together to further any purpose they have in mind, provided the purpose is not harmful. The difficulty is to decide what is harmful, or what is so harmful as to outweigh the harm of preventing people from exercising an important right. What is more, even when harmfulness is so defined by law and interpreted by the courts as to put relatively few *legal* obstacles in the way of people who want to exercise this right, it can still happen that many, or even most, citizens are so placed that they cannot exercise it, or cannot do so to much effect. For example, they may, for one reason or another, be unable to form organizations having access to higher levels of government; they may lack the skill or the time to do so. Or they may be unable to make their views known to their fellow citizens, or to get the information and advice needed to put their case persuasively. It is not enough that citizens should all have certain legal rights; it is also necessary that they should be able to exercise them.

No criticism of political communities that claim to be liberal and democratic is more familiar than this one. It is often well founded and formidable. But it needs to be qualified. If, in a country as large as Britain, any number of citizens, no matter how few, who joined together for the purpose of influencing makers of policy in Westminster or Whitehall had a right of access to the men they wished to influence, these men would have no time to do the business they are elected or appointed to do. So, too, if every citizen could ensure that other citizens had to listen to his opinions, nobody would have time to think to good purpose about public issues for being overwhelmed by the views, often uninformed and ill-digested, of his neighbours. Rights entail obligations. If everyone has the right to be heard, does it then follow that everyone is obliged to listen to anyone who chooses to speak? If God had intended us to take such undiscriminating notice of one another, he would surely have provided us with a more complicated brain and with many more than two ears. Rulers, even democratic rulers, need to be protected from their subjects, and citizens even in a democracy need to be able to shut their doors and their ears to one another.

It is a good thing that most citizens do not in practice form associations or call meetings or publish opinions likely to influence their rulers or more than a handful of their fellow citizens; and yet it is essential to democracy that they should have the right to do it, if they have the ability and the opportunity. The right to be heard is the right to speak to willing listeners or to listeners whose duty it is to get the information or to hear the views that the speaker can give or express. The right to form associations is the right to take an initiative to which others may or may not respond. Can we say that the right is annulled by their failure to respond to the initiative? Does not our willingness to say so depend on the reasons for the failure? If others would like to respond but are afraid of doing so, then we are inclined to say that the right is annulled; but if they are merely indifferent, then we are not. But it may be very much their interest to respond, and their failure may come of their being too ignorant to see that it is or too busy earning their meagre livings to have time to respond. If the failure is due to their lacking opportunities which they ought to have, we are inclined to say that both they and the men to whose initiative they fail to respond have a right merely on paper. It is notoriously difficult to define these opportunities.

It is not only inevitable, it is also desirable, that only a minority should be founders and managers of associations having a considerable influence on the government or on the people generally, or should be able to publish their opinions widely. This is desirable not only because the founding and running of these organizations and the publishing of these opinions are often whole-time occupations, and because there are other kinds of work that need doing in the community, and because these are enterprises calling for large resources; it is desirable also because people who have decisions to make in complicated situations, be they leaders or ordinary citizens, must not have more information and more advice thrust upon them than they can take in and act upon.

If democracy is to be genuine, this minority of managers, leaders and persuaders must not form one organized group nor be controlled by any one group. The associations that this minority form and manage must cover all sections of the people, and there must be freedom to compete for popular support between them and sometimes even inside them. The conditions of this freedom are not easily defined, but we cannot prove that there is no freedom simply by showing that established leaders (the men at the top) placate troublemakers by bringing them into their own ranks, unless we show that they do so without meeting the popular grievances and demands that the troublemakers exploit.

If there is to be democracy, citizens when they make political choices must have intelligible, relevant and genuinely different alternatives to choose between, and the men who put the alternatives to them must have sufficient motives for putting alternatives of this kind. The organized bodies making demands on the government on behalf of different sections of the people should between them make demands on behalf of all sections, and the demands should be in keeping with popular aspirations. There should also be widely publicised discussions of major issues of policy between persons who are neither competing for public office nor making demands on behalf of specific groups.

If 'the will of the people' or 'the will of the majority' is a myth, so too is 'the will of the minority imposed on the majority'. It is a myth everywhere except in what are called 'totalitarian' states, where government is controlled by some organized group dedicated to a doctrine that only the group may define and no one may challenge, a doctrine supposed to be a guide to all official policies; and it comes close to being a myth even in them. Arguments of the kind used to show that there is no collective will of the people in a vast community of millions of citizens can be used just as effectively to show that there is no collective will of a politically active minority of thousands of leaders. To be sure, in a totalitarian state, this minority of leaders can all, or nearly all, be relied upon to give the same answers (at least in public) to a considerable number of questions of a type to which political leaders in a democracy would give different answers. But then the same is true of the people; they too in a totalitarian state can be relied on to give on appropriate occasions the same answers to a whole lot of questions to which they would give different answers in a democracy. Fear is a great leveller.

In a totalitarian state the leaders are rather more reliable in this respect than the people are; they are better trained politically and know better what responses are required of them. But this does not make their responses any more expressions of a collective minority will, even when they make the responses willingly in the belief that this show of unanimity helps to maintain the system to which they owe their privileges and their power. Even then they do not have a collective will of the kind that, say, Schumpeter was thinking of when he denied that the people have such a will. We know that there can be, that there has been, widespread and most cruel oppression in totalitarian states. But this oppression, though it is of a majority by a minority, is not therefore an imposing of the collective will of that minority on the majority.

To establish that a political community is democratic, we do not have to show that there is no minority inside it who do the organized political persuading, the political negotiating and bargaining, and who take the important governmental decisions. There always is such a minority in any but a small community, no matter how democratic it is. Before we can decide whether a community is democratic, we must know how this minority are recruited, and in just what ways their power depends upon their having popular support. We must know how the organizations run by this minority are related to one another and to the groups whose interests they claim to promote or whom they seek to persuade. The closer the members of this minority are to forming one organized body or a set of such bodies controlled by one among them, the less they need take account of popular wishes and interests, and the less likely it is that the people will acquire definite political opinions and firm beliefs about their group interests. If there is to be genuine democracy, parties competing for power should be independent, pressure groups should promote a wide variety of interests and beliefs covering the whole population, and the mass media should express and discuss many different opinions. These are broad and familiar generalities. Defining the rights and opportunities which men must have if these general principles are to be realized is a long and difficult business. At the moment I am concerned only to say that it is a business of defining rights and opportunities and not of defining the optimal conditions for the maximizing of 'want satisfactions' or the 'allocation of values' or 'goal achievement' or even 'happiness'. It is also a business of explaining what kind of politically active minority is compatible with democracy.

Free elections and competition between parties

If elections are to be free, voters must not be bribed or intimidated, and they must be able to choose between candidates nominated by independent nominators or between policies sponsored by independent sponsors. It is not enough that voters should have real alternatives to choose from. After all, a dictator could put forward several genuinely different proposals and invite his subjects to express their preferences between them without either bribing or intimidating them, and could do so with the intention of taking account of their preferences in making his decisions. To ensure that, as far as possible, voters are presented with candidates or policies attractive to them, any group of persons who wish to must be allowed to nominate candidates.[1]

The theorist seeking to explain what free elections are must take

[1] The rule that candidates (or those who nominate them) should pay a deposit which they are liable to forfeit if they get less than a certain small proportion of the votes is, presumably, made either for the benefit of the voters, so that they do not have too many alternatives to choose from, or to reduce the risk that governments will be unstable and ephemeral. To contest elections costs time and money, and these costs act as deterrents to wouldbe candidates and nominators. The stronger their beliefs, the more willing they are to pay these costs: and the more widely they are supported, the more easily they can find people to contribute to these costs. Moreover, success attracts money and collaborators. There need not be many groups putting forward candidates for election; it does not matter that there should be only a few, provided that other groups can be formed easily and cheaply as soon as there is a will to form them.

care to be properly abstract; he must try to determine what conditions must hold if elections are to be accounted free. He must not just take a number of countries in which elections, so he believes, are free and decide that the electoral procedures common to them are necessary conditions of elections being free. He must not do this, even though he is right in believing that elections in those countries are free; for some of these procedures may be unnecessary to freedom, or necessary only in some circumstances and not others. American and British political theorists often say that, if elections are to be free, there ought to be at least two parties competing for power. But to explain what is involved in holding free elections, we need not speak of parties at all. In small communities candidates for office can be nominated by groups that hold together only for as long as the elections last, and are therefore not parties as we ordinarily use the word. In some large communities, there may be only one party, or only one giant party among several pygmies, and yet voters may have a choice between candidates put up by independent groups. Even where the real contest is for official nomination as the party candidate, the conditions of political responsibility may be satisfied.

If any organized group that endures through several elections and puts up candidates is to be called a political party, then clearly that term has a wide connotation. One party can differ very greatly from another in organization and methods of work. The Soviet Union is a one-party state and India was close to being one for several years after she gained her independence. But the Communist Party in the Soviet Union has always differed greatly, in organization and in spirit, from the Congress Party in India; and both these parties differ greatly from, say, the Democratic Party in South Carolina. Elections can be either free or unfree where there are no parties, where there is only one, and where there are two or more. The democratic theorist can define free elections without speaking of parties, and can then go on to consider under what conditions having only one party, or only one party of a certain kind, or only two parties, or more than two, or none at all, contributes to or detracts from the freedom of elections.

If elected rulers are to be responsible politically to the people, citizens, when they vote, must understand the significance of what they are doing. They must believe that there is, and there must in fact be, real competition for their votes. They must have some knowledge of how the candidates soliciting their votes differ from one another. The man who votes Labour rather than Conservative may perhaps understand only a little about how the policies of the Labour Party differ from those of the Conservative Party, but if he knows that the Labour Party relies on the support of the trade unions as well as of the majority of working men, and if he believes that it has a stronger incentive than the Conservative Party has to take account of demands made for the benefit of manual workers, he makes when he votes a relevant choice. The choice is equally relevant whether he is himself a manual worker or merely someone concerned that more should be done for manual workers. He has beliefs about the Labour Party which the leaders of that party have an interest that he and others who think as he does should retain, and they therefore do their best to ensure that he and they do retain them. They try to retain the confidence of their supporters despite the efforts of their Conservative and other rivals to destroy it.

If all voters decided how to vote by tossing a coin, then no matter how free elections were there would be no democracy. There would be no point in holding free elections because, owing to the people's refusal to make genuine choices, the criteria of political responsibility would not be met. There would be no competition for the people's votes by candidates whose ability to get electors to vote for them depended on their retaining or winning their confidence. There would be no getting or losing the right to govern by gaining or losing the confidence of the governed.

It is not a condition of political responsibility that all or most electors should understand the policies of the candidates or parties competing for their votes. Or if it is, then political responsibility, and therefore also democracy, is unattainable in a vast, intricate and changing community, even though most people inside it are highly intelligent and well educated. If to understand a policy is to be able to describe its likely consequences and to give good reasons for holding that they are likely, then, in communities as large, diverse and rapidly changing as our Western democracies today, no one understands the policies on major issues of any candidate or party putting forward more than two or three such policies. Not even the candidate understands them, nor any leader of his party. Indeed, it is unlikely that, even between them, the leaders and their advisers understand all the policies of the party on major issues; for usually they understand at least some of them differently. But if the leaders understand a policy in different ways, in just what sense is it *the* policy of their party? It often happens that leaders hit on a formula that excludes some courses of action and yet can be interpreted in several ways. It also often happens that, once their party is in power, the formula comes to mean something different to them as they see more clearly the difficulties of applying it.

Political decisions differ greatly in kind, and it is much easier with some kinds than others to decide whether or not the persons who make them are well-informed or rational. The Minister of Education has to decide, say, whether to build more schools or to improve facilities in existing schools. He has, let us suppose, a policy; he knows what resources are available to him, and he has a variety of experts to advise him. We may differ about the wisdom of his decision, and still agree that, given his policy, he has, or else has not, taken notice of the relevant information and made the correct decision. Or, if we disagree on this second point, our disagreement is likely to be the smaller the more we know about how he took his decision and the situation in which he took it. The Minister of Education, in carrying out the duties of his office, takes one decision after another, some having much larger consequences than others do, but most of them taken after a good deal of consultation. In assessing his decisions, we take notice of the policy of his government and of his official intentions; we are not concerned with his private intentions or his ambitions.

The mere voter takes few political decisions, for he votes at long intervals. He is not an officeholder whose official duties are pretty well defined and whose official intentions can be ascertained. The obvious, the incontestable, fact about the voter is that he does not himself take policy decisions but takes part in deciding who shall take them. That, at least, is what he does if he understands what he is doing when he votes, and he can hardly be said to be casting a vote if he does not understand that. Even if he cares nothing about the personal qualities of the candidate he votes for, and votes for him only on account of the party he belongs to, he makes a deliberate choice. But his understanding what it is that he does when he votes is not enough to make his vote *rational*, not at least in the sense that writers about democracy have in mind when they enquire whether or not the citizen does (or even can) vote rationally. Whatever they mean, they mean more than just that.

The difficulty is to discover what exactly they do mean. For though many of them agree that it is absurd to hold that the people elect representatives to carry out policy decisions which they (the people) have made, they still speak of the vote as if it were, or ought to be, something more than taking part in deciding who is to make policy decisions. The citizen ought, after all, to take an interest in matters of policy, and if he does take an interest, the conclusions he reaches will influence him when he decides what candidate or party to vote for. He will want some policy decisions made rather than others, and in that case it is rational for him to cast his vote in such a way as to increase the chances that they will be made. Everyone agrees that this, as far as it goes, is rational. But this, after all, is not all that the voter wants. He may not know what he wants done about other issues, although he knows that they too are important and wants wise decisions made. He cannot vote on every issue separately, and yet if he votes, his vote may help to determine how an issue that he knows nothing about will be decided. He votes at long intervals for and against candidates and parties who, if they get power, will have to take a wide variety of decisions.

When we look at the decisions that political leaders take, we are quite often satisfied that they are (or are not) well-informed and rational, but when we contemplate the decisions that the ordinary citizen takes when he casts his vote, we are much more puzzled what to say about them. We admit that some citizens are better informed and of better political judgment than others, and yet we are hard put to it to define criteria of rationality that can be applied realistically to ordinary citizens. We concede that the voter ought to be rational, to the extent that he can be, and yet we doubt whether he can be to any great extent. And so, when we compare leaders and voters as political agents, we slip easily into speaking of leaders as if they were more rational than the citizens they lead without noticing that we are comparing what is not strictly comparable. For the decisions that leaders, whether in or out of office, take differ in kind from the decisions that mere citizens take when they cast their votes. On the one hand, we have President de Gaulle at his best, gradually and judiciously preparing the French people, at least cost to their national pride, for the inevitable separation from Algeria taking, one after another, political decisions that are well informed and reasonable; while on the other, we have Citizen de Gaulle at Colombey-les-Deux-Eglises, making an altogether different kind of political decision, casting his vote at a general election, less puzzled perhaps than most Frenchmen how to use it for his country's good, but not therefore necessarily making a more rational use of it.

Well-informed and rational political action

Thus, before we can decide what constitutes rational political behaviour, we must look rather more closely at the political role of the agent whose behaviour is in question.

If we take a leader (whether he holds public office or office of some other kind or puts himself forward as a candidate for office), we have someone who not only takes specific decisions but takes many of them, one after another. He is active continually within a fairly well-defined sphere of action. We can therefore point to the kinds of information relevant to the sorts of decision that he takes. To whom should he go for advice? Whom should he consult on the ground that they represent groups or professions likely to be affected by his decisions? To these questions we can often, if we take sufficient trouble, give precise answers. We can also look at the particular decisions that a leader has taken and enquire how far he has had relevant information and consulted the representatives of interested groups. If he has a policy to guide him as he takes his decisions, we can enquire how far, given that policy, he has tried to get the best available information and has taken reasonable decisions. We can sometimes do this even when his policy statements, taken in themselves, are vague; for we can interpret his policy in the light of his decisions as well as in the light of his declarations of policy.

Even if he changes his policy, we can enquire realistically whether he acted reasonably in doing so, given the circumstances in which he made the change and given also his other policies (if he has any) and the policies of his party or his superiors in so far as they impinge on his sphere of action.

If we turn now to the voter, we have of course someone who takes, at one level, a quite definite decision; he votes for one party or one candidate or even one programme rather than others. But as soon as we go on to consider why he votes as he does, what he hopes to achieve by doing so, we are either hard put to it to answer or hard put to it to explain how we would set about deciding whether he has made a rational use of his vote. This is so, except when all that he wants is that a few clear policy decisions should be taken and he votes for the party or candidate that promises to take them, if elected. But this is rarely what the voter wants, or all that he wants; nor is it all that champions of democracy think he ought to want.

Even on the assumptions that Downs makes the voter ought to want more than that three or four policy decisions should be taken, for he is affected in many different ways by what governments do. By voting for a party that promises to do X, Y and Z, which he wants done, he may bring into power men who, though they keep those promises, take other decisions that do him more harm than good. Therefore, according to Downs, he ought, as far as he can, to consider what other decisions the party making these promises is likely to take. But this, as Downs himself admits, he can hardly do in practice.

Even if we make assumptions different from Downs's, if we assume that the citizen should vote for the party most likely to govern in the public interest, or most likely to look after the interests of the groups he belongs to or cares about, we are still hard put to it to set up criteria to enable us to decide whether or not he has voted *rationally*, in the utilitarian sense of that word.

Thus, if what we want to estimate is how far the citizen's vote is correctly designed to achieve his aims, we are in a quandary. We can attribute to him a few precise aims, and so make it easier for ourselves to decide whether or not he has used his vote in the way most likely to ensure that they are achieved. But if we do this we are unrealistic. For the aims of the voter are not precise, or most of them are not; and hardly anyone supposes that they ought to be. Or we can attribute to him much broader and vaguer aims, and so make it much more difficult, if not impossible, to decide whether or not he has voted rationally. Or, more realistically still, we can attribute to him both precise and vague aims, though this makes it no easier to estimate how well his vote is calculated to further his aims.

The citizen, when he votes, indicates, among other things, what party or candidate he thinks is the most likely to govern the country well or to promote the interests of the groups he cares about or to uphold principles that he values. He expresses greater confidence in one party or candidate than in others, or (at the worst) less distrust of one than of the others. This may not be the whole significance of his vote, but it is usually a large part of it. The vote is above all a mark of confidence or of lack of confidence.

Now, we can ask of confidence, whether or not it is well placed. But a mark of confidence is not a prediction about what the man or the party that is trusted or mistrusted will do in the future. If I appoint a solicitor to look after my interests, I do not know beforehand what problems he is going to deal with on my behalf. At the best, I know only what kinds of problems. Whether or not he is worthy of my trust depends on how able and how honest he is in dealing with such problems, and the relevant evidence here consists of his past record, his character, his education. I may make a foolish appointment, but my foolishness will not consist in my miscalculations about his future actions and their likely effects on me; for, at the time that I appoint him, neither he nor I can foretell what those actions will be. We may be able to foretell some of the problems that he will deal with on my behalf, but only some.

What is true of a man in relation to his solicitor is true also, to a large extent, of the citizen in relation to the party or candidate he votes for. My analogy, I admit, is not perfect. The solicitor or doctor that I choose does not, in competition with other solicitors or doctors, tell me beforehand what he proposes to do about such problems or illnesses as are already upon me or are likely to come my way; he merely places his skills and his advice at my disposal. Also, of course, I can get rid of my solicitor or doctor, I can stop his taking decisions that bind me, as I cannot get rid of the man or party I helped to vote into office; I can only vote against him or it at the next elections, which may be a long way ahead and may go against my wishes. But, still, there is an analogy, and it is important. Whether or not a citizen casts his vote rationally depends hardly at all on his ability to predict the decisions of the party or candidate he votes for, let alone the consequences of those decisions.

But the ordinary citizen is no worse off in this respect than his leaders are. At the last elections held in this country, both Labour and Conservative voters had only vague ideas about the consequences for the country, and even for the classes and groups they cared about, of a Conservative rather than a Labour victory; and their ideas were, no doubt, much vaguer than those of, say, Edward Heath and Harold Wilson. But does it follow that their ideas, being vaguer, were also further from the truth? After all, the predictions of the two party leaders differed greatly. Even if they had been asked to make their predictions, not in public and with a view to affecting the result of the elections, but quietly in the privacy of their studies, they would still have differed greatly. Their forecasts and their reasons for making them would have been clearer and more detailed than those of most of their supporters. Many a Labour voter, asked to make a prediction, might have said something like this: 'A Labour government may find it no easier than a Conservative government would to improve industrial relations but will be readier to try new remedies which may prove effective, and in any case will be keener to help the poor and the aged and to raise the school-leaving age.' Pressed to go more into detail, he would probably have had much less to say than Mr Wilson would, or other leaders of his party. So, too, would the Conservative voter compared with the top men in his party. But would either the Labour or the Conservative voter have been more mistaken in his predictions than the leaders of his party in theirs? In saying this, I do not deny that the leaders of large parties competing for power are able men, fitter to rule the country than most of the rest of us are; I say only that there is little reason to believe that they are better able than we are to predict the consequences to the country of their own rule as compared with that of their rivals. Being better able than others are to deal with certain kinds of problems as they arise is one thing: being better able to predict the consequences to the country of having you deal with them rather than someone else is quite another.

In politics nobody knows all the answers nor even many of them. Experts give better answers than laymen only to certain types of questions. Political leaders who are not experts have a great deal of politically relevant knowledge that both experts and ordinary citizens lack. They too are better than other people at answering certain kinds of questions. But, then, neither the questions that experts are qualified to answer nor those to which political leaders give the best answers are the questions that we can reasonably expect the voter to put to himself at elections. The voter, when he casts his vote, does not take incompetently a kind of decision that the expert or the political leader takes more competently; he takes a decision of a different kind. We cannot apply to him the same criteria of understanding and rationality as we do to the expert or to the leader.

Sometimes, we say confidently of one man that he has greater know-ledge and better political judgment than another, even though neither is a political leader. In comparing the two of them, we probably take greater notice of what they say over a period of time about a variety of political questions which are widely discussed than of how they vote at elections and the reasons they give for voting as they do. But from being able to say of two persons fairly well known to us that one is better informed politically and has better judgment than the other to defining criteria and devising questionnaires that enable us to test the information and knowledge of a random sample of voters is a long step.

We can put only a limited number of questions to the voters in our sample. The information we try to get from them may be important and relevant, but there may be other information not less relevant and important. If we had put different but equally relevant questions, we might have got answers that would have required us to place the voters in a different order of merit. Even if we believe that their answers to our questions are such that we can tell both which of them are better informed than others and what they want the government to do, how do we go on to decide that they are or are not making a rational use of their votes? Do we, the investigators who put the questions and assess the answers; do we know enough to enable us to decide how it would be reasonable for a man to vote, given his wants and his information? Can we say, for example, 'The rational voter who wants X and who knows a, b, and c would vote for Smith and the Labour Party rather than for Robinson and the Conservative Party?' Can we say this, no matter what the X is, and no matter what the as, bs and cs?

Clearly, the man who makes a choice on the assumption that he knows what he does not know is unreasonable. But the man who knows that his knowledge and understanding are limited may still make a reasonable choice. For example, the citizen who votes for a party be-cause he has good reason to believe that it is keener than other parties to promote the interests of groups he belongs to or cares about makes a reasonable use of his vote, even though he is unable to explain just how the policies of his party will benefit these groups. If he knows that the party depends on the support of these groups, he has good reason to believe that it will do what it can to promote their interests, especially if he knows that its policies are exposed to criticism by others better able than he is to assess them. So, too, if he votes for his party because it retains the confidence of persons he trusts, he may have good reason for voting as he does. Their confidence may of course be misplaced, but it does not follow that his trust in them is also misplaced. In taking guidance from fallible guides, he is not unreasonable, provided that he has good grounds for believing that they are less likely than he is to be mistaken.

Political decisions often have very broad aims whose pursuit affects large numbers of people in unpredictable ways, and the same is true of decisions that are not, in the narrow sense, political—as, for example, the decisions of a military leader. Some writers have been much impressed by this fact and have drawn sceptical, perhaps too sceptical, conclusions from it. One such writer was Tolstoy. In *War and Peace*, General Kutuzov, giving orders to the officers standing around him, is reasonably sure that they will do (or at least try to do) what he tells them, but when he gives orders through intermediaries to his troops on the battlefield, he knows that some of his orders will never reach the men they are meant for and that others will be misunderstood or else simply irrelevant. The battle is too complicated and too quickly changing for anyone to control its course. For its course depends on innumerable decisions taken by persons who do not know each other and cannot predict one another's decisions, who make mistakes and have false beliefs, who see the battle in which they are all involved differently. Kutuzov, the wise and experienced general, knows that his business is not so much to control the course of events as to maintain the illusion that he is doing so; for on this illusion depends the morale of the Russian army.

After all, as Tolstoy himself admits, armies do fight one another; that is to say, battles are not a war of all against all but of one side against another. What is more, battles—or at least campaigns—are lost and won, and generals contribute something to victory or to defeat. And yet, obviously, generals do not win or lose battles as chess players do games of chess. For though, in a game of chess, neither player can be certain what the other's next move will be, each can see clearly the state of the game and can remember, more or less, what moves have been made. He can also have good reason to believe that his opponent is likely to make one of several quite definite moves, and can decide what move he will make himself in response to each of these alternatives. There are (so Tolstoy implies) conceited and self-opinionated generals who speak of battles and campaigns as if they were won and lost much as games of chess are. Or, rather, when things are going well for their troops, they take the credit to themselves, attributing this success to their own foresight and their ability to size up situations and take timely and correct decisions, though when things are going badly, they attribute the failure to circumstances beyond their control.

Many readers of *War and Peace* skip the chapters in which Tolstoy philosophizes, while others read them and are impressed. But if they reflect on what they read, it must occur to them that Tolstoy goes too far; though by just how much it is difficult to say. The French army got to Moscow, and not by accident; its advance on Moscow was organized, was a controlled operation in a way that its retreat from Moscow was not. Its getting to Moscow was not the unintended consequence of what a large number of men, independently of one another, decided to do. What is more, it was Napoleon, whose delusions of grandeur seemed so absurd to Tolstoy, who, much more than anyone else, was responsible for its getting there. Even if he had first intended to take St Petersburg and had then, owing to events outside his control, decided to go to Moscow instead, he would still have been responsible. To be in control of his army a general need not know in advance what orders he will give, nor even what he will do if one thing happens rather than another; but he does need to know what he can do with his army, what decisions are likely to be effective in this or that type of situation. Though he has aims and makes plans to achieve them, his control of his army (which is only a limited capacity to predict and control events) does not depend on his sticking fast to his plans. Indeed, to maintain this control he may have to change them. Even his main objectives may change with circumstances; if he wins unexpected victories, his ambitions grow, and they shrink if he is defeated.

The same is true of political leaders, even in a democracy, whatever the promises they make when they seek election. Coming to office for several years at a time, they cannot know beforehand just what problems they will have to deal with. They can only be more or less prepared to deal with a variety of problems, which they understand imperfectly and which change continually. From time to time, if they are wise, they make plans, but they have to modify them as they go along. What they have achieved when their term of office comes to an end differs greatly from what they intended to do at the time they were elected. If, on leaving office, they had to report on their stewardship, their assessments of what they had done, honest and intelligent though they might be, would almost certainly be inaccurate or misleading in important respects. Both rulers and subjects are fallible judges of what rulers have achieved, and it is not obvious that democracy makes them less fallible.

If elected rulers are to be politically responsible to the people, there is no need that either they or the people should excel as judges of governmental policies and actions. It is enough that they should owe their authority to getting or retaining the freely given confidence of the people. Schumpeter prefers to say that they must owe their authority to competing freely and successfully with others for the people's votes. It comes in the end to much the same thing. The competition, he says, must be for votes freely given. This means, presumably, that the voter must not just go through the motions of voting. He must understand the significance of what he is doing. He must also have real alternatives to choose between, and must know that they are real. If voting were merely a matter of responding to stimuli, there could still, in a sense, be free competition for votes; there could be freedom for stimulators to try, without resort to force or intimidation, to get the responses they wanted—just as there could be shepherds freely competing with one another for possession of a flock, each trying by gentle methods to get more sheep into his enclosure than the others into theirs.

But free competition for favourable responses, even though the responses are unforced, is not enough to create political responsibility; the responses must be acts of choice by people who understand the significance of what they are doing. For anyone to be politically responsible to others, the others must understand the nature of his authority (which does not involve their being able to predict how he will use it), and his right to exercise it must come of their having chosen him to do so (whether directly or indirectly) when they could have chosen someone else; they must be free to criticize his official actions, and there must be a term to his office when they are able, if they wish, to choose another person to take his place. These conditions could conceivably be met even where there was no actual competition for votes; because, for example, no one wanted to compete with the only candidate or to induce anyone else to do so. But, in practice, at least in large democracies, we can never be sure that the conditions are met unless there is competition for votes freely given.

Thus, in principle, fools can be politically responsible to fools, provided they have intelligence enough to understand the significance of what they are doing when they solicit votes or cast them. This is not to deny that democracy requires a considerable measure of intelligence in both electors and elected if it is to survive, if those who practise it are to remain attached to it. If all electors and all holders of elected office were fools, democracy would soon come to an end. But the conditions for the survival of a political system are not the same as the conditions of anyone standing to anyone else in a relation characteristic of the system.

We can imagine two conditions, both unattainable, though the second is less out of reach than the first. In the first, everyone has the knowledge and understanding he requires to pass well-informed and wise judgments on the policies and actions of those who rule or aspire to rule. It is a perfect democracy of the kind that Rousseau said was possible only among gods. In the second, everyone recognizes the limits of his own knowledge and understanding, and passes what are reasonable judgments, given his limitations. It is a democracy, not of the omniscient and omnicompetent, but merely of the wise.

No democracy known to us consists, even predominantly, of the wise; it consists of men and women who are both wise and foolish, with some of them considerably more wise or foolish than others. If it is to be really a democracy, even the foolish must understand what they are doing when they cast a vote at an election or what kind of authority is theirs when they take up an office; they must understand the rights they exercise and the obligations they undertake. They must, in particular, understand the rights and obligations peculiar to democracy if they are to be politically responsible to others or others to them. But we must not say that, unless they are well-informed and wise when they exercise these rights and perform these obligations, there can be no political responsibility among them. We must say rather that the survival of democracy—of the system in which the supreme makers of law and policy are politically responsible to the people—requires that information and wisdom should be pretty widely distributed.

Private rights and political rights

In representative democracies that are liberal, there is a high value put on a number of rights, some political and others non-political or private. The most important of these private rights are: the right to choose your career; the right to an education which enables you to make an informed choice of career and to acquire the knowledge and skills proper to the career you have chosen; the right to decide whom you will marry; the right to discuss and criticize anything you like and more especially all social rules and received standards; the right not to conform to these rules and standards unless your doing so is necessary to secure the rights of others or to provide services which the community must require of its members if it is to do for them what they require of it; the right to form organized groups for any purpose not harmful to others. I now speak of these rights only in the most general way; the business of defining their limits and of deciding how to secure them in practice is elaborate and never-ending.

The most important of the political rights are the right to vote at free elections which decide who the supreme makers of law and policy will be; the right to criticize them and their subordinates publicly; and the right to form organized groups to make demands on them and to recommend policies to them.

Some of these political and private rights, broadly formulated, overlap. For example, the right to form organized groups to influence those who govern is part of the right to form such groups for any purpose not harmful to others. Still, it is possible to distinguish the political from the non-political uses of these rights, and even to define the rights so that the political and the non-political do not overlap. These two kinds of rights, even when so defined as not to overlap, are closely connected. Each kind is a support to the other. The private rights are, on the whole, more secure in countries where the political rights are exercised, and the political rights cannot be exercised effectively unless many of the private rights are so too. But this need not mean that rights of either of these two kinds are valued primarily as means to rights of the other kind. Wherever the private rights are valued for their own sake, so too are the political rights; for the reason that they are both entailed by the some conception (or, if you like, philosophy) of what man is and ought to be.

Of course, in countries where these rights are valued, men have purposes, whether for themselves or for others, which they could not achieve unless the rights were valued and to some extent secured. But then, equally, they would not have the purposes unless they valued the rights; they are the purposes of men who have, even though they may not be able to define it precisely, a conception of man that entails these rights. They have other purposes besides these but these they have also. If we say that securing these rights to them helps them to achieve these purposes, we speak truly; but if we say that they value the rights only, or primarily, as means to achieving the purposes, we speak falsely. The purposes are often changing or vague, and the persons who have them are unable to describe them, or can describe them only when they have achieved them. The rights are often more easily defined than the purposes, and the conditions of their being realized more easily described. For example, in one type of society men and women attach much greater importance than they do in another to being able to choose their partners in marriage. Why do they do this? Is it because they expect something from marriage that men and women in the other type of society do not? No doubt it is. But it is much more difficult to define what they expect and to decide whether or not they get it than it is to define the right to choose one's own partner in marriage and to decide whether or not the right is exercised. Both the right and the expectation arise in the same social conditions and are related to the same philosophy, and neither is prior to the other. And yet, even when we want to justify a policy by pointing to its consequences, we can ordinarily do so more easily by showing that it secures rights and opportunities to more people than by showing that it enables them to satisfy the expectations connected with those rights and opportunities.

In some countries the private rights I spoke of are more extensive and more secure than the political rights. They are so, for example, in Yugoslavia. But where the private rights are valued and to some considerable extent exercised, the political rights, even when they are denied in practice, are affirmed in theory. In Yugoslavia the right to vote at free elections, the right to criticize the actions and policies of the government and the right to form associations to influence the government are all officially recognized. There may be practices and conventions, and even laws, which prevent or greatly curtail the exercise of these political rights. Nevertheless, they are affirmed; it is officially conceded that they are of the essence of democracy.

Though the private rights are more extensive and more secure in such countries as Yugoslavia than the political ones, they are less so than they would be if the political rights were respected in practice and not only in theory. (I have in mind here, of course, not all private rights but the ones I tried to define roughly when I spoke of two kinds of rights highly valued in liberal democracies.) For example, in Communist countries the right of young persons to choose their careers, though it is limited less by poverty than it is in some Western countries, is more limited in another way. The range of occupations they can choose from is determined by, among other things, their rulers' conception of what society should be like and their attempts to realize that conception. In liberal societies, citizens have a greater opportunity both to influence the policies of their rulers and to make a living in ways not provided for by those policies.

The case for liberal democracy (or, in other words, for Western democracy as it would be if it were true to its own principles) is that it secures certain greatly valued rights, some private and others political. The private rights are perhaps more highly and more widely valued than the political rights, though even they are not highly valued in all societies. Yet we can say (for there is, I suggest, strong evidence to support our doing so) that the private rights are apt to be the more widely valued, the more industrial and literate a society is, and the more varied the occupations and styles of life, and the greater the social mobility, inside it. We can also say (for again there is evidence, though less strong, to support us) that liberal democracy does more to secure these rights, where they are valued, than does any other form of government. The political rights, of course, democracy secures necessarily; for, if it did not secure them, it would not be democracy. In a democracy rulers are by definition responsible to the people they rule, which they cannot be unless these political rights are effectively exercised.

Both the private and the political rights are valued for what they are and not only for their consequences. But if I am right in suggesting that the private rights are valued more highly and more generally than the political ones, then it is likely that the political rights are valued largely as a means to the wider and more secure enjoyment of the private rights. In other words, it is likely that political democracy is more valued as a means than an end.

It is not a necessary truth that these rights, private and political, should be highly valued in industrial and literate societies. We can easily imagine circumstances in which this was not so. But, in the world as it happens to be, it is so. It was so, to begin with, in the West, where the first industrial and widely literate societies emerged; and it is fast becoming so outside the West, as industry and literacy spread. Their spreading is both a penetration into other parts of the world of Western industrial and commercial practices, and an irruption into them of Western ideas. Of course, these ideas change as they move out of the region of their origin. Marxism, for example, has changed greatly as it has moved eastwards, first into Russia and then into China. But whether we approve of these changes or not, we have to admit that the ideas that have changed came from the West and are still in some ways the same ideas. Wherever they have power, Marxists claim to be liberators of the peoples they rule, and they claim that their rule is democratic. Their ideas about freedom and democracy are still, I suggest, closely related to ours; they are so whether we look upon them as improvements on our ideas or as perversions of them.

Kinds of democracy

It is often said that there are in the world today at least two kinds of democracy. Sometimes the claim is that there are more than two. But, as far as my argument is concerned, it does not matter how many there are, for I am dealing primarily with ideas and only secondarily with facts. For the sake of simplicity, I shall take it that the claim is that there are two kinds: the Western and the non-Western or, as it is sometimes put, the liberal and the people's democracies.

This claim that there are two kinds of democracy could mean either of two things: that there are two kinds of political system differing greatly in their practices and yet alike in being democratic, in upholding and seeking to realize certain principles; or that there are two markedly different ideas of democracy. I shall interpret the claim in the second of these senses, for it is in this sense that it is most often made. Years ago E. H. Carr started a fashion by distinguishing two ideas of democracy, a Western idea of it as government *by* the people or responsible to them and an Eastern or communist idea of it as government *for* the people or carried on in their interests. More recently, attempts have been made to distinguish three ideas of it widely current in the world today. These distinctions are, I suggest, more misleading than helpful.

There are, of course, many more than two (or even three) senses in which the words *democracy* and *democratic* are used in the world today; there may well be two or three dozen or even two or three score. There are many senses in which the words are used in the 'liberal democracies', and many too in the 'people's democracies'; and the two ranges of meanings do not exactly coincide. Yet I doubt whether linguistic usages differ to the extent that E. H. Carr's distinction implies. For his distinction suggests that, for example, Stalin, when he called the Soviet Union a democracy was making for it a claim quite different from the claim that Roosevelt made for the United States when he called it by the same name. But the political vocabularies of these two champions of democracy against Hitler, though they differed considerably, did not do so to that extent. When Stalin called the Soviet Union a democracy, he meant, among other things, that its rulers were responsible to the people they ruled. Whether he believed what he said is not to the purpose, for we are concerned with the meaning and not with the truth or sincerity of the assertion.

Professor Carr's intention, when he made his distinction, was a good one; he wanted to prevent misunderstanding and perhaps also point-less disputes. And, certainly, if it were true that liberals and com-munists used the word *democratic* in quite different senses, they would be well advised to take notice of the fact and not waste their energies arguing at cross purposes. Now that the word is used every-where and often as a term of praise, and especially of self-praise, we could, by taking the trouble to understand how different peoples and groups use it, avoid giving and taking unnecessary offence.[1]

Misunderstanding and pointless argument are to be avoided, except by persons who enjoy the noise and passion of disputes without much caring what the disputes are about. But there is, I suggest, much greater room for genuine argument about democracy between liberals and communists than they are sometimes willing to admit. As I said earlier in another connection, the communist, when he calls Western democracy a sham or a bourgeois illusion, is not just saying that Western governments do not govern in the real interests of the people; he is saying also that they are not in fact responsible to the people, though there is a pretence that they are. So, too, when he says that the people's democracies are more truly democratic than the Western democracies, he is not saying only that they are governed more in the people's interests, or have fewer social inequalities in them, or recruit

---

[1] Not that people who have grown used to thinking of each other as inveterate enemies are particularly sensitive to one another's adverse judgments. Just because they take their enmity seriously, they take little notice of each other as critics; or rather they take notice of each other's criticisms only as moves in a war of propaganda and speculate about the intentions that lie behind them.

more of their leaders from the manual working classes; he is also saying that their rulers are more genuinely responsible to the people. He does not admit that elections in the people's democracies are not free, and that therefore the party that wins them cannot claim that it has the confidence of the people. He may have different ideas from those of the liberal about what procedures are necessary if elections are to be free, but he does not deny that they must be free if the persons who win them are to be accounted representatives of the people. Nor does he reject the private rights precious to the liberal. He does not deny that it is important that men and women should be able to choose their occupations in life, or their partners in marriage, or even that they should have freedom of association and of speech. No doubt, he always goes on to say that these last two freedoms (and others as well) must not be abused; but then so too does the liberal. His ideas about what constitutes abuse of these freedoms differ, of course, from those of the liberal. Nevertheless, his ideas of freedom and democracy are close enough to the liberal's for genuine argument to be possible between them.

I suggest that it as often happens that two parties to a dispute misunderstand one another and argue at cross purposes because they have similar but confused ideas as because they have different ideas without being aware that they differ. This is the more likely to be the case the less one or both of the parties to the dispute can afford to think clearly about the matters at issue between them. The more a regime that calls itself democratic is a sham democracy (the less it lives up to its own principles), the more people inside it are confused about those principles. In other words, the less they understand just what it is that they are claiming for the regime. This is not the *only* cause of confused thinking about principles, but it is one cause among others, and often a very important one.

There are many political theorists in the West ready to admit that our Western democracies fall considerably short of living up to their own principles and are, therefore, to some extent, 'sham' democracies. Whether 'the people's democracies' are greater or lesser shams does not, for the moment, matter. What I am now saying is merely this: if we find two regimes, each claiming to be more democratic than it is, engaged in ideological warfare, we should expect to see their leaders and their theorists often misunderstanding one another and arguing at cross purposes. And yet, if we looked more closely at their claims and arguments, examining their unspoken assumptions and implications, we might well find that their ideas of democracy had a good deal in common. In that case, we could sensibly enquire how far the two regimes fell short, in their practices, of common standards implicit in their ways of describing themselves and criticizing each other. We should not have to throw up our hands and say that there was no deciding how far they fell short of democracy, except by reference to standards that only one of them accepted.

For some considerable time now peoples outside the West have been involved in a course of change, social and cultural, which is often called—in my opinion properly, though the name is sometimes resented —Westernization. These peoples, before Western practices and ideas were introduced among them, differed greatly both from the Western peoples and from one another. Today, as a result of this Westernization, they are in important respects more like each other and more like the Western peoples; and yet the differences are still great and probably always will be. Nor are these differences all survivals from the past, for some of them are effects of Westernization, of a cultural invasion of a kind that the Western peoples have never undergone. One effect (or part effect) of Westernization has been communist rule, something so far unknown in the West;[1] and this rule has deeply affected the peoples subject to it. Every Communist party subscribes to doctrines born in the West, and uses ideas that have no meaning except where there are practices and conditions that first appeared in the West. The translation of these doctrines and ideas to regions different from the region of their origin has, of course, changed them considerably, and yet they are still in many ways recognizably the same.

Thus, though Red China differs greatly from the Soviet Union, just as the Soviet Union does from what any Western country would be like, if it were to go Communist, Marxism everywhere still bears the marks of its origins. And what is true of Marxism is true also of nationalism, another Western ideology that has spread far beyond the West. Many Asian and African peoples are now much more nationalist than the Western peoples are, and their nationalism takes a different form as well as being more intense. This is partly because, like the Marxism with which it now quite often runs in harness, it is largely directed against the West. Yet it owes a great deal to ideas which arose first in the West. Communism and nationalism have come with the growth of trade and industry, with the spread of literacy, with the movement of people from the villages into the towns. They have come with industrialization, giving an impulse to it and getting strength from it. There may be no necessary connection between them. It is conceivable that economically backward peoples could industrialize rapidly and yet not take to either of these ideologies.

[1] Except in some countries bordering on the Soviet Union whose peoples still think of themselves as Western (for example, Poland and Czechoslovakia) and in East Germany. But these are all countries in which there would be no Communist rule if the Russians had not imposed it on reluctant peoples.

But the fact is that they have taken to them, to the two together or to one alone. And both these ideologies have a democratic bias. The bias is there, even though the peoples who take to the ideologies, or whose leaders do so, do not practise democracy. These peoples are, in some important respects, more concerned for the individual than their ancestors were. It may seem absurd that I should say so. Are they not either communist or nationalist, or both together? And do not communist and nationalist governments make large demands on their subjects? No doubt, they do, but then so, too, in their different ways, do the liberal governments of the West. All governments bear much more heavily on their subjects than they used to do in the past. These communist and nationalist governments are certainly more illiberal than Western governments are, and are also in some ways more oppressive than the governments they superseded. But all this, though true, does not prevent the peoples they govern being more individualist than their forefathers were; not in spite of what their rulers do to them, but largely because that is how their rulers want them to be.

Among these peoples children follow in the footsteps of their parents much less than they used to do. They are encouraged to choose their careers; they are given opportunities that older generations never had. They are taught to put aside what is customary and traditional, and to aspire to what is now offered to them on the ground that it is better worth having. They are, so their rulers tell them, being *liberated*, not only from the foreigner and the imperialist, from the landlord and the moneylender, but from the narrowness and the lack of enterprise of old ways of life. For the first time since their species acquired capacities raising them above the other animals, since they became properly human, men have, so they are told, the chance to live as human beings, as creatures capable of knowledge and self-direction, ought to live. It is dinned into them that they can, provided they have the courage, the intelligence and the self-discipline to go through with it, create for themselves a new kind of society with not only more equality but also greater freedom than any before it.

Their rulers may drive and oppress them, and may forbid them to question doctrines and policies officially approved, but they also educate them and teach them to think critically. They teach them science; and in learning it they learn that theories supersede one another, that what one generation takes for granted may be rejected by the next. Their rulers encourage them to compete for the new opportunities offered to them; they assure them that it is up to them to make what they can of their lives. In some ways at least they increase their hopes and their self-reliance.

There are also, of course, the plans requiring large sacrifices, the persistent indoctrination and the harsh external discipline. But the planners, the indoctrinators, the disciplinarians, are all men and women who have rejected the customary and the time-honoured in the name of reason and progress. Their philosophy is that human beings can transform their environments and themselves by taking thought and working intelligently together. They appeal to reason even though they also forbid certain kinds of criticism; they look for willing cooperation and preach that nothing worth while can be achieved without it, even though they also intimidate and deceive. In the past everyone accepted a social order which nobody dreamt of reconstructing. Today everyone is called upon to take part willingly and intelligently in establishing a more just and rational order. The leaders call themselves, and to some extent believe that they are, the representatives of the peoples they lead. The doctrines they propagate and to which they appeal to justify the sacrifices they require from others—and sometimes even from themselves—teach that leaders and led must trust and support one another if they are to remain true to the doctrines, if they are to use them effectively as guides to policy. Communists who lose the confidence of the workers (so the theory goes) cease to be their spokesmen and guides, the interpreters of their 'true' interests.

The same is true of leaders who are nationalists. They do not put themselves forward (whatever they may think privately) as Platonic guardians or philosopher-kings whose superior wisdom enables them to discover what is good for the people without consulting them, or who consult them only, as doctors do their patients, to get at facts which they alone are competent to assess. Rather, their public image of themselves is of trusted leaders solving one problem after another in collaboration with the people, discussing these problems with them in the light of a doctrine of which they may have the firmer grasp but which needs to be reinterpreted as the lessons of experience are learned. They claim to be teachers and yet also learners alongside those they teach. Their teaching is not salutary unless the people understand and accept it; which they will not do unless it makes sense of their endeavours and their sacrifices. The people are not subordinates of whom no more is required than that they should understand the orders given them; they are partners who must be satisfied that there are good reasons why they should do what is required of them. And the final proof that there are good reasons is that the people to whom they are offered see that they are good. Leaders and led learn together from experience as they interpret it in the light of the doctrine and interpret the doctrine in the light of experience.

This is the theory. In practice, no doubt, things are different. There is much less give and take between leaders and led than in principle there ought to be. The dialogue between them is apt to be onesided. The leaders reserve to themselves the right to prevent the workers or the people being misled. They admit that they must appeal to reason in them and must gain their confidence, but this, so it appears to them, requires that they should be able to silence corrupters and deceivers, 'lacqueys of the bourgeoisie' or 'neo-colonialists'. Here, so it may seem to us, there is a contradiction. I do not say that there is not. But whoever contradicts himself asserts both the contradictory opposites. The appeals to reason, the calls for sympathy and understanding, for intelligent and willing cooperation, are made despite the oppression and the suppression. The leaders do not claim to be merely guardians of the workers' or the people's interests; they also claim to be their spokesmen. They claim to be their leaders in a work of construction and liberation in which all men of good will are both learners and partners. They do not deny that they deal harshly with the subversive and the recalcitrant; they admit it and even take pride in the admission. They claim to be doing what has to be done if the attempt to build a just society is to succeed. But this, so they say, does not preclude their being learners alongside the people whose guides they claim to be; it does not even preclude their learning from the people. They can, so they say, learn nothing apart from the people.

We may call this muddled thinking, though it has also been called, more perceptively, 'double-thinking'. Not just *double-talk* but *double-think*. The double-talker may know himself for one; he may be consciously a fraud. The double-thinker, if he is truly such, does not know that he is one; he is sincere. He deludes himself. And his unconscious motive for doing so need not be personal ambition; or, even if he is personally ambitious, he may be public-spirited or patriotic as well. Deluding oneself, taking to an illusion, is often, as Marx saw, not just a personal matter; it can have social causes affecting whole categories of persons. It can be a condition of their carrying out their social functions adequately. It can be what Marx called false consciousness. The bourgeois, he said, have a false conception of the role of the bourgeois state; it is in fact an instrument of class domination but they think and speak of it as if it were an impartial protector of rights. For the bourgeois state to function as it does, those who run it must have illusions about it.

Now, it may be that what Marx said of the bourgeois in his day is true of Communists and the extremer nationalists today. It may be that they cannot achieve what they set out to achieve unless they have illusions about themselves in relation to the peoples whose aspirations they claim to express. They must say, and to some extent believe, that they are democrats; they must put themselves forward as believers in both equality and freedom, as men who respect these things as far as it is possible for them to do so, because their avowed aim is to create a kind of society in which, eventually and for the first time, freedom and equality are achieved.

It has been said that people, whenever they achieve a high material standard of living, come to aspire to freedom. I doubt whether this is true; and even if it were, I should not point to it in support of my present argument. There have been in the past wealthy classes that have not aspired to what we call freedom, to the rights, private and political, of which I spoke earlier. There has long been considerable wealth as well as a great deal of poverty in the world, and yet this sort of freedom has come to be valued, even in the West, only in the last two or three centuries. In both Greece and Rome there were moralists who spoke of wealth as if it were destructive of freedom. And though the Greeks and Romans of antiquity meant by freedom something different from (though related to) what we mean by it, I see no reason for believing that the desire for freedom, whether in our sense or in theirs, is either weakened or strengthened by the mere increase of wealth.

Nor do I see any reason for holding that the poor, merely because they are materially worse off than the rich, care less than the rich do for freedom. There is no evidence that they are more indifferent than the rich are to other 'moral' or 'spiritual' values: to dignity, loyalty to family and friends, trustfulness and generosity. Rich and poor have many values in common, and I see no reason why freedom should not be one of them. Indifference to what are called 'non-material' or 'moral' or 'spiritual' values is no more common among the poor than the rich.

Nevertheless, there are opportunities and rights that people have come to recognize and to value only as society has grown more industrial, more urban and more literate. These opportunities and rights are not, I think, valued because they make easier the accumulation of wealth or the pursuit of other things to which men turn their minds *after* they have become wealthy; but they are in fact closely bound up with ways of life peculiar to a certain kind of society.

Though society could conceivably become industrial, urban and literate and its members care nothing for these opportunities and rights, this is not what has in fact happened. Industry, large towns and literacy seem everywhere to have encouraged similar aspirations; and to have done so as much where the rulers are Marxists or nationalists as where they are not. In all these societies striving to catch up with or to surpass the West, many of the rights precious to the Western liberal and democrat are affirmed. They are both affirmed and denied, though not both on the same occasions or in the same contexts. Hence the tensions to which rulers and peoples are liable in these societies. Arguments for democracy mean something to them. The accusation that what they practise is not democracy touches them nearly. Just as it touches us when it is brought against us. We mean by democracy substantially what they mean by it; we have in mind what are at bottom similar rights, private and political. We may differ from them about the institutions needed to secure the rights but we agree about the rights. They may say about us that our institutions secure the privileges of the wealthy and the well-organized under the pretence of securing rights that everyone shares. We either deny this confidently, or, when confidence deserts us, we pretend that things are different from what they really are or we seek to change them. We may say about them that their institutions secure the ascendancy of an organized minority bent on transforming society to meet some ideal of their own regardless of the people's wishes; but this they strenuously deny, though they sometimes admit that they have to resort to harsh measures to ensure that the economic and social conditions of equality and freedom are solidly established. The claims they make for themselves are quite inconsistent with the view that in their opinion democracy, as they practise it, is not government *by* the people but only government *for* the people.

So, in principle, a genuine argument is possible among the peoples who claim to be democratic or to be moving towards democracy. And today nearly all peoples do that. Or else their leaders do so. The opportunities and the rights they say they care about are broadly similar. But what can be done in principle is sometimes in practice difficult to do. Rulers who claim to be democratic and who use undemocratic methods do not listen to their critics and try to prevent their subjects doing so. Peoples who have come to think of themselves, as their ancestors never did, as in some ways backward because they have been the last to acquire aspirations acquired by other peoples before them, look with suspicion and dislike at these other peoples. They are not the less suspicious of them for believing that their own revolutions and struggles for independence have put them in other ways in the van of progress. There are many reasons why peoples who are or who claim to be democratic do not listen to one another; why they believe that they have nothing to learn about democracy from peoples whose political practices differ greatly from their own. I do not underestimate the strength of the motives which cause them to close their minds to one another; I merely suggest that, if they opened them, they would be compelled to take one another's arguments seriously because, for all their muddled thinking, they often have in mind much the same opportunities and rights. This world in which nearly all political leaders now speak of democracy in order to praise it is not ideologically quite the Tower of Babel that it seems to be. These leaders still speak what is in important respects the same political language. Some speak it more clearly than others do, and some more sincerely, though they all at times find it expedient to speak it obscurely or to fail to understand other speakers of it.

Index